Powerhouse

Powerhouse
The Life and Work of Judith Chafee

Christopher Domin and Kathryn McGuire

Princeton Architectural Press · New York

"Abstract art, then, is like a powerhouse without practical use.
It is bursting with energies which, once set to work in the practical
context of life, might well influence life on a tremendous scale."
—Alexander Dorner, *The Way Beyond "Art"* (1947)

Published by Princeton Architectural Press
202 Warren Street, Hudson, NY 12534
www.papress.com

Editor: Kristen Hewitt
Designer: Benjamin English

Special thanks to: Paula Baver, Janet Behning, Abby Bussel,
Jan Cigliano Hartman, Susan Hershberg, Stephanie Holstein, Lia Hunt,
Valerie Kamen, Jennifer Lippert, Sara McKay, Parker Menzimer,
Wes Seeley, Rob Shaeffer, Sara Stemen, Jessica Tackett, Marisa Tesoro,
Paul Wagner, and Joseph Weston of Princeton Architectural Press
—Kevin C. Lippert, publisher

Library of Congress Cataloging-in-Publication Data
Names: Domin, Christopher, 1967- author. | McGuire, Kathryn, author.
Title: Powerhouse : the life and work of Judith Chafee / Christopher
  Domin and Kathryn McGuire ; introduction by William J.R. Curtis.
Description: First edition. | Hudson, NY: Princeton Architectural Press,
  [2019] | Includes bibliographical references and index.
Identifiers: LCCN 2019001593 | ISBN 9781616897178 (hardcover:
  alk. paper)
Subjects: LCSH: Chafee, Judith, 1932-1998. | Architects—United
  States—Biography.
Classification: LCC NA737.C369 D66 2019 | DDC 720.92 [B] —dc23
LC record available at https://lccn.loc.gov/2019001593

The creation of this book has been a journey from peripheral awareness to acute realization.

Clarity of purpose drove Judith Chafee to define her path in architecture as an unrepentant modernist, an environmental steward, a social justice advocate, and a demanding teacher. Chafee's architecture combined sensitivity to place with an uncanny ability to employ brutalist materials with sophistication, grace, and indigenous influences. Her translation of architectural concepts inherited from architects preceding her, as well as from her contemporaries, has now been generously entrusted to future generations. Judith Chafee's life was enriched by many layers of complexity: a rough and ready southwestern childhood in the context of an erudite social order, a mature cadre of acquaintances with the intelligentsia of the arts and architecture world, long, endearing friendships with strong and unwavering personalities, and extensive travel undertaken with the purpose of comprehending other cultures and constructs.

In-depth research has revealed just how important teaching was to Chafee's cosmology, even to the detriment of maintaining her office. The work was important, but it had to be good enough to be a lesson for others in how to live and build in the world.

Sometimes Chafee would muse about getting away to the ocean so she could see and feel the water. But the desert always completed her. Per her request, her dear friends placed her ashes in the Tucson Mountains, north of Wasson Peak.

This book covers a lifetime and would not have been possible without substantial support and encouragement. The Graham Foundation for Advanced Studies in the Fine Arts provided important financial support and project recognition. Additional financial support came from the University of Arizona Provost's Author Support Fund. Early financial support and assistance came from the Maynard Dixon Chafee Fund; Dr. Seymour M. and Marcia L. Sabesin; Sandra Helton and Norman M. Edelson; and the Judith Chafee Research Project. We thank Jane Weinzapfel, FAIA, and Max Underwood, President's Professor at ASU, for their encouragement and letters of support for our project.

The University of Arizona, School of Architecture in the College of Architecture, Planning and Landscape Architecture generously supported both travel for research and lectures about Chafee's work, and sponsored a recent return visit and lecture with William J.R. Curtis to continue his shared perspectives. We are also grateful to R. Brooks Jeffery for initiating the reception of Judith Chafee's archives into the College of Architecture, Planning and Landscape Architecture.

The authors thank the University of Arizona Libraries Special Collections, where Chafee's archives are now housed. Director Steve Hussman and his administrative assistant, Kathy McCarthy, afforded us access and time to review many documents while they were reorganizing the Chafee archives under the stewardship of Bob Diaz, Associate Librarian. Bob generously shared his time and resources, and developed a sincere appreciation for Chafee's story, which culminated in his curation of an exhibition in the Special Collections Gallery, and coordination with the School of Architecture and local chapter of the AIA to present scheduled lectures about Judith Chafee and her work and writing.

The authors also thank the Arizona Historical Society in Tucson, the Arizona Historical Society Library and Archives in Tempe, and Yale University Library Manuscripts and Archives for their library resource assistance.

Princeton Architectural Press responded to our book proposal within hours of delivery, initiating a compelling partnership that brought this work to a higher level of refinement. The careful editing, respect for content, and sophisticated graphic attitude of this publishing team sets an exceptional standard for professionalism. The impact of Jennifer Lippert, Kristen Hewitt, and Ben English on the development and artifact of this project is significant.

We are indebted to photographer Bill Timmerman, who started documenting one of Chafee's projects in the Upper Peninsula of Michigan that had never been photographed, was about to be sold, and as a result could have become unavailable to photograph. Bill, along with Christopher Domin and an assistant, flew to Michigan to experience his first Chafee photo shoot. When Christopher described the bigger project, a book on Chafee's work, Timmerman said "count me in." He photographed eight more houses as they became available and ready for photographing on weekend excursions, pacing out a few projects each year. Some of the houses have been well-lived-in for thirty, forty, fifty years, with significant changes made in furnishing and the adjacent landscape; this often provided challenges in accessing views of the exteriors, with mature vegetation creating more obstacles. Despite this, Bill persevered. His discerning eye and positioning was in sync with Chafee's work as he followed the paths she designed for the natural lighting of the spaces. This book would not have been possible without him.

Diana Brock-Gray was a student, employee, and close friend to Chafee. Her contributions were invaluable. And we are especially grateful that she called on her friend Jennifer Thomas—the two became very able volunteer assistants for Bill's photography work, traveling from their home bases in Seattle and Phoenix to Guilford, Sonoita, and, on several occasions, Tucson.

Over the past four years, owners of the houses have been welcoming and hospitable as we took over their homestead from sunrise to late evenings for photography weekends. All the activity was quite disruptive, with five to six people on walkie-talkies turning lights off and on, rearranging art on the walls, and moving chairs from one room to another before returning everything to its original placement. We are very grateful to Paul and Meg Johnson, John Biklen and David Streeter, Jane London, Joan Jacobson, Judith Hydeman, David Russell and Susan Randolph, Dr. Seymour and Marcia Sabesin, Sandra Helton and Norman Edelson, and Adelyn Hansen for allowing us to photograph their homes. We also thank other owners for answering knocks on their doors and welcoming us to come in and talk about their Chafee-designed houses: Anne Maley and Tim Schaffner, Barbara and Jorge Albala, Karen and Bill Shumacher, Audrey Merriman, Terry and Bill Bendt, Annemie and Don Baker, Jack Grossi, Mark Hydeman, Renee Morton, Lisa Ryers, Neena Ryers, Dr. Peter Ryers, Dr. Peter Salomon, Debbie and Tom Collazo, and Dennis Decker.

The authors are grateful to the architects, engineers, former students, friends, and family for generously sharing their time and experiences: Chuck Albanese, Kevin Alter, Ray Barnes, Sheila Blackburn, Will Bruder, Jerry Cannon, Hercules Christofides, Jack DeBartolo 3, Bob Earl, David Eisenberg, Brian Farling, Barbara Grygutis, Diane Hastings, Joshua Edwards, Luis Ibarra, R. Brooks Jeffrey, Rick Joy, Eddie Jones, Helen Kessler, Diane Lewis, Larry Medlin, Bob Nevins, Anne M. Nequette, Robert Peters, Elliott Price, Ann and John Price, Charles (Corky) Poster, Teresa Rosano, Mark Ryan, Thomas Spendarian, Robert A. M. Stern, George Stevenson, Bob Swaim, Stanley Tigerman, Robert Vint, Les Wallach, Joseph Wilder, A. Richard Williams, Scott Woodward, Canan Yetman, Carl Abbott, Pat and Briggs Ackert, Caleb James Alvarado, Janet Bloom, Inge Brown, Paul Brouard, Bryant Conant, Richard Chafee, Caroline Emerson (daughter of Judith Chafee), Joan Geller, Neil Goodwin, John T. Hill, Don and Jay Irving, Raymond Liston, Susan Bloom Lobo, James McNeely, Gordon Meinhard, Paul Mitarachi, John J. Molloy, Tim Prentice, Kevin Roche, Lily Rothenberg, Bourke Runton, Mark Sublette, Patti Van Leer, and Yung and Ming Wang.

How fortunate we are to have the introduction by William J.R. Curtis, who gave Chafee encouragement and exposure within an international community, speaking the language of architecture. His appreciation for her work is gratifying, and his memories of Chafee are profound and endearing.

Kathryn McGuire thanks Norman Rubin: He is the kindest, dearest person, and she considers herself fortunate that he is her husband. His "laid-back" retirement has had him traveling around the country on their research schedule and checking out the local museums while the authors scanned through archival material. Norm has transported, fed, and helped out in the photo shooting cadre. He has been an honest sounding board, very tolerant of prickly behavior and supportive during deadline schedules (including McGuire's time in Judith Chafee's office). McGuire is grateful for her understanding and supportive family and friends, in particular for Lynn Saul's generosity and sage advice.

Christopher Domin thanks Diana Chen for sharing in life's adventures and providing the critical insight required to bring the Judith Chafee story into the light for all to learn from and enjoy. Eleonora and Maximus gave inspiration, as citizens of the latest generation, who must grow up in and learn to nurture a region of the mindful heart.

Principles and Forms:
The Architectural Vision of Judith Chafee

William J.R. Curtis

"We should attempt to bring
nature, houses and human beings
together in a higher unity."
—Ludwig Mies van der Rohe[1]

There are no recipes for good architecture. Invention follows no set rules, and there is always the spark that brings a building alive. Works of a high order communicate before they are understood, touching mind and senses and revealing new dimensions of experience. Such buildings transcend time and refuse to be limited by the passage of fashionable agendas. They are like microcosms distilling ideal visions of life, or constructed myths fusing many precedents yet engaging with the contradictions of contemporary reality. They combine the unique and the universal, drawing upon diverse pasts and opening the way to unexpected futures. They give shape to spatial concepts, images, and ideas. A highly resolved work may reveal unexpected dimensions in a site or a view; it may even intensify the presence of nature. Architecture speaks its own language in silence, enhancing human life, stirring subliminal memories, and suggesting alternative realities. It uses all the means at its disposal: form, function, space, light, material, structure, and meaning, yet the result is more than the sum of the parts. There is a higher sense of unity, a poetic sense of order, which makes itself felt directly.

My initiation into Judith Chafee's work and world occurred on a sunny winter's day in the early part of 1984, and it took the form of a revelation. I had come to Tucson to deliver a talk in the school of architecture and the next day was taken on a tour through landscape relatively close to the city. The raking sunlight picked out lines of shadow on plants, cliffs, and buildings. The vertical tubes and prickles of the saguaro cacti seemed to vibrate. As we drove along, I caught sight of a horizontal roof hovering above the desert vegetation in the middle distance. This gesture established a line of calm against the surrounding drama of small hills and valleys, eruptive crags, and vertical cacti. There was the suggestion of a delicate frame structure through which one could perceive the sky and the surroundings. The building was at ease in its desert setting and almost seemed to breathe alongside the plants around it. It filtered light and air while floating above areas of shadow. I realized at once that I was in the presence of a remarkable architectural work. My eyes were fixed to the spot.

As we approached along a track, the structure revealed more of its anatomy. The hovering horizontal roof proved to be a slender wooden shading device combining planks and slats. It was held aloft on a grid of evenly spaced cylindrical wooden poles: timber relatives, perhaps, of Le Corbusier's concrete pilotis. The perforated roof cast an ever-changing pattern of shadows and striations of light over the lower parts of the dwelling. These were defined by whitewashed walls weaving in and out of the plan. Planar yet textured, they anchored the building to the ground in a manner recalling traditional adobe construction. The sheltering roof spread out toward the surrounding vegetation as a long horizontal plane over the landscape. The desert floor seemed to move in under the building, which supplied shaded zones of transition. Edges and boundaries were ambiguous. The interlocking planes and voids combined geometric harmony with a liberating sense of space. Above all, I was struck by the aura of the building—its tranquil presence and its curious fusion of modern architectural abstraction and southwestern

Ramada House,
Tucson, Arizona

desert rusticity. While of its time, it touched memories from the past, even evoking a sense of origins, but without recourse to bogus folklore or nostalgic imagery.

The building into which I had stumbled without prior knowledge was the Ramada House by Judith Chafee, designed and constructed in the mid-seventies. It was one of a series of her designs attuned to the desert environment and to the aspirations of an emerging clientele in the region. Chafee's work fused diverse influences in an abstract yet resonant architectural language. The ramada was a traditional shading device in Spanish colonial architecture usually formed from branches and twigs held up on crude timber poles. It in turn echoed a type of Native American shelter (of the Tohono O'odham tribe) found in the Sonoran Desert, combining structures of sticks and dried fronds of saguaro or ocotillo over walls half-buried in the ground—in effect two desert archetypes, the one nomadic, the other sedentary. There were modern reminiscences as well, such as Le Corbusier's shading parasols in his Indian works (especially the Shodan House in Ahmedabad, 1953) and Frank Lloyd Wright's timber roofs over platforms at Taliesin West (1937), even of Rudolph Schindler's floating pergolas in the El Pueblo Ribera Court apartments (1924). The Ramada House reinvented the modernist free plan with its structural grid and curved partitions while revealing debts to Alvar Aalto's sensuous use of wood and lime-washed brick. But whatever the "sources," modern or ancient, they were completely absorbed into a work possessing its own internal life and sense of unity. In effect, Chafee here crystallized her guiding vision of the ideal desert dwelling: she aspired toward a type.[2]

Throughout her life, Judith Chafee extended basic ideas from the modern tradition and adjusted them to local circumstances. She rejected facile postmodernism, with its skin-deep historical references, and spurned neomodernist academies with their formalist references.

Chafee dug deeper in search of principles, starting at Yale, where she was strongly influenced by the teaching and buildings of Paul Rudolph, who had himself established a modern tropical regionalism in his Florida houses of the 1950s. Chafee also worked with Edward Larrabee Barnes and Eero Saarinen in the 1960s, both architects combining intellectual rigor and a sense of craft. Her breakthrough building was surely the Merrill House in Guilford, Connecticut, of 1969, an astute fusion of shingle-style reminiscences and a modernist expression of abstract volumes and planes. This building immediately propelled her to fame and was published on the front cover of *Architectural Record* in the mid-May issue of 1970, but Chafee broke with the world of her formal education and departed from the lush landscapes of New England to rediscover herself in the Sonoran Desert of her childhood, with its fierce heat, sparse vegetation, stark geology, and distant horizons. She did not take the forms of the Merrill House with her, but she did transport the underlying principles. She worked along the knife-edge between the local and the general but in an utterly different climate and natural setting.

When one looks back over Judith Chafee's entire oeuvre, one is struck by the uniqueness of each work but also by her consistent ways of thinking, imagining, and designing. She did not possess an obvious signature style, but she did have deeply embedded patterns of visual and spatial organization that informed her overall production even as she invented contrasting designs. These recurrent mental structures and spatial types were rethought in each case so as to solve the unique problems of each site, program, climate, and landscape. In section, her buildings often combine superimposed zones, each with its own character. She refashioned the ground as a domestic landscape of interlocking levels, steps, and shelves, which propel the eye to the surrounding landscape through judiciously placed openings. Interiors were often lit through shaded apertures to the south and high-placed horizontal slots to the north. Chafee's roof forms varied considerably from flat to angled, depending on the surrounding topography, the direction of the wind, the likelihood of rain, and the desired interior character. In her dwellings, Chafee was acutely sensitive to the filtering of light, the provision of shade, and the need to establish spaces with a tranquil mood.

When designing a new project, Judith Chafee immersed herself in the topography and microclimate of each site, walking back and forth like a prospector looking for a source of water with a divining rod. While involved in this deep reading of the site (which no doubt drew upon memories of her times in the Sonoran Desert as a child), she was ever attentive to the changing directions and angles of the sun throughout the seasons of the year, the prevailing breezes in each arroyo or valley, the character of existing vegetation, and the potential views of landscape near and far. In a similar fashion, she digested and analyzed the client's program, seeking out the main connections, the balance between public and private, and the areas of communal gathering. Her plans resemble maps of human relationships or diagrams of family dynamics with variable areas of intensity. Private rooms were established at the perimeter where they offered intimate views onto the small plants, sand, and pebbles of the desert floor, or carefully framed views toward vast panoramas of hills and mountains in the distance. And these interior and exterior spaces were explored over time: there was usually an architectural promenade linking a sequence of perspectives, incidents, and events.

To realize her house designs, Judith Chafee needed clients who were willing to take some aesthetic risks, as her work departed dramatically from the Pueblo Revival–style dwellings that were often built in and around Tucson. Viewpoint, constructed in 1973, was for relatives of Chafee and in a sense was midway in its expression

between the Merrill House and the Ramada. It was a compact plan under horizontal roofs, which were suspended between stepping wall planes at the ends. While the north side admitted light through wide windows and horizontal skylights, the south and east sides were protected by overhanging rectangular "eyebrows" made of concrete. What no photograph can capture is the variety of interior spaces and the harmonic rhythms between horizontal elements at different scales including steps, window ledges, and shelves. Chafee was able to make a small house into an entire world with an aura of its own. It was as if she captured a piece of the desert landscape and then released it here and there between abstract planes. The setting is perceived through a series of carefully framed apertures as in a camera. The experience of nature is intensified.

The Rieveschl Residence (1983–88) was the grandest of Chafee's realizations, a large compound of interlocking concrete frames and horizontal platforms jutting from the hillside and affording spectacular views in all directions.[3] Resting upon a grid of slender cylindrical supports, this dwelling was conceived as a sort of sky house, a continuum of spaces of variable character floating above the sloping terrain. Chafee established a central spine of interior circulation running the entire length of the building. This provided access to private rooms laterally while culminating in the generous and transparent public living areas and open-air terrace at the far end. As in so many of her houses, Chafee orchestrated a ritualistic sequence, which begins with a curved approach by car, then continues into the interior, where it is guided by astute level changes, diverse sources of natural light, and interior perspectives. In effect, the Rieveschl Residence took over the Corbusian themes of the free plan and the architectural promenade and gave them a new charge of meaning. Chafee's curved partitions—whether the rough stone hearth or the fully glazed bar—

responded to the body in space and launched the eye from the interiors toward the horizon. With this symphonic work, Chafee provided her answer to several grand villas in the modern tradition: Le Corbusier's Villa Savoye (1928–31), Mies van der Rohe's Villa Tugenhadt (1928–30), Wright's Fallingwater (1935–37), and Aalto's Villa Mairea (1937–39). These were not overt references; rather, they were part of the artist's internal dialogue with exemplars in her tradition.

Each Chafee house, while unique in spirit and atmosphere, embodied a consistent attitude and ethos. This extended to the use of materials and the design of built-in furniture. Chafee liked to express materials directly, enjoying the interplay between naked concrete, rough timber, clay tiles, glass, and adobe. She rejoiced in the presence of everyday objects, such as tiled bathtubs or heavy wooden doors recalling those of Spanish missions. In her celebration of domestic rituals, she treated kitchen slabs as altars and naked metal extract pipes as cult objects. Her towers and cascades of bookshelves conveyed the air of antique libraries or massive Spanish colonial furniture but through forms nourished by abstract painting and sculpture. The Russell-Randolph Residence of 1983 was constructed from brown adobe brick, while the ceilings combined timber beams and thin struts of dried saguaro. The inherent density of the material was offset by a long clerestory gap admitting a crack of daylight. Wide lower openings were cut through the thick walls, their depth emphasized by massive wooden frames and generous sills. The pièce de résistance was the book tower at the center, a contraption that could have been extracted from a Renaissance painting of a scholar's library. Great attention was devoted throughout to joints and details, such as steps, door frames, shelves, and railings. These established a strong physical presence while reiterating overall themes at a smaller scale.

With each design, Chafee established a clear central idea, then explored the best means of giving it spatial, formal, and material expression. She was always concerned with proportion and the interplay between solids and voids. The off-white textured walls of the Ramada House were expressed as abstract planes sliced off cleanly at the top to distinguish them from traditional masonry punctured by openings bridged by lintels. They were realized in a "slump" concrete block with soft edges and corners giving the feeling of adobe. Transoms and frames in anodized bronze were recessed from wall ends to reinforce the overall theme of weightlessness. These visual effects would have been impossible without the legacy of cubism and abstract art—the floating planes of Piet Mondrian or Gerrit Rietveld for example. Chafee was acutely aware of the inheritance of modern architectural masterpieces, which were here "rethought." In her brief text on the Ramada House she wrote: "The elevation studies used the Modulor of Le Corbusier as a study tool and the problem of solving the relationship between the columnar system and the other building elements returned my thoughts often to the Miesian thinking of the period of the Tugenhadt House and the Barcelona Pavilion."[4]

When I first saw the Ramada House on that key day in early 1984, I had no prior knowledge of the architect. The building spoke to me directly through architectural means, without the intermediary of theories or the impedimenta of movements. When it came to "positioning" or "situating" the Ramada House, I was much interested at the time in ways in which modern architects might respond to local climates, cultures, and traditions. The

first edition of my book *Modern Architecture Since 1900* (1982) had already explored transformations of modernism and regional identity in developing countries.[5] In 1986 I published "Towards an Authentic Regionalism," an article that explored seminal buildings in Mexico, India, and the Middle East attempting to reconcile modern and traditional, local and international. I included Chafee's Ramada House as a rare example of a building in North America embodying just such a synthesis:

> At its worst regionalism may degenerate into a skin-deep instant history in which ersatz images of the vernacular are combined with pastiches of national cultural stereotypes. At its best regionalism penetrates to the generating principles and symbolic substructures of the past then transforms these into forms that are right for the changing social order of the present….The hope is to produce buildings of a certain timeless character which fuse old and new, regional and universal.[6]

The second edition of *Modern Architecture Since 1900* came out in 1987 with an addendum titled "The Search for Substance: Recent World Architecture."[7] As a counter to postmodernism, the essay asserted that the "seminal works of the modern masters touched deep levels in tradition even as they innovated: their lessons continue to be extended, criticised, transformed, regionalized." In this case, the Ramada House was discussed in the company of works such as Balkrishna Doshi's Sangath and Geoffrey Bawa's studio in Sri Lanka. The text leading to the section about Chafee's work declared the following:

> Regionalisms draw sustenance from the aboriginal wisdom and craft of peasant vernaculars, even when these are fast disappearing; they also try to deal with the extremes of climate through direct architectural means. Even in some advanced industrial nations there are pockets of regionalist

consciousness which hold out against cosmopolitan fashion. These tend to occur at the fringes where native habitats are still visible even if native culture has been undermined. In these circumstances the best work eschews direct imitation and uses abstraction to go deeper.[8]

The third revised edition of *Modern Architecture Since 1900* was published in 1996. An entirely new part IV, "Continuity and Change in the Late Twentieth Century," explored the notion of a modern tradition as a delta with different streams. It concentrated upon seminal buildings that provided convincing architectural solutions to general problems of the time while achieving long-term quality. Chafee's Ramada House appeared in the new chapter 34, "The Universal and the Local: Landscape, Climate and Culture," alongside later buildings, such as the Koshino House in Japan by Tadao Ando, the President's House for Illustrious Guests in Colombia by Rogelio Salmona, and the Ball-Eastway House in Australia by Glenn Murcutt. The text insisted upon the power of individual works to transcend movements and crystallize fresh visions while returning to fundamentals:

> Theoretical post (and pre-) rationalizations are one thing, works giving shape to ideas, insights and intentions, another…The Ramada House in Tucson, Arizona by Judith Chafee combined the space, structure and abstraction of modernism with a recall of ancient methods for dealing with the hot dry desert climate and fierce sunlight of the American Southwest…Chafee rejected the term "regionalist" as too limiting: the Ramada House captured the spirit of a place using means from near and far, interpreted natural conditions through the inheritance of myth, and engaged with the very idea of architectural origins.[9]

Early Practice

Essay by Christopher Domin

From the start, Judith Chafee (1932–1998) threw elbows with some of the most significant architects of the twentieth century. Her education at Yale University with architect Paul Rudolph, a thesis adviser, came at a momentous time when the best of a generation gathered in New Haven to debate the future of architecture. Thriving in this competitive male-dominated environment, Chafee established herself in the Northeast and practiced for a decade in the offices of Walter Gropius, Sarah Harkness, and Ben Thompson at The Architects Collaborative; Kevin Roche and John Dinkeloo at Eero Saarinen and Associates; Edward Larrabee Barnes; and Paul Rudolph. In 1969 she broke away and soon found recognition for her early design projects, as well as a fellowship at the American Academy in Rome, with Charles Eames as resident director. Her inaugural independent project landed on the cover of *Architectural Record* in 1970—the first Record House Award cover to feature the architecture of a woman. [1]

During her first decade of independent practice, Chafee became celebrated for her finely tuned buildings carefully situated in iconic desert landscapes. These houses brought form to priorities that are now widely embodied by the sustainability community and mindful designers worldwide. A close reading of Chafee's early training and built work provides a unique understanding of the making of architecture that is both regional and far-reaching—an architecture that leverages limitations to stimulate an identity.

Chafee's creative and industrious energy was not limited to architecture. She was also a productive poet throughout her life, played the piano, and composed elaborate meals for friends, guests, and clients alike. In her writing Chafee found inspiration in quotidian moments and often elevated daily routine to ritual importance as she did in her architecture through the careful creation of space, modulation of light, and recognition of regional intelligence.

Migrations

Judith Chafee began her life as Judith Davidson in Chicago, the only child of Christina Affeld Davidson (1901–1992) and Dr. Percy B. Davidson (1895–1932). Affeld and Davidson married in 1928, during an optimistic moment in their lives just before the Great Depression. At the time, her mother framed marriage in these egalitarian terms:

> Men today do not expect a woman to submerge her personality when she marries. I think that I owe it to myself and to cultivate my mind all that I can…I can satisfy my inner urge best by studying and improving myself.[2]

Christina began college at the University of Wisconsin, Madison, majoring in English and playwriting under Professor A. Eustis Hayden, who also held the position of visiting pastor at the Unitarian Church in Madison. Christina left the University of Wisconsin in her junior year to focus on a stage-acting career, which led to a leading role with Lionel Barrymore and significant press dedicated to her subsequent dramatic roles. After her marriage to Davidson, the couple continued an active schedule of work and life in Cambridge, Massachusetts, under increasingly difficult financial burdens. Christina matriculated at Radcliffe College to study anthropology and continued writing and directing plays for regional theater productions. Percy, who had previously been an instructor at the University of Wisconsin, practiced in Boston and had an instructor position at Harvard Medical School as well as clinical posts at several institutions where he focused on tuberculosis and gastrointestinal research. In an essay for the *Annals of Medical History*, he positioned current social issues within a historical framework:

> There are periods in the history of any science when not only the various theories and procedures must be re-evaluated, but when the science itself must be the object of pragmatic procedure. In an era, such as the present, characterized by

a shifting of methods of study of disease from the mechanical approach of a century ago, through the microörganism of more recent times, and the recent chemical attitude, one might, with advantage, look back upon the history of the science as well as the art of medicine, not only for the purpose of orientation but also for prediction of its ultimate development. Further, in the age of essential utilitarianism, when medical education is becoming reduced to a clock-work procedure in many instances, one might do well to speculate upon how best to reconcile the training of a highly efficient physician with the attributes of a man of culture. The study of the life of a great physician, philosopher, humanitarian, scholar, and classicist may assist us in formulating a more satisfactory point of view.[3]

Judith's father's essay focuses on the art and science of a discipline in a way that would indeed strike a chord with the future architect, who often embodied this duality through her concomitant interests in philosophy, humanism, and classical studies. Percy balanced a busy schedule of academic and clinical work at multiple hospitals and universities in the Boston area for five years. Just before his death in 1932 at age thirty-nine, he accepted a position as an associate professor of medicine at Tufts University, with a slate of research articles soon to be published. The peripatetic schedule that often kept the couple apart

Christina Affeld Bloom and Benson Bloom, Tucson, Arizona, 1930s

Judith D. Bloom's childhood in Tucson, Arizona, 1930s

stabilized with the new position, but when Percy underwent what appeared to be a routine appendectomy, a more complicated diagnosis emerged. He died soon after surgery, just months before he would have met his new daughter. Instead of focused planning for a new baby in the spring of 1932, Christina Davidson laid plans for a funeral, which took place in Boston. Numerous condolence letters arrived afterward that illustrated the substantial impact that Percy Davidson made on the profession of medicine during his short career. The shock of Percy's death and single parenthood necessitated a move back to Chicago for Christina, where she and baby Judith could be closer to family and a strong social network.

Christina and Judith spent the waning years of the Great Depression in Chicago and its suburbs, with mother and infant adapting to circumstances beyond their control. As the economy was showing signs of recovery, Christina met a young Johns Hopkins University School of Medicine graduate named Benson Bloom (1901–1985), who was establishing his medical career as an intern at Michael Reese Hospital, an institution well-known for research and teaching, located in the Near South Side of Chicago. In 1929 Benson also began a relationship with the Desert Sanatorium in Tucson at the request of Dr. Allen Krause, and the next year he returned as

physician-in-charge of sanatorium patients and thirteen interns. Bloom, himself a tuberculosis survivor and pulmonary pathologist, helped others find relief from respiratory ailments. At that time, well-heeled patients sought relief from respiratory diseases in Tucson's dry and cool nights.

Christina and Benson's marriage ceremony in Tucson signaled a strong commitment from both partners to their new home in Arizona. Judith D. Bloom, now a part of the Bloom family, moved to Tucson as a young girl in 1934. The family soon came to embrace the Sonoran Desert with a passion akin to religious fervor.

Many transplants from Chicago, like Judith's family, settled in Tucson during the 1930s and created a community steeped in progressive ideas that were shared by neighbors from other locales. As Chafee's stepfather continued work at the Desert Sanatorium, her mother, applying her training in anthropology, immersed the family in the indigenous culture of the place, along with New Deal politics and programs. The family became part of a community of medical professionals and academics linked to the University of Arizona, which functioned as a progressive cultural satellite for the recent arrivals. The Bloom family linked their political agenda with a keen interest in modern design that embraced the vernacular building heritage of the region.[4] They assembled a community that easily crossed over established boundaries while forming a new social collective that confronted the civil rights issues that plagued Tucson as much as other regions in the country. As a physical expression of this, the Affeld / Bloom family purchased, expanded, and brightly painted the interior of a two-story adobe with cobalt-blue floors on Martin Avenue, which they named Casa Colorida. The house is located along the arroyos of the Catalina Foothills in the Richland Heights neighborhood where Judith spent her childhood under the close direction of her mother. In this context, a primary-school-aged Judith learned how to make adobe

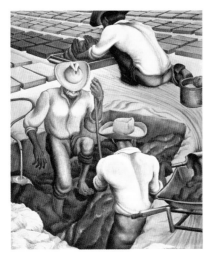

Adobe Makers,
painting,
M. P. Ventres

natural (as a girl) to be involved in building. My mother didn't have a sexist point of view; quite the contrary. She would send me out to help make bricks.[5]

The family quickly connected with other progressively minded transplants including activist and Planned Parenthood founder Margaret Sanger, who moved permanently to Arizona in the late 1930s. A combination of desert empiricism, intellectual curiosity, and social activism provided an early education in life essentials and a toolbox of strategies for the future. As a writer, she looked back on her Tucson childhood:

> My perception of what should be built in the desert stems from having grown up in the desert. I grew up going up and down arroyos and knowing where it was cool and where the breezes blew.
>
> We would spend a lot of time at Old Pasqua, spent a lot of time at San Xavier; we would go to the state museum. There was a lot of talk in my childhood home about traditional cultures here and respect for them.[6]

Tucson is among the oldest continuously inhabited areas in the United States. Migration through the Santa Cruz River Valley dates to circa 10,000 BCE, and evidence of agricultural settlement near central Tucson exists from 1,000 BCE. Development of the modern city center aligns with the completion of the Presidio, a fortress built by the Spanish in the late 1700s, the Gadsden Purchase (1854), and the arrival of the transcontinental railroad (1880). From 1867 to 1877, Tucson was the territorial capital of the region, and during this period building in the city center expanded. Desert scholar Joseph Wood Krutch wrote about the Tucson environs and the unique qualities of the desert:

> On the brightest and warmest days my desert is most itself because sunshine and warmth are the very essence of its character.

blocks by hand, which the family used to expand their home, and spent hours playing and exploring the arroyos in the surrounding neighborhood. The desert arroyos around her house became an exploratory playground where plants and animals revealed the mystery of survival in this harsh environment. These lessons of the Sonoran Desert were formative experiences that helped Chafee negotiate the complex vicissitudes of her life. Chafee remembered the following:

> It was one of those wonderful old Tucson houses where a room or two got added every year. It changed all the time. I could come home from school, and my mother would be moving the kitchen to another room. It gave me an attitude about being freewheeling instead of having false, formal images in the house.
>
> It was also a very modern house. It didn't look like other people's houses. It was not cutesy. The bare concrete floor, the modern furniture…There was a north patio where you could have violets, and on the west my mother built huge ramadas. One was very aware of the house's relationship to the climate.
>
> Building the house was the most interesting thing going on…There weren't other kids in the neighborhood making things. Also, it never occurred to me that it wasn't completely

Margaret Sanger at Bloom family birthday, Tucson, Arizona

In this country "inclemency" means heat. One is "sunbound" instead of snowbound and I have often noticed that the psychological effect is curiously similar. It is cozy to be shut in, to have a good excuse for looking out of the window or into oneself. A really blazing day slows down the restless activity of a community very much as a blizzard does in regions that have them. Without one or the other any society, I imagine, would become intolerably extroverted. Where there is either, a sort of meteorological sabbath is usually observed even by those who keep no other.[7]

The building culture in southern Arizona has invariably been a hybrid construct, drawing on a range of sources, from the design of Hohokam settlements that upheld contact with trading partners in the Yucatán Peninsula to influences of the transcontinental railroad, which increased dialogue along the east-west route of travel. The early part of the twentieth century brought a new influx of people, ideas, and financial capital to the Tucson region, as people gravitated to the Sonoran Desert for its climate and as a respite for respiratory ailments. Tent cities emerged north of the University of Arizona, and more permanent settlements established themselves around facilities like the Desert Sanatorium at the eastern edge of town and St. Mary's Hospital and Convent to the west.

In 1935, Benson Bloom entered private practice with Paul Holbrook and Donald Hill, and built an office in a newly developed medical center in the neighborhood adjacent to the luxurious Arizona Inn. Many of his early patients became friends for life and partners in the fight for social justice.[8] During this period, he was often called to the Arizona Inn to see guests in need of medical care, but as a Jew, even though from a prominent family, Bloom was required to enter through the kitchen to see his patients, an indignity that continued well into the 1960s. It was intimately clear to the Bloom family that the battle for civil rights was not complete. Christina became involved in reproductive-rights debates through contacts in Benson's medical community and through her friendship with activist Margaret Sanger (1879–1966). Sanger worked professionally with Bloom and was a frequent guest at their home, including at birthday celebrations for Judith and her new half-sister, Janet. Sanger would include the Bloom family in gatherings she hosted for dignitaries, including Eleanor Roosevelt and Frank Lloyd Wright, who made a strong impression on a young Judith.

The Blooms were also involved in school desegregation efforts in Tucson, with Judith and Janet attending neighborhood public schools. Christina was elected to the local school board and soon discovered that the schools did not meet the rigorous academic expectations of the family. Consequently, Judith was sent to the Francis W. Parker School in Chicago, Christina's alma mater, to complete high school. Parker School, as it was referred to, modeled itself on the ideas of education reformer John Dewey, who espoused a program of instruction based on the relevance of empiricism, primary source material, and social equity. Judith's life of action and learning through doing first took root in the politically engaged community of Tucson in the 1930s and 1940s; it continued logically into the milieu of Chicago's Hull House, and the legacy of activist Jane Addams, which acted as a pedagogical extension of Parker School for Judith and her cohort.

Parker School

At Parker School, Judith, or Judy Bloom, as she was known on campus, joined the newspaper staff, becoming an editor in her final semester. She spent many hours working on the production, layout, and written content of the publication, giving her an excellent introduction to publishing and printing houses. During her time at Parker, Judith boarded with different sets of married teachers. A letter from one, requesting that she get back at a respectable hour, called out behavior that her hosts found challenging but that seemed perfectly normal to Judith, having lived a somewhat unrestrained and precocious childhood in the Southwest. She enjoyed going to jazz clubs and sociopolitical lectures—it was in this context that she learned about and became a lifelong fan of Paul Robeson for his art and his politics. Her time in Chicago was formative.

The final Parker School academic year was perennially busy with schoolwork, extracurricular projects, and college board exams. Judith's college applications focused on two selections, Bennington College on the East Coast and Reed College on the West Coast, at a time of significant change at both institutions. During the application process, Judy became enraged that school counselors shared students' religious affiliation with the colleges because she knew that the review process was not wholly merit based; most institutions placed a cap on the number of Jewish students admitted to each class. After this experience and other altercations with Parker School's administration stemming from her work on the school paper, Judith celebrated graduation day by excoriating the principal with a final salvo, "Fuck you Mr. Smith."[9] Thankfully, she was accepted at both schools, chose the Bennington offer, and decided to spend that summer interning at the Hull House, perhaps feeling the continued influence of Margaret Sanger. At eighteen years old, she began to strike out on her own with ideas that expanded upon early influences. A new generation was taking over at Hull House, and it focused on the economic and racial inequality in Chicago's neighborhoods, such as the Near West Side, with educational and recreational programs including art and music that were well suited to Judith's education and avocations.

Francis W. Parker
School, high school
graduation, Judith
Bloom, middle row,
fourth from left, 1950

Bennington College

Now known as Judith Bloom, she matriculated during the fall semester of 1950 at Bennington College in Vermont. She quickly integrated into an activist community, even traveling in September to Pittsfield, Massachusetts, to help the Congress of Industrial Organizations, a federation of unions of industrial workers, with an election. At the meeting, the workers and students sang union songs while bonding over a common cause. That first semester she registered for classes in piano, music theory, literature, and art history, including the Language of Visual Arts, taught by Alexander Dorner (1893–1957), who became a mentor and friend. At the end of November, faculty comments were delivered including this observation from Francis Golffing, the language and literature instructor: "An excellent student; her mind seems to be capable of both force and subtlety, and she writes unusually well for a freshman." And this evaluation from Professor George Holt in the painting studio: "Judith has worked well and made real advance. She exhibits imagination and independence in her painting and is gaining technical skill. She tends to take criticism in a negative rather than constructive way; that it is a method designed to hurt rather than to help." That year English historian Edward Carr visited the campus to speak on his work *The Twenty Years' Crisis*. Judith found him to be "perfectly magnificent," and said he "spanked us all gently and made complete fools of everyone who talked fight in Korea and war in Europe." Even though she still had reservations about her choice of college, life at Bennington was rich with new experience, its faculty engaged, and the decidedly intellectual culture of the Northeast was thrilling and immersive. Thus, Judith ignored ongoing efforts by Reed College to lure her away from Bennington.

Her artwork at this time often referred back to southern Arizona. When painting, she could not bring herself to depict scenes from her new base in Vermont. Tucson flora and fauna prevailed in her paintings and prints. Adobe building was an essential link to the culture of Tucson that set the region apart from Chicago and the Northeast, and Judith continued to explore its primal impact on her identity through writing and art projects. In her childhood home of Casa Colorida hung a painting by M. P. Ventres titled *Adobe Makers*, which inspired the reverence of Judith's entire family, along with paintings by Maynard Dixon and a portrait of Dixon by Ansel Adams. The cadre of artists created a new narrative for the life the family was composing in the West and its intimate place in the landscape.

Working on assignments with poet Howard Nemerov (1920–1991) at Bennington, Judith mined her personal family history for inspiration. In her poem "Jesu Fimbres," Judith evokes both the romantic and the pragmatic reality of her Casa Colorida:

The heavy timbers Jesu Fimbres bore brought us to him.
Fort Little, which had held the land for white men in its prime,
was coming down and Jesu Fimbres owned the ancient wreck,
that ancient monument to days when even trees were better built.
He dragged its massive beams through land which now stands desolate
and dry, which cannot force such greatness from earth that's turned to die.
His wood was many men's lengths long and many men's hands wide,
about a man's head deep, and was the skeleton of home.

So Fimbres' twelve men came in different colors of faded blue,
each garment bought on different days in different months and years.
The Levis were the same [as] the blue shirts all from Sears, the men
all golden brown from birth and men from being Mexican.
They made a great hole in the earth and ran the water in
so that the thirsty ground could drink and show its strength again.
Then proud to see the earth content, they rolled their blue pants up,
their fiercely kind legs mixed the mud and forced the water to
each dusty particle until the brown of calf and mud
were one great plastic surge of life and ready to be bound.
Now golden bands of straw were scattered through the dark and raw
adobe, pushed down by dexterous feet—then forced up by them—
when, being thoroughly involved, there was no place to go but up.

Then even mud and glistening straw was thrown by shovelful
into the waiting wheelbarrow above, and carried off
a little way to dry earth now perused by the maestro.
He had laid a ladder on the ground so that its four large steps
ran horizontally from ladder end to ladder end,
all even on the sweetly swept and blotter-like dry earth.
The maestro's hands now dipping in the barrow judge by length
of proud experience, that brought him up to the maestro's rank,
the just amount of mud to fill each ladder's step—without
the air he slowly kneads from it until—each inch itself—
it firmly fills that step. The next step and the next and next
his clay-cleansed hands knead out in just proportionality.

Admiring eyes watch anxiously to see
The magic of the maestro as he hesitates—
Then shakes the mold spasmodically, and lifting at that time
he leaves the raw adobe firm and free.
His great mosaic stretches on
for half an acre in successive tone of drying brown.
The fading browns as numerous as faded blues,
on the brown men who made them, show the different minutes they
were offered to the sun to strengthen and solidify.

When, baked for days, the blocks were light in weight—so light to see
that they belonged in color to the dusty earth they were,
the peons of the earth and masters among men again
took up their tender labor, cared still for the infant house;
began to set adobe on the earthen blueprint, marked
by sticks, and strings, and trenches lined with silvery concrete.
The trowel in the gritty mortar scraped and shrieked when spread
upon the then laid brick to bind it with the weight its kin
persistently enforced from just above—and many rows'
heights hence. The loving wall grew peacefully caressed by hands
that smoothed the mud and loved the imperfections of the fleshy
roundness and hollows, loved them as they loved their own.

The walls all raised up on the thorny desert now—the twelve
with Fimbres' signal strained to lift the timbers from the ground.
A human throne, they weighed the timbers to the dobe top,
and resting there they told where sky would end—where human life
begin[s]. They lifted more wood up and crossed it with itself,
and called their crosses beams, and nailed less sturdy stuff to them
'til underneath—completely separated from above—
was house and ready to begin the job of being home.

La Casa Colorida, the house of many colors,
radiant as Maria's face, generous giver of warmth—
'Til last year, Jesu Fimbres died, we stiffened and moved out.
And when you come into [a] house salute it,
and if the house be worthy let your peace
come upon it; but if it be not worthy
let your peace return to you.[10]

Century Plant,
by Judith Bloom,
Bennington
College, 1952

While Judith idealized her home in Tucson, relations at Casa Colorida were fraying. After the first year in Vermont, letters from Judith's mother began to arrive from Northfield, Illinois. Christina had left Tucson, and Benson Bloom, with Judith's younger sister Janet in tow, and returned to the Chicago area where she would soon begin a career at Carson Pirie Scott in the contract interiors department. The family stayed in touch through active and candid letter writing—each playing a part in the quickly developing installments of each other's lives. In March 1952, Judith shared an update with her mother indicating her continued respect for Dorner and his encouragement of her architectural studies at Bennington:

> The Sunday after I got here I went over to the Dorners' house and talked to him about my ideas for a major. He was very pleased and excited about them. He wanted me to take his current course—"Art and Science"—which I am now doing. I was very pleased to see how much of Dorner I have learned since I last worked with him simply by thinking about it and letting it soak in on its good old time.
>
> Dorner felt strongly that I should keep up my work with Kessler (Architecture and Design Studio). He also, by the way, wants me to speak with Hudnut or Gropius about my plans the next time I go to Cambridge.

Dorner had known Walter Gropius in Germany and stayed in close contact when Gropius moved to Harvard. Joseph Hudnut was the inaugural dean of the Graduate School of Design at Harvard and was instrumental in bringing European modernists to the institution, including Gropius and Marcel Breuer. With Dorner's encouragement and counsel, Judith continued developing architectural and design skills along with a broader education in the arts, literature, and museum studies. During this period, Bennington was gathering a healthy cohort of young faculty and immigrant intellectuals from Europe who had fled Nazi Germany. The college was transforming from its previous incarnation as finishing school to a site of cultural change and a center of intellectual and artistic production. Judith and her friends groused about the recent presidential election where Dwight Eisenhower won a landslide victory over their candidate, Adlai Stevenson. At Bennington, work progressed with Alexander Dorner, but also expanded into painting with Paul Feeley and more poetry with Nemerov. Judith now had three core advisers, and she attempted to gather all her influences into an integrated senior project, which began to coalesce around a professional interest in architecture and design.

Bloom often traveled to Chicago during breaks from Bennington to visit family and friends. During one of these trips, she met Zachary LeBolt (1915–2016), an engineer who was several years older, and the two would visit the Art Institute and attend the theater and social gatherings of writers and artists linked to the University of Chicago.[11] Unexpectedly, Judith became pregnant. With her deep childhood connection to Margaret Sanger, issues surrounding reproductive options were, no doubt, clear in her mind, but Judith decided on her own to proceed with the pregnancy and prepare for an adoption. During the spring of 1954, she completed a nonresident independent term in Boston, where she would give birth to a daughter. With the help of close family friend Ruth Merrill in Manhattan and Lydia and Alexander Dorner at Bennington, she continued her studies during the pregnancy, and prepared for adoption with the Boston Children's Friend Society. Because of the ongoing schedule of classes at Bennington, she was able to keep the pregnancy secret from her family. With great care, she outlined criteria for the adoptive family. She decided they must be professionals, well educated, interested in the arts, and nonreligious. The decision to give up her daughter for adoption was a pragmatic one, but would haunt Judith for the rest of her life. Adoption records were sealed during this period, and there was no chance for mother and daughter to meet.[12]

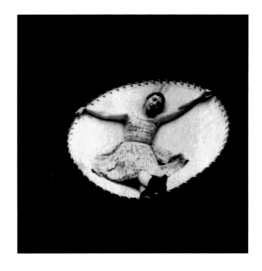

Gap Years

After overcoming numerous obstacles during her final year, Judith graduated from Bennington on time in 1954 with the help of her trifecta of advisers. She moved to a small rented apartment near St. Mark's Church in New York City, near Ruth Merrill, who was a short walk away. Judith pursued work in publishing and art production during this period, which was a typical rite of passage for graduates with strong liberal arts training, such as that from Bennington. Judith continued her design education with Alexey Brodovitch at the New School, who offered curriculum dedicated to design conception and technique. This course of study included such topics as advertising layout, contemporary furniture design, and interior display. Brodovitch's European- and Bauhaus-inflected curriculum logically expanded upon Judith's studies with Dorner at Bennington, and Brodovitch put Judith in close contact with leading design and publishing offices through his extensive network in the city. During this period, she worked in a small product-design office that included pasteup, layout, and toy design, along with architectural and interior design projects. Longing to remain in studio practice, she apprenticed to a furniture designer and honed skills in wrought-iron welding and woodworking. She, along with Ruth Merrill, also studied at the New School with sculptor Seymour Lipton, who integrated his interest in surrealism with the language of abstract expressionism. The sculptor shared with the students his material techniques for wood, clay, and stone, as well as his love of bronze casting, in a way that confronted both the how and why of a creative work.

A chair, which Judith designed during her tenure at Bennington, again became a focus during this period of her life and eventually culminated in a US government patent. The first working prototype captured the keen interest of Dorner to such an extent that he recommended to the art faculty that 150 chairs be produced for use at the school. Significant progress ensued during the post-Bennington period in Manhattan, where Judith balanced work on her own projects with what she described as "continuous work experience." In fact, this iterative development of related chair drawings and prototypes seemed to be the central creative focus of her life outside of employment in the New York design industry in the mid-1950s. The seed was planted at Bennington for multiple chair iterations that Chafee would learn and grow with for the next three years. She first developed small-scale wire and paper models, then transitioned into construction drawings, and, finally, executed the first full-scale prototype in welded iron and fabric. Another prototype of the chair focused on cast fiberglass construction techniques. A personal photo album from this period features a series of candid photographs, including one of her mother posing in a fiberglass shell chair, an image of friend Jim Campbell in a steel and canvas version set on a broad lawn, and Judith Bloom enthusiastically embracing her new creation. Ideas gleaned from making the first full-scale physical models sparked conversations with a consultant about pricing, materials, and methods of production. Judith cited the introduction of a financier with an experimental laboratory equipped for making more complete full-scale

Tilt Chair

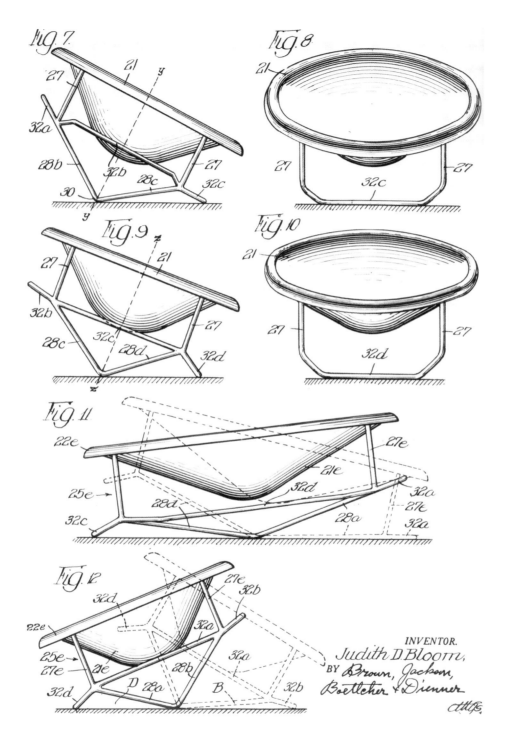

30

models. As work extended into 1956, drawings, photographs, renderings, and text were gathered for a patent attorney in Washington, DC.

In Chicago, Christina Bloom's reintegration was now complete, and she accepted the position of chief home fashion coordinator at Carson Pirie Scott, with an emphasis on the Scandinavian collection. Christina embarked on a new independent phase of her life and career in charge of curating the store's modern collection and designing interiors for clients. She regretted not studying architecture but harnessed a lifetime of related skills along with an impeccable fashion sense; with this, she created a new reputation in the Chicago scene as a respected designer of interior environments that combined elements from large to small, with antique to modern Scandinavian design elements.

With the encouragement of friends and family, Judith applied to architecture school at the Cooper Union for the Advancement of Science and Art, and Yale University. After being accepted at both institutions, Judith, then twenty-three years old, matriculated at Yale University School of Architecture at an auspicious time in its development as a program.

Yale University

Long under the shadow of Harvard's Graduate School of Design and its by-then-retired chair Walter Gropius, Yale School of Architecture was entering a phase of renewed vigor and inventive curricular development. By the time of Judith's matriculation, many significant architects gathered around the school in New Haven, including Louis Kahn, Edward Larrabee Barnes, John Johansen, Philip Johnson, Peter Millard, Paul Mitarachi, James Stirling, and Paul Rudolph. Because of a change in the admissions office, some gender diversity could be seen in the undergraduate School of Architecture student cohort of 1954. Four women were admitted, which was a significant number for Yale.

During the initial semester, a party was organized to welcome the first-year design students. Prominent faculty attended, including Philip Johnson, Louis Kahn, and Vincent Scully. Kahn delivered a slideshow of his current work, with a response from Johnson and Scully. Students found Johnson to be pompous, elitist, and dismissive of student comments. Scully linked Kahn's work to Greek and Egyptian precedent, and both agreed that architects should focus on the public realm and enter into city planning debates instead of focusing on single-family houses. Judith described Scully in a letter to her mother as the "favorite art historian here, a rigorous slob, but still a slob." The speculation among students was that Kahn would soon be announced as the new leader of the architecture school, but this would not come to fruition. Focusing on her studies, Judith threw herself into studio work every night on the top floor of the Yale University Art Gallery designed by Kahn, often staying until the building closed.[13]

Paul Rudolph began his first full-time academic position as the Yale School of Architecture department chair in 1958. To his advantage, he took leadership of a program in which he was already a visiting design critic and where he was highly respected by the students.[14]

When Rudolph arrived, the program was in transition; he reorganized the visiting faculty roster and reinvigorated the design studio. The new leadership offered what some students viewed as the ideal dual-natured architectural education in the hands of two skilled educators: Louis Kahn and Paul Rudolph. Yale graduate David Niland observed the following:

> Kahn was a poet, he was a metaphysicist, he spoke about architecture as if it were a religion. He was interested in meaning, in the symbolic content, and [in the] impact of architecture. Rarely could you get him to talk specifically about how he was trying to implement. It was very broad, and almost had a kind of personalized morality to it that was very stimulating but also very frustrating for students because as any student I wanted to know how he did it. I wanted the key. Rudolph, on the other hand, I considered and still do consider to be the absolute genius of architectural tactics and architectural techniques—I am talking about design techniques.[15]

During third year, faculty member James Stirling defined the program for a hotel in New Haven, and architect Mies van der Rohe led a two-week sketch problem for a small office building in an urban context. As this cohort advanced in the program with increasingly professional drawing and model building skills, select students in the school of architecture, including Judith Bloom, James McNeely, and Stanley Tigerman, would also work for Rudolph's office during the night and evening hours as deadlines increased for Rudolph's rapidly expanding practice. This experience allowed the students to pull the curtain back and understand more about Rudolph's personal definition of architectural practice and how the life and work of an architect like Rudolph were inseparable.

Next semester, Judith became a student of studio leader Paul Mitarchi who thought that she was a "good student, very serious, dedicated to architecture." Third year included enhanced technical content, and Mitarachi emphasized what he called "social architecture." Projects included a housing problem, a church, and a hospital competition sponsored by Koppers Company. Architect Paul Nelson was invited as a guest critic and hospital expert, based on his reconstruction work in France and his later hospital competition projects that balanced functional concerns with larger issues of architecture and urban design.[16] Judith's studio project won a hospital design award from Koppers and was later published with other winners from across the country.

Along with her forthright design prowess, Judith was known as an exceptional cook. She hosted dinner parties in New Haven that attracted students and faculty alike. Her custom-made western clothes and canine companion Zeus left a memorable impression on the Yale community for years.[17] In her third year at Yale, Judith D. Bloom became Judith D. Chafee, after her marriage to fellow architecture student Richard Spofford Chafee. With little time for a honeymoon, Chafee could soon be found again in the School of Architecture design studios. From the lived perspective of many students, the location on the fourth floor of Kahn's Yale University Art Gallery Building was ideal. Studios were open and spacious, and the museum's innovative cast-in-place triangulated roof looming above the desks seemed to personify many of Kahn's potent provocations about structure, program, and materiality. Fellow students in Chafee's graduating baccalaureate class of 1960 were fortunate to have Rudolph directing their thesis projects and Kahn offering a master class in the studio adjacent to their first-year studio. Overhearing Kahn's master class was, for some of those undergraduates, an education in itself. This training, bookended with Kahn lecturing about essential conditions of architecture at the beginning of the program and Rudolph coordinating design techniques and urban planning in the final semesters, provided a rich and varied intellectual scaffolding.[18]

During the thesis year, Rudolph's skill as an educator and leader of the program became evident in the work of Chafee's cohort. For the first time in Rudolph's tenure as program chair, he oversaw the direction of the baccalaureate thesis studio. Students in the class of 1960 were encouraged by this personal attention and excited about the prospect of developing their own site and program for the final project, which included the US Embassy for Afghanistan (James McNeely), the Shakespearean Theatre for Central Park (Tim Prentice), the Apartment Tower in Chicago (Stanley Tigerman), and the Building for the Visual Arts at Bennington College

(Judith Chafee). Students could expect at least one formal desk critique from Rudolph each week during the development phase of the project. Chafee's colleague James McNeely vividly remembers the experience:

I had my first [thesis] crit from Rudolph and was bowled over by the eloquence, the understanding, the perspicacity of the man. He set my head spinning over the ground he could cover in a few minutes. Most important of all, he taught me a methodology for studying the problem— listing all possible alternatives in plan and section at the tiniest scale (but not inaccurately) and checking off various ones for various advantages. Obviously, in this way he gets through the entire conceptual stage of the problem very quickly. It seems very important not to bog down at this point—to try everything very quickly. Why do I move along so slowly on my own? Now I must begin the quest for detailed knowledge of (1) soil moving and retaining walls, (2) pre-cast concrete details, (3) plans of Middle Eastern compounds, i.e., Khorsabad, Persepolis, Pataliputra.[19]

A photo of Chafee's final undergraduate thesis review shows Rudolph and Johnson at the center. On the far left is Jean Paul Carlhian, principal at Shepley Bulfinch Richardson and Abbott. The juror hidden behind Chafee is Henry Pfsisterer, former program chair in the Yale School of Architecture and Rudolph's structural engineer for several of his significant buildings during the 1960s. Chafee's project integrated an existing campus road into a pedestrian circulation path through the building flanked by large open studio spaces, which allowed for ample daylighting. Massive walls to the east and west define the edge of the studio modules. The entire composition culminates in a smaller wing that steps down the hillside, effectively allowing the campus to extend beyond its existing boundary. Chafee is highlighted in a series of photos from her

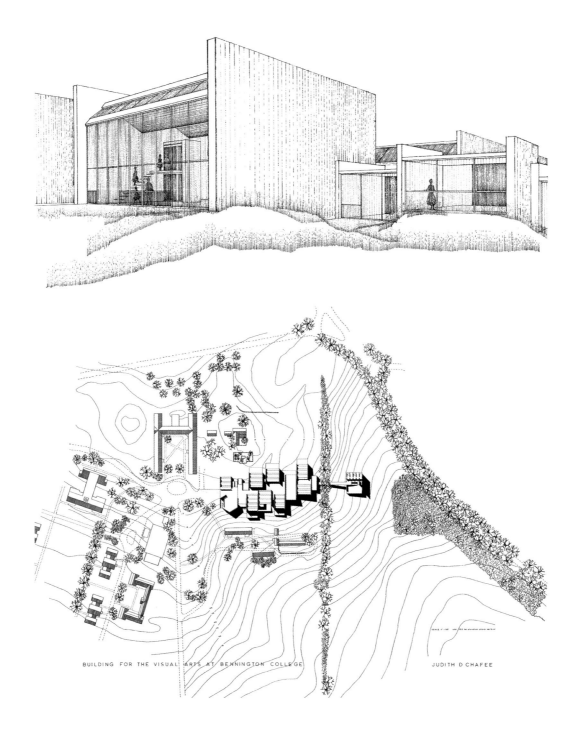

Building for the
Visual Arts at
Bennington College,
Yale School of
Architecture
Baccalaureate
Thesis Project (left)
and Thesis Review,
(opposite), 1960

BUILDING FOR THE VISUAL ARTS AT BENNINGTON COLLEGE   JUDITH D CHAFEE

Contextual Modernism

After graduation Chafee remained at Rudolph's firm and worked on the development of the Yale University Art and Architecture Building and Married Student Housing during grueling studio *charettes*. Later she was named job captain for a residential project in Baltimore, which required her to select and then coordinate with the engineering consultants and to lead the design development process. Chafee took charge of delivering the contract documents on time and ready for construction.[20] As the only woman in her graduating class and one of the few in the professional office setting, it is not surprising that she would often work from her New Haven apartment away from the male-dominated culture of the studio.

In seeking more stable employment, Chafee expanded her search to include larger offices in New Haven and Cambridge, including The Architects Collaborative (TAC), which was started by Gropius and a younger generation of architects. She visited the Gropius House during her tenure at Bennington and wrote about the experience:

thesis review armed with the tools of the architect and taking questions from the distinguished panel. Her face reveals a range of emotions from triumphant satisfaction to dejected frustration. The final semester review was a grand event in the school and was well attended by students and an elite group of guest critics—formidable practitioners from Boston, New York, and London. Fellow student Stanley Tigerman, who documented the final review process through candid snapshot photography, remembers Chafee as a talented designer and that Rudolph offered high praise for her thesis project. Chafee chose to reside in New Haven after graduation, which allowed her to work with Rudolph in a professional capacity as she charted a course for the next phase in her life and work.

A brilliant Autumn afternoon and a feeling of widespread belonging, outsinging the Volkswagen with a loudly-belted-out, old Paul Robeson song— "and the little bridge at Concord where [freedom's] light began." Then an exuberant turn towards the Gropius house where I was picking up a friend. Walter Gropius came across the lawn with a beautiful white skyrocketing chrysanthemum which he pressed into my hands. "I used to be too shy to give flowers to girls," he said. Halfway across the yard I was grabbed abruptly and sternly stared to silence so that we might observe some particularly prized bird visitor. Inside the front door on the stairs, just at eye level, a crystal bowl of flowers sat strangely and powerfully supervising the space.[21]

Because of her respect for Gropius's work at the Bauhaus, Chafee reached out to the firm for an interview.

36

Also, in the summer of 1962, Judith's husband, Richard Chafee, departed for Germany on a research trip, at a time when the couple was growing apart and the two were beginning to lead separate lives, which culminated later in divorce proceedings.[22] Judith accepted a job in Cambridge with TAC and started work on academic projects for Radcliffe College and Brandeis University. She also worked on an unbuilt restaurant design for the Pan Am Building (now the MetLife building) in New York, which was in the final phase of construction.[23]

In the office, Chafee's mentor was Sarah Harkness (1914–2013), who became a lifelong friend and coteacher in design studios at both MIT and the University of Arizona. With her home base still in the New Haven area, Chafee spent one year in Cambridge before returning to Connecticut for a position at Eero Saarinen and Associates in nearby Hamden. Kevin Roche and John Dinkeloo were now in charge of the office after Saarinen's death. Saarinen had a close connection with Alexander and Lydia Dorner, which made this office a logical setting for Chafee. The working process in the Saarinen studio provided a strong education in rigorous technical practice with a model-based design development process, which attracted a strong international cohort of young architects to the area. In that office, Chafee led the training program for professional architectural registration and even participated on a panel dedicated to the topic at Yale. Along with her preparation for professional licensure, she helped Roche, who was not yet registered as an architect, study for the exam.[24] While in the office, she worked on projects for Cummins Diesel in Darlington, England, and was on the team designing the international terminal for the TWA Flight Center at JFK Airport.[25]

Chafee's most significant professional experience during her tenure in the Northeast came at the Edward Larrabee Barnes Office in New Haven, where she worked for five years. At the time, Chafee was also running a small private practice and working concurrently on the Ruth Merrill Residence (1969) in Guilford, Connecticut, and the Robert Funking Residence (1972) in Stockbridge, Massachusetts. Since graduation she had advised and worked on displays for Carson Pirie Scott with her mother, often reminding Christina that she should be paid for her design work. The May 1966 edition of *Mademoiselle* magazine included an article on the pros and cons of young women entering the architecture profession. In the article, Barnes's office is singled out for its "integrated male-female setting," and Chafee is prominently depicted with a model of the Yale University campus and the Sterling Memorial Library. This publication offers one of the few instances of Chafee discussing the role of women in architecture:

> From childhood women are concerned with maintenance of the family; we are trained to provide comfort for those around us. When we cook, knit or arrange a room, we are—as in architecture—involved in a selection of tools and textures. A natural extension of traditional female concern for individuals is an interest in the city. As architects, our chief concern must not just be the relationship between buildings, but also the relationship between buildings and people.[26]

ARCHITECTURE IS AN EXCITING FIELD FOR THE GIRL WHO IS TALENTED AND

A BATTLEGROUND OF THE SPIRIT

Judith Chafee, architect in the office of Edward L. Barnes,
looks over a cardboard model of Yale University. Miss Chafee grew up in Tucson,
was graduated from Yale's School of Architecture in 1960.
Since then, she has worked for such
leading figures as Paul Rudolph,
Ben Thompson, Eero Saarinen.
Now a registered architect, her special project at
Barnes is the redesign of Yale's Sterling Memorial Library.

BY EDITH ROSE KOHLBERG

DUANE MICHAELS

When the new building of Yale's Art and Architecture School was opened in 1963, a giant statue of Minerva, Goddess of Wisdom, was lowered through the skylight into the drafting room. "Her arrival was like the opening of *La Dolce Vita*," said one male student. "We like the old girl. And we like having a woman or two among us. It sets a better tone."

Women are definitely welcome at all but one (Princeton) of the 79 major architectural schools in this country, 57 of which are presently accredited by the National Architectural Accrediting Board.

They make up, however, merely 3 per cent of the 30,000 registered (i.e., licensed) architects in the United States. This is in contrast to the Soviet Union, where the figure is 24 per cent, or to Greece, where more than half the number of practicing architects are women.

The reasons for this are hard to understand in a country that is spending about 65 billion dollars annually for construction; a proliferating variety of large-scale urban-renewal projects, cultural centers, trade and business centers, skyscraper developments, educational complexes, is rapidly changing the face of the country. The major reason for the small number of women may be that architecture is an undermanned profession compared to law (225,000 practitioners), accounting (430,000), or engineering (975,000). Walking down the street, one would have to pass 4,500 people on a city block before meeting an architect.

Both a creative artist and a technologist, an architect can no longer simply design an isolated building and supervise its construction. The technical and human complexities of 20th-century living make it imperative for him to relate his work to the social, economic, and cultural needs of the community. And women architects can make a much-needed humanizing contribution to the monolithic quality of urban design. For, as Judith Chafee (*see photograph*) explains, "From childhood, women are concerned with maintenance of the family; we are trained to provide comfort for those around us. When we cook, knit, or arrange a room, we are—as in architecture—involved in a selection of tools and textures. A natural extension of traditional female concern for individuals is an interest in the city. As architects, our chief concern must not just be the relationship between buildings, but also the relationship between buildings and people." Clothiel Woodard Smith has brilliantly exemplified this concern in the pacesetting homes for the "new town," Reston, Virginia, and in her design for the modern, almost trafficless residential community in the La Clede Town area of St. Louis.

Other women architects iterated this conscious desire to improve the world around them—for their future and their children's. A call, if you will, such as doctors have. "I wanted to do my thesis about Welfare Island," said Lynn Phohl Quigley (Harvard '62, the only girl to graduate with her class), "because I hate to see those ghastly nursing homes to which elderly people, still healthy, are driven in despair by automation and unemployment."

In addition to this concern, a woman can bring to architecture other peculiarly feminine, but needed, insights and aptitudes. Elliot Willensky, director of Cornell's intensive one-semester program in New York, feels that they "bring a desire to use their creativity here as they do in their homes and in other areas where they function as women." Just as women architects have an instinctive flair for designing domestic interior spaces—such as kitchens, closets, bathrooms—so also are they needed to personalize schools, hospitals, public housing. "What woman doing a school would design a kindergarten in a huge space?" asks a young woman architect. "She would know that small children need closeness, intimacy."

Architectural training is long, arduous, and expensive, three reasons it is comparatively few practitioners. Dean Olindo Grossi of Pratt Institute feels that the decision to pursue architecture

is precarious enough to warrant telling interested young people beforehand about it. Each year, Pratt's faculty and students meet with teen-agers and their parents during a one-day high-school competition. They try to clarify for them what the study and pursuit of architecture involves. Eighteen-year-old Barbara McKinnon, now a sophomore at Pratt, doesn't regret her choice. For her, architecture is "a craft that is as personal as poetry or sculpture."

The daughter of a U.S. diplomat, Barbara has lived and gone to school in Belgium, in the Philippines, and in several African posts, including Ouagadougou. A voracious reader, she discovered in high school that she liked various subjects—mathematics, physics, art, and English; architecture was the place where she found she could combine them all. During her last years of high school, spent in the United States, she realized that Africa, with its great need for architects, was the place she wanted to work. (She feels she will easily combine this career with domestic life.)

At most schools, the usual course is five years and leads to a Bachelor of Architecture degree. This is the length of the course at such schools as Cornell, M.I.T., Pratt, and Oregon. Columbia, Yale, and Harvard, however, do not take students straight from secondary school; they require four years of undergraduate work and a B.A., before admission to their courses, which are three and a half to four years long. Entrance requirements are sometimes flexible. Columbia, for example, will occasionally admit a student who has had only two years of undergraduate work. All graduates of whatever architectural school are awarded the same bachelor's degree, considered a "first" professional degree. Master's and doctoral degrees in architecture and planning are also offered at most schools.

Students are required to take two years of courses in English, the humanities, the social sciences, math, and the physical sciences; the professional part of their training includes design (the central subject in the curriculum), architectural history, art, engineering, and building technology. (Clichés to the contrary, most girls don't find engineering difficult.) The range of technical knowledge that must be acquired extends from the principle behind the Roman arch to the latest wrinkle about the tensile strength of steel. A student must learn the moisture content in wood, the basic chemical properties of new materials like Epoxy, and, when she works onsite between semesters, how much the watchman gets an hour. One girl said, "just keeping abreast of all the properties of concrete is a job in itself."

As the course continues, the concentration on design intensifies. At first, a student is asked to do a small picnic area or a tiny chapel. Then he progresses to a house in the city for a family of four, say, and is given these facts to work with: "The wife's hobby is painting; the husband, a lawyer, does carpentry. The children are of school age. There is little traffic on the street; the lot slopes and has a drainage problem. The climate permits lots of outdoor living. The family income is $15,000 a year." Gradually, the assignments take on greater complexity in preparation for the final-year's design thesis, usually an involved scheme such as "Revamp Fort Worth."

Student architects are always "*en charrette*," i.e., making a design deadline. (*Charrette*, or cart, goes back to the 19th-century days of Paris' Beaux Arts School when students literally sat on a

cart, frantically finishing work that was being collected for their instructor.) Regular criticism by staff members takes place about once a week.

At Yale (which has seven girls enrolled this year—four in the bachelor's, three in the master's program), a criticism session was observed. The student tacked his graphic work to a wall of the drafting room, and placed his cardboard model on the floor. The instructor was surrounded by about 20 lucky students, who were relaxed because they had finished this particular assignment (the redesigning of a Puerto Rican estate into a resort area) the day before.

"Why did you put the offices on the third floor, where they're so inaccessible?"

The student defended his plan by explaining he felt the lower-floor areas were more logically used for recreational space.

But the teacher continued needling. "That's a screwy way to do a parking space. Whatever made you design it like that?"

Nothing is left unquestioned. "And we have to learn to take it. They rip into us as hard as they do into the men," said a girl. "They don't," protested a second-year man. "They do, too," said another girl. "I cried like a baby the first time, but I wouldn't have wanted him to pull his punches because I'm a girl." Lynn Quigley says of this toughening process: "When your work is torn apart, you must learn to defend the logic of what you are trying to say graphically."

Criticism by juries, often made up of visiting VIPs from other schools and other countries, comes every few weeks and requires agonizing preparation. "The tension before, the letdown afterwards," said Susan Green, "are awful. We are wrecks. I don't even care how my hair looks."

A man pounced on her. "But we do," he said, "we don't like

the way the art majors look. They're sloppy. Our girls aren't."

All schools require work in architecture during vacations. Often, these temporary jobs lead to permanent ones after graduation. If they can manage it, many students travel, especially to Europe, not only to see the old masterworks, but the more recently built as well. It is sad but true that there is greater belief in the social value of good design among Europeans than among Americans.

The apprentice period, a three-to-four year state-required prerequisite for a license, follows graduation. It is often equated with a beginning internship in medicine. But, since architecture—unlike medicine—is not standardized, this can be a hard time for the young architect.

She is ready for a job as junior draftsman, which has a salary range of $80-$110 a week (West Coast salaries are higher than those in the East). From there, she progresses to senior draftsman and then, in the large firms, to "job captain." This means that she now heads a team of two or more men and is responsible for a design or a set of working drawings for a large project. At this point, her salary has increased to about $200 a week.

There are two major nondesign jobs in an architectural office: specification writers who describe in exhaustive detail the quality and dimensions of all the materials and workmanship required by the project (a good design, without adequate, legally air-tight specifications, literally resembles the proverbial house built on sand); and construction superintendents who check onsite to see that the contractor correctly interprets and executes the architect's drawings. Some women have become chief "spec" writers but, while site supervision is useful for a rounded background, it is usually a for-men-only job.

A beginning architect can only realize [continued on page 209]

On Thanksgiving Day of 1966, Judith Chafee furiously typed an eight-page letter directed to Ed Barnes. With the development of the Yale Library project not progressing to her satisfaction, she outlined a litany of serious concerns about the project and the studio hierarchy. With the Barnes office transitioning from residential scale to larger public buildings and master planning projects during the 1960s, direct participation by Barnes was significantly curtailed. It also became clear to Chafee that even the Barnes office bestowed leadership positions more readily to male architects.[27]

I am deeply troubled by the long talk that you and Herb and I had among the dwindling breadcrumbs and glass rings yesterday…I do not believe that our talk yesterday dealt with problems of architectural solution at all. It had rather to do with factors contrary to good work such as fear, evasion of responsibility, and lack of trust.

She concludes:

I have one more thing to say. I am very tough with myself and with others about doing good work. I spend full time on my work because I cannot escape constant thought and concern about it. I am conversely very thin skinned and sensitive about having the stability and very existence of work upset and confused. I have made personal and economic commitments in New Haven including moving, lease signing etc., based on the assumption that I would follow through on this job I had agreed to undertake. During this entire year,

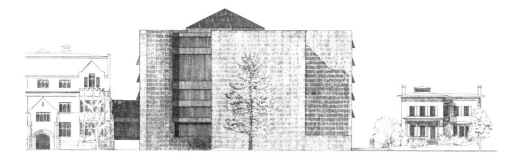

no sooner would work be progressing in a positive way than you would question whether you really wanted to do the job. Since we were doing it I was forced to take all the anxiety on the chin, hide your questioning of it from the clients and the people in the office except Herb, and manage to find ways alone to make clear progress.[28]

The Barnes office employed many female architects on staff, but the project leadership remained decidedly male throughout the 1960s. Chafee accepted a limited leadership role in the studio, focusing mainly on renovation projects and interior design work for clients with whom she had a strong personal connection.[29] Judith Chafee's résumé at the office includes projects at Yale University, such as work on the Campus Master Plan and an addition and renovation of Sterling Memorial Library. At Bennington College, she completed significant work on the new dormitories, including design of the interior environments and custom furnishings. In the late 1960s, Chafee's small private practice in Hamden expanded significantly in scope, including houses for Merrill, Funking, a competition entry for the Yale Mathematics Building, and a studio residence for herself in Tucson. Despite Chafee's reservations, she remained in close contact with the Barnes office, employed full-time, and later as a consultant, until her confident departure for Arizona.[30]

Private Practice

Judith Chafee's ten-year apprenticeship on the East Coast had provided valuable practical experience and a tight network of professional contacts, but in 1969 she decided it was time to move back to Arizona, where she established her private practice in one of Tucson's oldest neighborhoods. She combined her interest in the Sonoran Desert landscapes of her childhood, endemic building techniques, and the experimental outlook that she embraced during her time on the East Coast. To further examine the roots and physical manifestations of vernacular building culture remembered from childhood experiences in Tucson, she reconnected with the community from her youth and went on to develop friendships with a new generation of creative minds. As was her habit, Chafee explored her concerns through writing poetry and prose—shaping her thoughts about the manicured landscape of Connecticut within the frame of her desert experience:

BUILDING TYPES STUDY:
RECORD HOUSES OF 1970
PLUS APARTMENTS OF THE YEAR
TWENTY EXCEPTIONAL HOUSES AND EIGHT MULTI-FAMILY PROJECTS
SELECTED FOR THE 1970 AWARDS OF EXCELLENCE FOR DESIGN

ARCHITECTURAL RECORD
1970   A McGRAW-HILL PUBLICATION

> I flee along the suburban Connecticut road with the Volkswagen on a high whine. In the woods are perfect glass houses, in the villages priggishly perfect white churches. The sides of the road are perfect. Placed stones, considered fences, ground covers and orange day lilies. The trees are beautiful, they crowd over the road and touch above. I think that I will drown in the green muck. I think that I will lose myself, my purpose, if I can't see something beautifully naked and clear, if I do not see the edge of space—the horizon. I go to the seashore and find the space of the desert.[31]

A concern for essential conditions of site, culture, landscape, and endemic materials had often been in opposition to the dominant architecture culture that was taking shape in the northeastern US. Chafee was increasingly interested in an architecture delicately tuned to its environment, where the making of a good room was an end in itself, and the quality of light signaled the

time of day and season of the year. In this context, seemingly ordinary moments and objects were imbued with ineffable and often sacred qualities. Later in life, Chafee framed her return to Tucson in this way:

> I decided to return to Tucson in 1969 as a direct result of the advent of "Post-Modernism." I thought, perhaps, to deal with real climate problems, and an interesting history, and social situation involving several cultures would be a way to use modern disciplines honestly.[32]

Back in Tucson, and throughout the formative years of her private architectural practice, Chafee focused on strategies for reengagement with Sonora on both sides of the border, with the goal of creating a meaningfully

Merrill Residence,
Architectural Record
cover, 1970 (opposite)
and Judith Chafee,
late 1960s (right)

situated life of action. A group of row houses, four connected buildings in the fabric of historic downtown Tucson, in what is now known as the El Presidio neighborhood caught her attention. With the purchase of this property and an investment of sweat equity, she carved out a home and studio for herself in one of the oldest continually inhabited parts of the US. This complex would house Chafee's practice for the remainder of her life and anchor its second phase in the American Southwest. In the opinion of people who were close to her at this time, Chafee was not retreating to Tucson; rather, she was drawn there *toward* something essential. Chafee wrote of this migration and the lure of her home place:

> One lives in a secure area defined by certain geographical powers, often mountains, that relate one's body to the environment. I fully feel this. In Tucson, where I grew up, the Catalina Mountains are North, traveling north toward a certain point in their facade is "going home." The Rincon Mountains on the East are where Lake Michigan is in Chicago and the shore in New Haven; South is Nogales Sonora, Hull House, and Ostia Antica.
>
> One should always live in view of where one's umbilical cord is buried. My umbilical cord flew as polluting matter with odors of the stockyards over Chicago and perhaps contributed one pinpoint of grey to the grave of Louis Sullivan. The first connection must be respected and then we who have gone far afield, albeit taking the Catalinas and the Rincons with us for reference, must accept that our umbilici feel their former adhesion to what scholars have long called the "birthplace" of this and the "cradle" of that.[33]

Chafee had returned to the city of her childhood, but it no longer contained a family home; kinship with the place needed to be rebuilt. The city she knew was also in the process of being reorganized in front of her eyes.

The Pueblo Center Redevelopment Project of 1965—a multiyear plan to clear a portion of Barrio Viejo and replace it with a convention center, city government buildings, and performing arts venues directly south of her neighborhood—was well underway.

She continued, from her base in Tucson, to work on the Merrill Residence (1969) and Funking House (1972) in the Northeast, creating a dual existence for Chafee as the Arizona practice was established. As construction concluded in Guilford, it was clear that the project was a significant work of art. *Architectural Record* and *House Beautiful* both photographed the final project, with its interior design by Christina Bloom. With *Architectural Record*'s award of the Merrill Residence as a Record House in 1970, Chafee achieved a level of recognition that placed her private practice on the architectural map. With an even higher level of magnitude, the editors of *Architectural Record* chose the Merrill Residence for the magazine cover.

During this period, Chafee reconnected with her cousin Susan Bloom Lobo, a student of anthropology at the University of Arizona, and they embarked on a series of trips that would help the architect frame the direction of her expanding practice. They headed south into Sonora along the Mission Trail and spent time at

Old Pasqua with family friend and eminent anthropologist Edward H. Spicer. The Pasqua Yaqui Easter Ceremony had made a strong impression on Chafee when she visited as a child with her mother, and after returning full-time to Tucson as an architect, the ritual continued to inspire reflection and realizations in her building projects. Susan Lobo remembers:

> Judy went with us to the Pascua Semana Santa celebration often, as well as other public celebrations. I think that what was really crucial for her work after she returned to Tucson were the many, many times that she and I went to Old and New Pascua, as well as out to various Tohono O'odham communities such as Sells and San Pedro to just informally drive around, look around, and visit families that I might have been working with in one way or another. Both she and I were fascinated with the ingenuity of construction details and use of materials, many of which were based on long-term traditional knowledge of the desert environment...especially seeking or creating shade, or knowing when and where specific breezes flowed during the hottest months.[34]

Chafee and Lobo benefited from the scholarship of Spicer along with the insights of a younger generation of anthropologists who gathered in Tucson during the 1960s, including Bunny Fontana and Jim Griffith, but it was Chafee and Lobo's own insight forged from direct experience that made a lasting impact on their work. Susan Lobo continues:

> We often would stop the car after visiting a village on the Tohono O'odham reservation and discuss what we had observed, such as the positioning of a house in order to catch the breeze coming off a hillside or along a dry wash, or...that [a] ramada was placed in such a way that it was covered by the house's afternoon shadow when the family was perhaps most often cooking outside, eating, etc. We noticed things such as why the feet of the tables outside under the ramadas often were placed in "Hills Brothers" coffee cans. When asking around, it was to fill them with water so that ants could not

Chafee's Fiat with San Xavier del Bac
in background (opposite left), San Xavier
del Bac with ramada (opposite right),
and Great House (Sivan Vah'Ki), Casa
Grande Ruins (right)

climb up the table when there was food on it. We both were intrigued with all of the ingenious uses and reuses of building materials such as the multi-uses of baling wire, for example in securing the horizontal ramada beams or the common use of large pottery ollas to keep water cool (which you hardly see any more). I think that these exploratory trips [improved] her architect's eye and mine as an anthropologist [and] were important times in bringing us together as cousins and friends.[35]

Growing up with, and maintaining, a nonreligious theology, she was inspired by this coexistence of church and more ancient mythologies, set to a structured ritual with music and dance through the time of Lent, culminating with an Easter day "Gloria" at Old Pascua. Each ceremony followed a ritual sequence but also was particular to that year, rooted in oral history, of a journey through the structure of the celebration. Attending the Pascua Yaqui Easter ceremony became an annual tradition for the Chafee Studio, and new friends were invited on the pilgrimage throughout Chafee's life.

It was not unusual for the Chafee office to hire students and young architects for individual projects. Charles (Corky) Poster had just graduated from architecture school and was looking for temporary work for six months until his job with the Tucson Community Development and Design Center could start. After a brief conversation, and without even looking at his portfolio, Chafee hired him to start the next day. He wrote, "Judith was an unrepentant snob and the fact that I had graduated from Harvard Graduate School of Design was reason enough for her to hire me on the spot. Working for Judith was a profoundly informative experience for me, an ideal position for an inexperienced designer."[36] Although Poster had a brief initial stint at Chafee's office, he would return to help Chafee on special deadlines for a few years. He noted:

The production system for architecture in Judith's office was extraordinary. We drew everything in the building. We spent an unusual effort on the interior elevation of the building, drawing each and every one. On each elevation we showed everything including light switches and outlets. In my later practice on my own, I understood Judith's maxim, "If you don't draw it exactly the way you want it they will screw it up." Judith was precise, demanding, and thorough in all of her work. When we designed for An Evening Dinner Theatre [1974] in New York for Robert Funking, a former client, she had me build a full-scale mock-up of the terraced seating design in the office, including the wooden levels, the recessed lighting, the carpeting, the tables, chairs, flatware, dishes, stemware, tablecloths, and napkins. It sat in the back of the office for some considerable time later. The theater was a great success.[37]

The owners of the theater were pleased enough with the work to hire Chafee to design An Evening Dinner Theatre II in 1990 at a new location. It has been equally successful. In fact, Funking was a long-term Chafee client and close friend from her time in New Haven. In the late 1960s, Funking commissioned a house from Chafee to be located in the Berkshires of western Massachusetts. The initial design scheme was compact in plan and tower-like, rising vertically into the conifer forest canopy. Stacked

Funking Residence, interior (left) and first version sketch (right), Stockbridge, MA, 1972

program elements ascended around a central fireplace core, terminating in a built-in seating area that doubled as expanded guest sleeping quarters. The final version decentralized the program into a composition of discrete volumes, each sited in close communion with the local landscape at ground level. When published in a 1972 edition of *Architectural Record*, the house was included with the works of other like-minded architects across the country under the heading "These houses go beyond good design to expression of place." Chafee described the project as "simple as a grouping of children's blocks,"[38] but of course it was not this straightforward or effortless. As with many clients, Chafee was a demanding presence and unrelenting advocate for both people and the integrity of her projects. She acted as both friend and architect for life.

Chafee hired Ray Barnes during the summer of 1973 as a student intern. With careful drafting and model-building skills, he complemented Chafee and another Yale-trained architect, Myron Silberman, who was also well versed in structural engineering design, with a degree from Columbia University in civil engineering. Barnes noted:

There were small window and door openings in the office. Myron [Silberman] called [them] "punched," because of the thick adobe walls, the doors, and windows [that] could be recessed toward the interior side of the exterior wall. The recessed windows and doors were in the old tradition of maximizing sun and weather protection. The thick adobe walls performed reasonably well in the hot arid climate.... Judith had her office in the southeastern most room. She had her own window (or windows). She had a flat table like everyone else. Her office door was generally open, so we could hear her conversations. Judith called our skylight "north light."[39]

Barnes noted the daily rhythm of the office, starting promptly at 8 a.m., when Chafee unlocked the studio door. At midday, the entire office moved to the table room for a communal gathering:

Lunchtime at the Chafee dining table meant two important things. The first was that we watched the Watergate hearing. [There] was a small TV—in black and white as I recall—in the upper part of the southwest corner of the dining room. The only time I ever watched the Watergate hearings was at Judith's office. Watergate was important to Judith and not just for something to do during lunchtime.[40]

For Chafee and many others in the Arizona activist community, the monitoring of the hearings became an

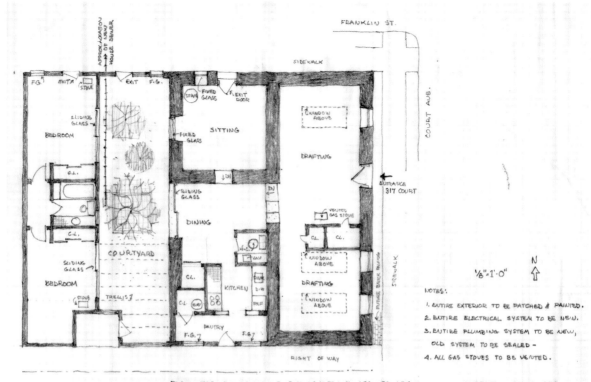

PLAN FOR REVISION OF 317 COURT AVE, 180, 182, 184 FRANKLIN STREET. OCT 13, 1970.

exercise in good citizenship and a reminder that the hard political and civil rights work in the 1930s and 1940s required ongoing maintenance.

The Chafee Studio Residence (1971) often blurred distinctions between public and private—the space of the office and that of the residential quarters, which exclusively occupied the western row house. But the residential area also extended into the courtyard and sitting room, adjacent to the studio space. When clients arrived for meetings, Barnes remembers that the small studio was reordered to accept the guests:

When clients came to visit, Judith knew when they were coming and would greet the clients personally at the door. Formal presentations for clients were done on brown line prints from Tucson Blueprint. The orders for Tucson Blueprint had to be for "medium background" but the medium terminology lacked a consistent quality standard. Judith pinned up the presentations along the west wall of the main space where Myron and I worked. Judith always presented with two or three elevation options [so] the client could choose one or parts from more than one. Her presentations to clients did not have slick graphics, nor fancy terminology, but she kept the attention and respect of her clients. They listened a lot and asked a few questions. I got the impression from the couple of presentations [that] I experienced that the clients knew they were receiving information from a master. There was just that air of mutual respect when clients came. Referring to her clients, I have never seen her give so much respect to people before. She cared for her clients like relatives.[41]

Judith Chafee
Studio, early 1970s
(left), and Viewpoint,
Construction
Document, 1972
(opposite)

Barnes and Poster both provided assistance with a small residence in central Tucson. The Putnam House (1975) was an economical design for a paraplegic military veteran. Here Chafee applied the kind of creative thinking her teacher Paul Rudolph demonstrated in his early Florida houses. Lightweight, modest materials, such as the plywood in a custom-cut arching truss system, provide open interior spaces with minimal doorways and accessible functions. The building is scaled to its context of a community of moderately sized houses on close building lots. For privacy, high windows provide natural light, and the indoor therapeutic swimming pool serves as an internal oasis with a partial courtyard and garden. Throughout her career, Chafee met the challenges of accommodating exceptional health-care issues. Many

years later, the Putnam House was purchased by another paraplegic veteran who recognized the value of the original design principles and their continued value to a life well-lived.

The conjoining of art and daily life is an aspiration that is often discussed but rarely achieved. Discipline, thoughtful presence, and time are all requirements for the translation of factual knowledge into reflexive action. Applied knowledge takes on many forms, but in the case of Judith Chafee, a careful balance was achieved between the prosaic, poetic, and spiritual dimensions of human existence that extend from the domestic sphere into public life. The ability to focus on local materials and the expression of their unadorned qualities certainly appealed to Chafee. Much like Rudolph, she developed an adaptive reuse project for her home and studio that respected the historic form of the existing urban context but expanded the interior to graciously allow for an architect's studio and residence to coexist in close proximity.

Chafee continued her private practice in Tucson designing finely crafted buildings suited for their Sonoran Desert setting. She carefully sited projects to gather light and direct breezes through the living areas, actively drawing on vernacular building examples. Each space was graciously tuned to the needs of her clients and the surrounding landscape. She followed the lead of her teachers, who practiced commonsense healthful design strategies that harnessed sun, wind, and water based on an ethic of economy and aesthetic intelligence. She employed materials that required minimal maintenance and provided a clear performance benefit in a hot and arid climate. Early projects forced Chafee to think beyond her existing practice and reimagine the scope and responsibility of the work of an architect related to the health and well-being of interior spaces. Another example of this prioritization is the Viewpoint Residence (1972) for her mother, Christina, and Christina's new husband,

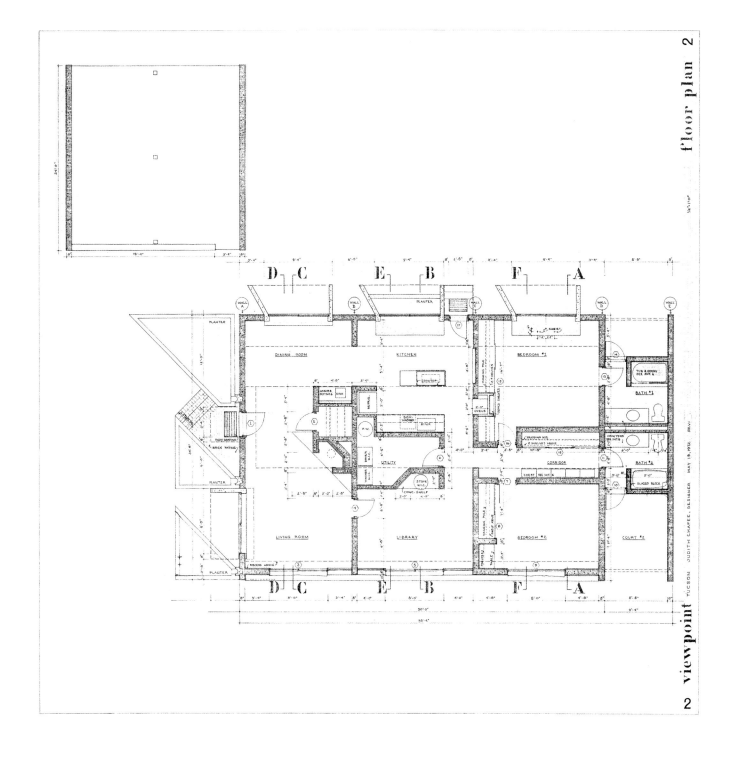

Earl Johnson, as clients, another collaboration between the architect daughter and interior designer mother.

In 1973 Chafee continued her long-term engagement with education principles as a visiting critic at the University of Arizona School of Architecture. She was the first and only woman on the faculty for eight years until an associate professor, Linda Sanders, joined.

Chafee was initially perceived as an outsider with East Coast credentials and politically liberal, frank, and opinionated. In 1977 her status was changed to adjunct professor, a role that engaged her in the design studio three afternoons a week from 1 to 5 p.m., and theoretically allowed her time to maintain her office. Then the requirements to participate in meetings and advise students were added for which a shared office space was provided. It was not unusual for Chafee to also offer extra review time during the summer for students with legitimate misfortune who were unable to complete their semester project on time. As a nine-month contracted adjunct professor, she was not paid for this altruism. Most classes Chafee was assigned to teach were third- and fourth-year levels. She was rarely assigned the early studios or senior thesis classes. In 1978 she addressed the pedagogical objectives as follows:

> The evolution of the student's intellectual desire to be involved in architecture, into emotional and physical involvement with architecture, is my prime concern. A sense of self and others moving in scaled places created by scaled materials combined in the solution of human, functional, environmental, mechanical, and structural necessity is what I wish to instill first. The hardware and mechanics of problem solving which is being learned concurrently with the development of architectural emotional growth is a tool of that growth. To view buildings as the culmination of a concept about a place for people, constructed in a logical mechanical or physical sequence of materials that all have

dimensions and special characteristics and appropriateness is the beginning of operating as an integrated person who can be an architect. Coupled with this power of observation, a highly developed critical sense must become an almost immediate response, so that forms, uses of materials, [and] response to site that do not fulfill the requirement of rational development are noted immediately as a reinforcement of the student's own approach to the next problem.[42]

During this period, the Chafee studio was immersed in the design and construction of the Ramada House (1975). In this building Chafee fully embraces the massive material technology of the desert, but replaces traditional adobe with concrete slump block finished with a light mortar wash as walls rise out of the Sonoran Desert floor. A roof deck and large glass openings in the walls are protected from above by a sheltering roof canopy that Chafee likens to a Tohono O'odham ramada or vernacular shade structure. An embrace of vernacular building culture is evident, as is a respect for the later work of Le Corbusier (1887–1965) in the modular organization of columns, as seen in the plan and secton drawings. Historian William J.R. Curtis was a welcomed guest in Chafee's El Presidio studio. Knowing Tucson well, he is quoted as having "a mystic reverence for the surrounding desert landscape." Curtis included Chafee's work in his widely read *Modern Architecture Since 1900* and helped position her southern Arizona practice in an international context of like-minded architects:

> The best of these buildings seem able to draw upon indigenous wisdom, but without simply inhabiting vernacular forms: to penetrate beyond the obvious features of regional style to some deeper mythical structures rooted in past adjustments to landscape and climate.[43]

When Chafee would allow herself the time, she would have sensational dinner parties for guests, a tradition

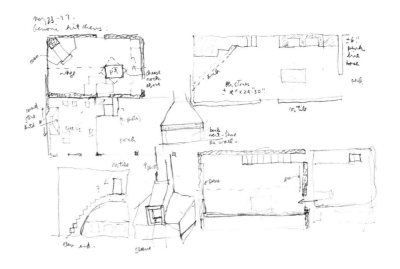

she learned from Margaret Sanger that she carried through to Yale. Yung and Ming Wang, who were classmates at Yale and remained good friends after, traveled with Chafee in China and later visited her in Arizona, enjoying her Tucson hospitality. They said, "Judith was always her own person."[44] They met when she rented part of the little house next door to them in New Haven, and when they would get together, they never talked about architecture, which they all had enough of in their regular life. They would talk about food, recipes, travel, and life. Chafee gave extravagant parties that were "designed from procession to presentation." She invited professors and bosses, and was on first-name basis with everyone. To their amazement, she would refer to her mentor as Paul, while everyone else would say "professor" or "Mr. Rudolph."[45]

When Chafee submitted her application for the midcareer fellowship with the American Academy in Rome, the Jacobson Residence was under construction in Tucson, and architect Edward Larrabee Barnes sent a letter of recommendation, carefully handwritten from New York:

> Judith Chafee is an excellent designer—very thoughtful, not at all superficial. She worked with me in my New Haven office so I know her well. She is intelligent, continuously well read, a solid technician, and a good architectural historian. Now in Tucson, she has her own small office and a teaching job at the Architectural School. She is a dedicated teacher interested not only in design theory, but also in the individual student. Her work and teaching all runs together, and she has developed a style and field of interest appropriate to the Southwest—environmental architecture directed to solar and wind power and patterns of living that try to work with nature. Judith Chafee is bright, charming, imaginative, and curious.[46]

In the spring of 1977 Chafee, having been awarded the fellowship, departed Tucson for the American Academy in Rome. As an established architect and teacher, Chafee

pined for a sabbatical to provide critical distance from her expanding practice in order to critique current work, correct deficiencies, and define goals for the next phase of her practice and teaching. In her application, she emphasized the necessity for reflection:

> Several months of firm unrushed time in which to consider one's work, communicate with others involved in scholarly and creative endeavor, study many architectural theories, and product[s] of the past and present, [and] experiment with formal and graphic ideas would be of inestimable value at this time.[47]

In Tucson Chafee studied vernacular architectural antecedents—low-technology examples of limited resource building methods, along with the adaptation of plants and animals to a hot and arid environment. At the American Academy, she outlined her task accordingly:

> The study of ancient and indigenous building and planning techniques primarily as they related to control of sun and wind in an area centered in Rome would contribute to the formulation of attitudes about the function of these phenomena as form determinants, and the proper place of newly conceived low-technology structures in our sophisticated but perhaps over-standardized and overspent standard construction in

simple structures such as non urban and remote housing. I would propose to spend the major part of the fellowship period in the study of the climatic determinants of regional building forms.[48]

The outcome of her work would focus on the climate-adapted domestic stone architecture of Sardinia and Apulia in an attempt to further understand regional adaptation in hot, arid environments. She arrived in Cagliari, Sardinia, on May 1, 1977, with memories of repeatedly reading D. H. Lawrence's *Sea and Sardinia*, with its vibrant images of the city and its people. She endeavored to arrive on May Day in order to stand in front of the Cagliari Cathedral to witness the formal processions from the surrounding mountain towns into the city, the citizens dressed in customary attire, with statues of patron saints leading the way. It was the lives of the people and the architecture of daily life that attracted Chafee to Sardinia and Puglia. The modest structures that she drew while visiting were constructed using mainly stone technology—both corbelled and vaulted—and very little wood. Upon Chafee's arrival at her hotel, she was handed a note announcing that Sardinian-born artist Constantino (Tino) Nivola and his wife, Ruth, had arrived in town for May Day as well. Arrangements were made for a meeting. During her travels, she found inspiration in Nuoro Piazza Sebastiano Satta sculptures of Tino Nivola, likening them to secrets hiding in plain sight. From a distance, the sculptures take on the monumental quality of geology, and at close inspection a finer level of detail presents itself in the work. For Chafee and Nivola, a central question is often present—how to live in the larger world and to make better work for your home place.

Chafee's use of writing as an analytic tool is in evidence during this period as she mined early architectural influences, seen in this poem written while at the American Academy:

To Louis Sullivan

I've thought a lot about you recently,
While far from all accustomed books and notes,
The filled and shelved familiar images,
That give, if not the answers, then the peace
of knowing they are safely near to seek
the secrets which enfolded there were you.

The long and shaded gaze from Ocean Springs,
The torso close to motion, which I think
will hold a hint of strut, But most of all
the tree, the rough and tough and rigid rod
exchanging equal thrust with hand that curves
in gentle ease returning force—just there.

The seed germ put, as only Yankee would:
A simple process to become all life's
complexity, has split this Spring abroad.
Unfolding in this kindergarten's yard,
I watch it grow in different centuries
Of soil, and start to learn all things again.

Remembering you in the joy of forward thrust
brings pain, old guilt, from the white clouds wherein
I sit, that said the seed germ didn't count,
and spread its deadly pallor over you.
My presence means the cloud is fading now,
and fronds of our own growing shall mature.

I send these thoughts to you beneath your tree,
to say that you have come to Rome with me.[49]

The opportunity for a sabbatical from which to view teaching, practice, and her relationship to Tucson anew allowed Chafee to continue her steadfast process of layering influences, inspiration, and research into a unique palimpsest or system of ideas. The outcome was akin to a theory of pragmatism, and her use of inquiry to clarify ideas and attempt to resolve doubt continued the tradition of Socratic discourse that Chafee embraced at Parker, Bennington, and Yale. Her friendships were also an integral part of this ongoing search, as she wrestled with increasingly intertwined professional and personal complexities.

Architect Diane Lewis (1951–2017) remembers her immediate affection for Chafee after the latter's arrival at the American Academy and that she was struck by the physical presence of Judy Collins and the attitude of Dorothy Parker embodied by Chafee. After spending time together, Lewis initially thought of her as a "wounded bird," but she later came to see her as fully human in her range of concerns and empathy for others, counting Chafee among her inspiring mentors.[50] As an established architect in private practice with teaching intertwined in her daily ritual of work, Chafee provided counsel to Lewis as the two bonded over shared aspirations for a life in architecture as well as their overlapping networks of New York–based friends and colleagues. In 1977 Charles Eames also arrived as a resident architect and began a study of Rome that would find its way into films later developed by the Eames Office. Lewis began a detailed study of Michelangelo's large sculptural series of slaves at the Accademia Gallery in Florence, and Chafee was occupied with her study of traditional domestic architecture in the more remote hot and arid regions of Italy. These projects were later displayed at the annual Academy exhibition. With the residency complete, both women booked flights for the United States. Lewis, with financial assistance for travel from Chafee, soon returned to Manhattan to practice architecture in large firms, including I. M. Pei & Partners Architects, before becoming a respected educator and practitioner at the Cooper Union. Chafee's homecoming to Tucson placed her in one of the most productive periods in her professional life, with design awards forthcoming, the Jacobson Residence (1977) in the final phase of completion, and the Blackwell Residence (1980) soon to begin.[51]

Chafee's attitude toward her practice is redolent with Puglia, Sardinia, Kahn, Rudolph, and Le Corbusier, but is most influenced by the vernacular landscapes of southern Arizona itself and the Mission Trail leading south into Mexico. The fabric of her buildings is informed by tracking the sun throughout the day and from season to season in order to provide logic to fenestration and establish the placement of rooms. Tucson's local building techniques, refined over centuries of trial and error, became Chafee's palette as she defined a unique way of building that was simultaneously tough and refined, local and universal. She developed a building culture that respected landscape and climate and relied on a deep regional precedent. The implementation of massive materials, including concrete block, traditional adobe, and earthen construction techniques, was explored through systematic iterative project development. Use of passive solar strategies

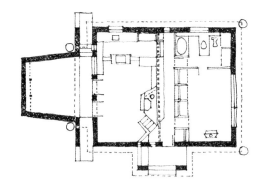

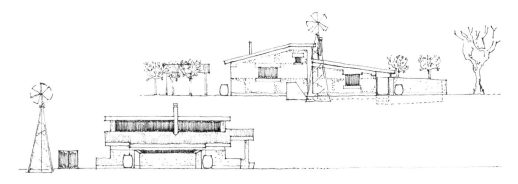

52

and emerging active methods of environmental control provided a prescient case study of practice and research conjoined. Chafee believed that a modern building program could logically coexist with the local tradition of massive earth building. Her work was widely respected for its integrity, honest use of materials, and rigor. The massive walls sheltered inhabitants from the extreme desert climate with grace, but the work did not appear to fit into the conventional architecture tastes of the period, which typically included applied stucco finishes and red terra-cotta roofing materials. The Blackwell Residence (1978–80), for example, was the focus of prolonged adaptive reuse efforts and a contentious public preservation debate that played out in the local newspapers. The house has always existed in the memory of a sympathetic hardcore following, and now that current taste is shifting back to the physical and metaphoric weight that can be felt in the massive quality of Chafee's architecture, the void that is left by the demolition of this house takes a positive turn, as noted by Tucson writer Charles Bowden:

> Judith Chafee came out of this community and was in part influenced by Margaret Sanger who spent her later years here. Chafee's work shows this influence of place and character— a kind of severe modernism that somehow roots itself in the

forms and ideas of pre-historic Native American designs. All this is evident in the Blackwell house which seems at first to speak to a new era (and an international style) rather than an old one, but which incorporates an ancient ethos with its passive solar design, its flue for heating and cooling, and its eerie ability to seem a permanent and natural part of Gates Pass. To put it another way, it is a relatively recent building which states a heritage that has grown more and more silent here for well over a century. A healthy town neither forgets its past nor becomes a slave to it, but rather constantly grows and changes while rooted in this past. The Blackwell house belongs here and grew out of the conditions of life that dominate here. Tucson is first and always a desert city and anything which denies this fact will not persist.[52]

Judith Chafee was compelled to craft a unique course for her career, which took her from New Haven to New York and Cambridge and, finally, back to Tucson. Her independent projects of this period embrace geographic precedent, aesthetic research, and energy imperatives. Chafee soon became associated with dialogues in regionalism that integrated principles introduced during her sojourn in the Northeast with a foundation of pragmatic lessons abstracted from the landscapes of an Arizona childhood, including the Mission San Xavier del Bac, Tohono O'odham ramadas, and pueblo building complexes. The Best Residence project began in 1972 and developed over several compelling iterations that embodied many of the principles that Chafee espoused, but within the grassland landscape surrounding the site in Patagonia, Arizona, the range of vernacular precedent significantly expanded to include new materials and landscapes in the large ranches found in the region south of Tucson. In honor of the project, and for the love of her clients, Chafee wrote this poem:

House in a Remote Area

Into the eighties and the hills with; [*sic*]
Rammed earth walls and tin roofs,
Passive solar heat and earth insulation,
Home generating plant and water pumped
by windmill, Solar heated water and
soft water barrels, fruit orchards and
wood burning stoves.[53]

After completing several house design iterations for the site, it became clear that the project would never be built. Only the poem exists, as do the design drawings and experiments in rammed earth construction. Of course, all the completed design work is research for future projects. The later Hydeman Residence (1983) in Sonoita, Arizona, and the clients who commissioned the house would significantly profit from the experience.

Conclusion

With each new project, Chafee merged sensible vernacular siting strategies and material building innovations into her architecture without ever turning to nostalgia or visual pastiche. As the only woman in her graduating class at the Yale School of Architecture, she worked with a passion for equity of opportunity and dedication to excellence in her creative output, which deepened over time into an architecture of substance that continues to inspire architects and an expanding population attuned to environmental intelligence. As her earliest projects reach the fifty-year mark, historians are examining the legacy of her work, the relevant criteria for preservation, and the sociopolitical repositioning of a woman architect in the context of gender equity. The Ramada House is now listed on the National Register of Historic Places, and Chafee's work still provides an intellectual scaffolding and a tough-minded, independent practice model for the Arizona School of Architecture.[54]

Merrill Residence

Guilford, Connecticut, 1967–69

Exterior, looking
northeast

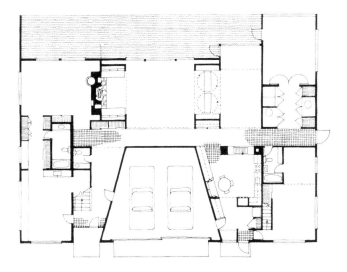
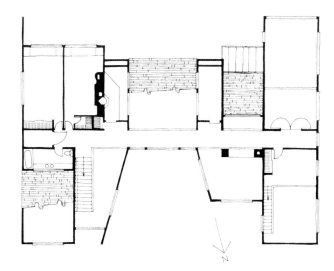

For her design of the Merrill Residence, Chafee won what would be the first of three Record House Awards and became the first woman architect to appear on the cover of the annual Record House edition of *Architectural Record* in 1970.[1] This milestone coincided with the decision to close her small practice in Hamden, Connecticut, leave the Northeast, and begin anew in Tucson, Arizona.

Ruth Merrill, who commissioned the project, was a close friend and classmate of Chafee's mother, Christina Bloom. As evidenced in bold, glamorously curated Bloom-family photographs, Merrill often joined the family on their trips throughout the American Southwest during Chafee's youth. In her early adulthood, while Chafee attended college and architecture school, the two women developed a close bond over frequent visits to Merrill's Greenwich

Village and Gramercy Park apartments. Merrill also kept a weekend house in the leafy idyll of Meriden, Connecticut, that the Bloom women dubbed the Bridge House. It was during gatherings at these homes that Merrill, Bloom, and Chafee conceived the idea of collaborating on the creation of a new home for Merrill in which Chafee and Bloom would form a mother-daughter team as interior designer and architect. This new residence would combine the urbanity of Manhattan with the quality of sanctuary that the Bridge House inspired.

To this end, in 1967, Merrill purchased a waterfront lot in an exclusive recently subdivided area in Guilford, Connecticut, set in a protected cove along a rocky coastline overlooking Long Island Sound.[2] The three set to work on what would prove to be a challenging process, led by the youngest among them, Chafee. This intense and at times conflict-inducing odyssey would test the depth of their friendships. The result is proof that the steep price they paid to realize Chafee's vision—strained and lasting tensions between Merrill and her design team—was worth it. Upon completion, the Merrill Residence represented a total work of art to all involved. A *gesamtkunstwerk* in stone and wood.

The house is quite large at 7,500 square feet of enclosed volume, but it feels intimately connected to the six-acre site, its exposed geology, and the rhythms of daily life. The influence of Alexander Dorner's regional building research and Vincent Scully's work on the shingle style are indeed evident, as is the contextual modernism of Edward Larrabee Barnes. But this house can also be seen as a wolf in sheep's clothing with its traditional New England vocabulary of weathered shingles masking a dynamic composition of interlocking volumes and rotating walls. The elemental external forms frame an elaborate spatial interior with a sophisticated procession of varying height volumes, a gallery with bridge above that runs the length of the house, and a double-story porch facing Long Island Sound. From Chafee's perspective, the Merrill Residence is "imbued with the severity with which traditional New England houses return to rectangles in elevation and in plan...the Merrill House also has nostalgia for pueblo forms in the way it is stacked on the mesa of the large south-facing, sun-collecting deck."[3]

The location of the house and orientation of the drive, which leads to an entry court surrounded with dense foliage, allow no preview of the dramatic waterfront landscape and view along the rocky coast that lie beyond the volume of the house. U-shaped in plan, the house wraps around a trapezoidal garage at ground level providing additional area for car egress for when Ruth Merrill's health issues required her to use a wheelchair. This unexpected geometry also provides an intimate entry vestibule that opens broadly into the central living area of the house. An abundance of care was given to the entry area that includes an adjustable door assembly with vertical slats that can be modulated from opaque to a compelling pattern of open and closed, light and dark. A rope tied to a simple bell inside is used to announce visitors. Each element engages the body haptically, leading to a full-body sensory experience from the moment one enters the house. A room is never framed as a distinct space unto itself, but one that logically leads to another area or that creates conversation with seemingly disparate areas of the house and, of course, the local landscape and stunning distant views.

For the cover of *Architectural Record*, the editors chose an image of the living room showing the bridge, secret reading alcove above, and inglenook beyond—a surprising view of domestic tranquility for a professional magazine. The inglenook is an updated version of Frank Lloyd Wright's lovingly scaled fireplace arrangements and functions as a psychological "cave" contrasting the open volume of the high-ceiling central living room. In this house, Chafee accommodates the large group as well as reclusive individuals, providing a variety of ways to inhabit spaces. The granite of the fireplaces was quarried nearby at Stony Creek Quarry and connects the interior to rock outcroppings found throughout the property and along the coastline. Chafee designed a flexible interior with cabinets on the opposing side of the living room that pivot from open to closed on large rotating hardware components.[4] This kinetic device allows the dining area and solarium to connect directly to the living room or to remain discreetly linked to the kitchen and outdoor patio. The greenhouse/solarium functions as an extension of the dining area and winter sitting area and provides the sensation of being both inside and outside on a cold winter's day bathed in the warmth of the house.

Exterior, looking
northwest

Entry drive (left)
and entry vestibule
(below)

Living room
and inglenook
from above

62

Although the kitchen contains many elements typical of successful domestic arrangements, Chafee programmed this space as a total reflection of the client's needs, each component imbued with meaning that makes this area of the house worthy of further consideration. The wood-fire grill occupies a central position with a sizeable sculptural flue above as an interpretation of a New England fireside kitchen where guests gather and share stories as food is prepared. The exposed gallery walkway overhead allows balanced natural light to enter deep into the space. Oak and Plexiglas cabinets are lit from below, which allows for subtle adjustments to the task lighting. Quarry tile on the floor and other well-used areas offer easy maintenance with a tough but elegant modular surface. An Aalto table and chairs are arranged next to built-in seating. The two-story maid or assistant suite lies just beyond the pantry, the angled wall from the trapezoidal garage logically compressing space again, this time at the secondary kitchen entry before opening up into the communal kitchen.

Ruth Merrill's bedroom and painting studio are located directly behind the first-floor inglenook, with the majority of the second floor zoned for guests. An inclined lift at the central entry stair is provided, when necessary, for assistance navigating the stairs. The gallery bridge on the second floor is the primary circulation space for the upper floor and overlooks the living area below, a device reminiscent of the widow's walk found in New England coastal communities and that is also possibly related to Paul Rudolph's Art and Architecture Building at Yale, where a high bridge overlooks the design studios.

Two intimate spaces can be found on the second floor as well, with their small triangular openings connecting to the living room below.

Chafee associated the large deck facing south toward the water with a broad Southwestern mesa affording great prospect from house to cove beyond. A warm-weather screened porch anchors the western end of the patio with a large-scale rolling screen enclosure, with sections of screen woven together by the architect to avoid any obstruction of the view. An expansive fin wall at the rear deck to the west provides privacy from the main road and protection from sun and wind. The house is oriented to magnetic north, which protects the open northern elevation from unwanted direct exposure during the long summer days.

The house is set on concrete piers with a wood frame and cedar shingles that cover the entirety of the walls and sloped roof forms. Exposed copper joist vents, along with windows and frames painted black, further unite the building composition. Chafee even provided a cedar-shingle-clad structure for storage of firewood that deftly emulates the building vocabulary at small scale. Ruth Merrill's art collection—an assortment of objects gathered from a lifetime of travel—was highly curated by the design team. At this point in the process, it is difficult to discern whether it was client, interior designer, or architect who drove the level of detail and care brought to this house, but it is clear that the synergy afforded by the interaction of these three strong personalities provided a dwelling of incomparable beauty composed for living in this unique place in the world.

Dining room
with cabinets in
open position

Judith Chafee Studio and Residence Tucson, Arizona, 1970–71

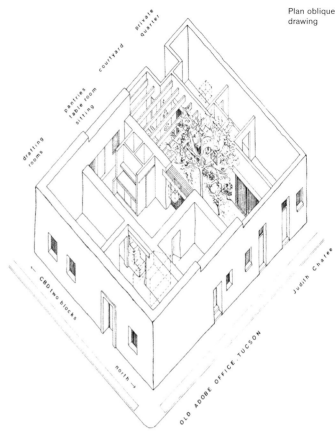

Upon returning to Tucson in 1969, Chafee began creating her studio, a live-work space in a neighborhood now known as the El Presidio Historic District. She purchased a dilapidated four-unit rowhouse complex at the intersection of Court Avenue and Franklin Street and began to shape the existing adobe and brick buildings into a compound that respected both its territorial period identity and its present-day urban environment. The two houses to the east are unstabilized adobe structures built in the 1870s, while the dwellings on the western end of the property are brick, constructed in the 1930s. Perhaps drawing from her studies at Yale and work in Edward Larabee Barnes's office, where the value of regional identity, craft, and materiality were etched into her, Chafee took painstaking care to respect the structure's urban form while repurposing it as an office and home with modern services like plumbing, electrical service, and cooling.[1] A need for additional daylight and exterior space led Chafee to sacrifice the interior square-footage of one entire unit to create an exterior courtyard within the complex. Ultimately, the final product paid homage to the existing cultural fabric, and the courtyard building typology she selected served as a vessel for all of the lessons she had learned to date—a calling card for her talents as an architect, and a fitting base for her next twenty-five years of practice.

For the Chafee Studio and Residence, the doors and windows were rehabilitated and exterior walls rendered with stucco to maintain a unified street appearance in keeping with neighborhood precedent and to announce that the place had become one unified entity. The architect created an urban form drawing that included elevations of all existing buildings along the main streets in the district, illustrating how her home and studio are integrated into the historic building fabric. At first glance, it is difficult to ascertain which structure houses Chafee's studio, but the composition at lower right (see page 71), with angular skylight announcing itself above the roof parapet, subtly

sets it apart from its neighbors while taking part in the ensemble of the street.

Architect Ray Barnes worked with Chafee during the summer of 1973 and fondly remembered:

Upon entering the office, immediately on the left was a very nice black leather lounge chair. I remember the chair as having a chrome framework. I also recall a large chrome, arching, floor-mounted, modern light fixture that was carefully situated next to the chair for reading. Occasionally Judith would sit in the chair specifically to read *Architectural Record* magazines. I never saw anyone else use the chair. Judith told me that reading "Record" was important to "keep up with what everyone else was doing." Around the time of my employment, Paul Rudolph was getting published in

El Presidio map

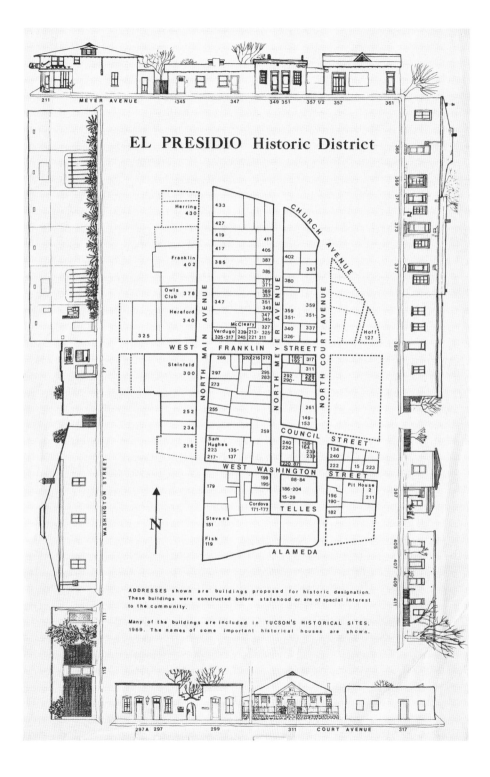

EL PRESIDIO Historic District

ADDRESSES shown are buildings proposed for historic designation. These buildings were constructed before statehood or are of special interest to the community.

Many of the buildings are included in TUCSON'S HISTORICAL SITES, 1969. The names of some important historical houses are shown.

Looking through
adobe wall toward
table room

Architectural Record. Paul Rudolph and Edward Larrabee Barnes, both of whom were Judith's former employers, had *Architectural Record* editorial connections. Their role with the magazine may not have significantly influenced her reverence to the magazine, but probably helped. The real significance of the two famous architects was that she had a personal connection to *Architectural Record*. She made summer trips to New York to visit Rudolph and Barnes, of course taking pictures of her work with her.[2]

Chafee placed her architecture office in the historic adobe facing North Court Avenue, the most public street. An asymmetrical opening carved in the earthen wall of the studio allowed for movement through a passage into the adjacent row house. The staggered threshold not only offered logical support for the roof structure above, but also provided a low shelf or bench while revealing the time-tested earthen wall. The newly exposed adobe is maintained using linseed oil rather than a new plaster application. Special client meetings and office lunches were often held in the dining area adjacent to the exterior courtyard, which created a clear public / private intersection in the building composition. Sliding glass doors opened to the abundant dappled light under the shade tree in the courtyard, and existing roof beams were left in place on the south side of the court, defining a discrete space that included an outdoor shower and offered shade adjacent to the architect's bedroom. The shared adobe walls of the building complex help to temper the Sonoran Desert climate and provided a daily reminder to Chafee that earthen architecture still has a place in contemporary architecture. She often shared her position, that "we could do more earth-sheltered design. At three feet (below grade), we have a temperate climate. We could also learn tremendous lessons from the desert plants, the nocturnal and burrowing animals. They have achieved quite a comfortable lifestyle."[3] Ray Barnes also noted:

The office was evaporatively cooled and seemed reasonably comfortable. The papers did seem to wrinkle, but not to the point of being a serious problem. Sometime during the early middle of the summer Judith had the evaporative cooling system replaced with a refrigeration unit. I did not notice a significant change in comfort, but the papers did not seem to wrinkle as much. Judith did not like having to install the air conditioning system. She let us know the change was expensive, but I got the feeling that the principle of using more energy and moving away from adequate simplicity was what bothered her.[4]

In the drafting area, the rehabilitated roof incorporates a sizeable north-facing skylight with corrugated C-panel roofing material. Interior modifications included a truss system over the work area with industrial pendants hung from old barn pulleys. To provide power and phone service to the studio, a raceway was built into a shallow storage shelf running along the adobe walls, allowing technology requirements to coexist with the historic earthen construction. A large-scale photo of Walter Gropius at his retirement party sat on the storage shelf for many years: the consummate teacher and practitioner keeping watch over the work of the studio.

Chafee found inspiration in quotidian moments and often elevated daily routine to ritual importance through the careful creation of space, the modulation of light, and the mindful recognition of regional intelligence. In this spirit, she carefully arranged each room in service of life and work intertwined. Light is brought into every space from multiple directions through existing openings and subtractions made in the roof plane. In the studio, the north-facing skylight illuminates the area of work, and a simple square opening near the dining table directed attention from the studio deep into the complex and the courtyard beyond. Updated mechanical equipment augmented the passive cooling provided by the original adobe walls—allowing new and old to coexist. Exposed headers were constructed of reclaimed wood from

Sitting room,
looking northwest,
with Leda

Private quarter
(left), and kitchen
(opposite)

the reconstruction work. Salvaged beams also found new use as shelves in the kitchen, suspended from the walls on slender cylindrical metal supports. The architect's sitting room included new concrete tile work, the Steinway grand piano from her childhood, Aalto chairs gifted from Alexander and Lydia Dorner, repurposed Navajo blankets, a Carl Gustaf Nelson painting, a ceramic Mexican stove for heating, and Hopi kachina dolls and Acoma pottery resting on a cherished Charles and Ray Eames prototype storage unit all integrated into the new context.

Here, Chafee experienced her own model of the architect studio and residence similar to the live / work compound Paul Rudolph built onto an existing building in New Haven upon his arrival as chair of the Yale University School of Architecture. Rudolph modeled a robust life of practice and teaching for the students, faculty, and a growing roster of international visitors. Chafee and other students accepted invitations as dinner guests as part of Rudolph's extended circle. It is also useful to consider that Rudolph, too, began his career off the radar, on the west coast of Florida, which was akin to the remoteness of Tucson, creating a model of regional modernism for a generation of students and practicing architects.

The spaces in her home and studio are internalized compositions but are never far from the local light that signals the time of day or season. Chafee's home and studio combines sensitivity to place with an uncanny ability to employ massive materials with sophistication and grace. Seemingly ordinary moments in these rooms provide a unique understanding of how to make an architecture imbued with tradition and innovation. In the historic building fabric of Tucson, Chafee encountered a built heritage with which a program of modern building could coexist.

Judith Chafee's first freestanding project in Tucson is the Viewpoint Residence, commissioned by her mother, Christina Johnson.[1] In 1969, Christina and her new husband, Earl J. Johnson, relocated to Tucson shortly after both retired from careers in Chicago.[2] The couple chose a multi-acre desert site on the west side of Tucson with unobstructed views of both the Catalina and Tucson mountain ranges surrounded by undisturbed desert and acres of ranch property. Memories of uncomfortable glare created by the robust Sonoran Desert sun in the Martin Avenue home of Chafee's childhood prompted the couple to prioritize spaces filled with balanced natural lighting and no glare.[3] Additionally, they directed that the house should graciously hold the lives of its inhabitants, embrace their love of cooking, and provide a safe shelter for their collection of furniture, textiles, pottery, jewelry, and paintings. Despite this broadly worded but demanding program, Chafee was given a budget that required restraint.

Until her retirement, Christina spent many years working in the residential interiors department of Carson Pirie Scott in Chicago, focusing on modern interior environments with a specialized interest in Scandinavian design. This sensitivity is evident in the exquisite arrangement of objects that the house exhibited. Photographs by Glen Allison from the mid-1970s display architecture and interior design visibly fusing into an inseparable whole. Soon after completion, the home was featured in the *Los Angeles Times* and won a coveted Record House Award from *Architectural Record* in 1975.[4] This 2,600-square-foot house has inspired architects in Arizona for decades because of its reputation for economy, environmental adaptation, and cultural connectivity. The importance of this relatively small house has consistently been inversely proportional to its size.

The house is sited on a high elevation near the far northwestern edge of the parcel. Primary vehicular access

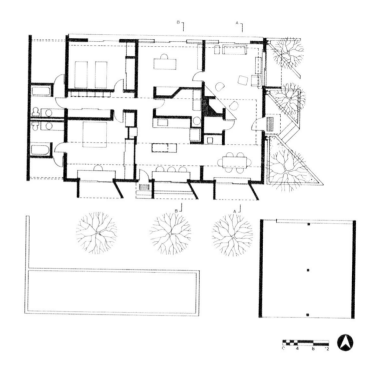

is from the southeast, with a curving drive gently moving through the low desert scrub until the southern elevation of the house appears in full view. The building displays its full height of over 20 feet along with uninterrupted clerestory glazing above and cast-in-place brise-soleil, or solar shades, at ground level. The drive directs guests to parking east of the residence and provides access to the eastern facing entry area. To respond to the harshness of the desert site, Chafee specified a light-colored mortar wash over standard 8 × 8 × 16-inch concrete block walls to reduce heat gain, which also presents a monolithic appearance from a distance and subtle modularity upon close inspection. The cast-in-place concrete solar shades limit direct entry of light, and exposed concrete rain leaders divert water into triangulated planters on either

Exterior, looking
northwest

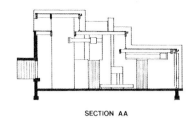

SECTION AA

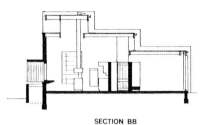

SECTION BB

EAST ELEVATION 0 4 8 12

side of the main entry.[5] With the spatial separation of the freestanding carport, visitors have a clear view of the stepped form of the dwelling rising out of the low-desert landscape. In morning light, the building appears white against the blue sky, much like the Mission San Xavier del Bac, a historic Spanish Catholic mission located fifteen miles to the south and a pilgrimage site for Chafee and her family since childhood. In fact, the house's distinctive rain leaders are cleverly adapted from examples found at San Xavier and link its unique building form to the cultural heritage of southern Arizona, San Xavier's Moorish origin in Andalusia, and as far east as the central mosque at Sana'a in Yemen.[6]

A humble but carefully constructed wood door provides access to the public area of the house, past the monsoon-rain-fed planters with herbs carefully located adjacent to the walk to stimulate a more fully rounded sensory experience. The scent of mint and rosemary marks the threshold from exterior to inner sanctum. The only nonnative additions to the landscape are in these entry planters; the remaining site is left to paloverde, creosote bush, cholla, and cacti. Once inside, the lofted interior volume serves multiple public functions, from food preparation to reading, in one grand volume. Spatial complexity is evident throughout, with each corner turned and every framed view composed with deliberation. The interior mortar-washed walls do not meet the ceiling, allowing the clerestory to diffuse light seamlessly into each quadrant. The public spaces—kitchen, dining, living, and library—are arranged in a logical four-square around a utility core. Low, sheltered openings to the south and direct access to the open desert on the north further balance the light. Exposed galvanized ductwork weaves through the upper reaches of the loft, creating the appearance of a sculptural, site-specific mechanical installation overhead. The living area is anchored to the desert floor by a large fireplace with a polished concrete

base that pulls the center of gravity back down to the Earth. The south side of this large room is dedicated to dining and food preparation. Along the exterior wall, an ample concrete shelf accommodates plants, casual dining, or even a workspace with a desert view.[7] The ingenious kitchen cabinet design mirrors the stepped profile of the building while meeting ergonomic and task lighting needs with unique grace. With this design innovation, Chafee brought abundant natural light to the work surface along with integrated task lighting as the storage cabinets decrease in depth from high to low.

All items in the house are carefully curated much like in the Merrill Residence and Chafee's own studio and residence. In this case, Chafee created six traced drawings of Glen Allison photos that outline the location and name

Exterior, looking
northwest

of each item in the house, including detailed captions
such as this one for the living and dining room drawing:

> The south clerestory and dining room window seen in this
> picture have very deep overhangs, permitting direct sun to hit
> the glass only in winter. 1. Levolor "Riviera" blinds in brushed
> aluminum, are concealed in the concrete lintel of the window.
> 2. Navajo rugs from Chinle, Arizona. 3. Mexican pigskin chair
> and ottoman. Cushions covered in handwoven Mexican
> cotton. 4. A pair of Finnish chairs with seats and backs of
> Herman Miller nylon hopsack, purchased in the Scandinavian
> Shop of Carson, Pirie, Scott, Chicago. 5. A Finnish record
> cabinet, imported from Artek in Helsinki, and also purchased
> at Carson's. 6. Antique American brass maple syrup kettle,
> used for wood. 7. Antique English, Irish and French brass
> candlesticks; a Sheffield stick; an American pewter stick and
> a miner's candle holder made of iron. 8. Indian pots from
> various pueblos and Hopi Kachinas, the wooden dolls they
> use for teaching children about their gods. 9. "Century Plant,"
> 1952 casein, by the architect.[8]

This type of documentation is more typically found
in interior design and decoration departments than in
architectural practices. Although this is the only example
of this drawing type in Chafee's archive, the level of care
and attention to the entirety of a room can be seen in
many projects throughout her career. The level of confident
eclecticism of sources and juxtapositions is reminiscent
of the Eames's home and studio or the art collection
of Albert C. Barnes as originally installed in Merion,
Pennsylvania, and is a testament to the educated and
confident eye of both mother and daughter. Documentation
of rooms created for display at Carson Pirie Scott under
the direction of Johnson illustrate a similar combination
of rigor and care that is evident throughout the Viewpoint
Residence—a sophisticated model for architecture and
interior design intertwined. Soon after construction, the

Indian rugs hung in the steep stairwell cheered us as we lived like mountain goats. Later, all went by elevator to a Michigan Avenue high-rise. In the Chicago years, the Dunbar sofa came along from a neighboring state. During many working trips abroad, the other modern things—some from as far away as Israel—found their way to us through the Saint Lawrence Seaway, and quietly slipped into place— back home in the Middle West.

Now, these old friends are, by plan, in a new house that provides them with a fresh, sophisticated, free-wheeling space for desert living.[9]

The public areas of the house are situated to the east, with bedrooms and baths to the west including an exterior shower alcove with desert views. Each zone has a dedicated HVAC unit and exposed ducts, and the general feeling is of movement from east to west, from openness and expansion to inward focus. To avoid excessive heat gain, there are no openings to the west and judicious openings to the south and east. During the early development of the project and in coordination with Richard Kesterson, the builder, Chafee was vetting options for sand-casting the "shade units," or brise-soleil, on-site as an homage to the sculptor Constantino (Tino) Nivola, whom she held in high regard for his own work and for his collaborations with Le Corbusier. In her work at Viewpoint, Chafee united some of the most powerful influences in her life with a building program that held her developing, but already distinctive, signature. In fact, the house graciously communicates its historic and personal lineage from exterior to interior, with each detail crafted from a unique narrative thread.

interior was the focus of several publications, and the client delighted in describing the lineage of its contents:

During the thirties and forties, rugs, pottery, and other Indian handicrafted treasures were brought home from trips to Santa Fe, the Navajo Reservation and Hopi Pueblos in Arizona and New Mexico. Needed furniture and glass were supplied during jaunts to Mexico.

This mix of Americanas was brought to a rear triplex in a brownstone on Chicago's LaSalle Street in the early fifties.

Ramada House   Tucson, Arizona, 1973–75

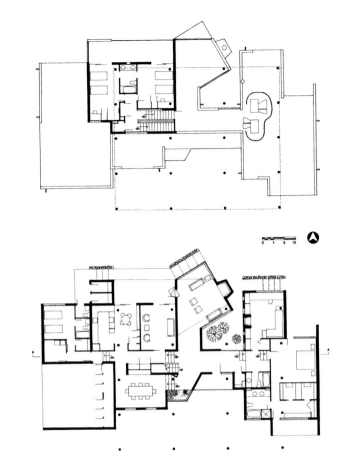

In 1972 a young couple from the Northeast looking to relocate to the Southwest began searching for a home with the "proper" architectural attitude in Tucson. At the time, a Josias Joesler–designed house was the obvious choice; Joesler had designed many of the premier Tucson residences of the thirties and forties. But after touring several Joesler homes, the couple decided his works felt like spaces intended for brief seasonal stays, unfit for the daily lives of a growing family. Eventually, their exasperated real estate agent, exhausted by their repeated disappointment, suggested to her clients that they turn their focus to finding the perfect empty lot on which to build a custom residence. After all, this couple had expressed performance criteria for their home that could not easily be met with the existing local housing stock. They took the suggestion, bought a desert property in the foothills of the Catalina Mountains northeast of Tucson and, in 1973, set out in search of a local architect.[1]

Several architects were interviewed for the job—all men—and, conforming to prevailing gender stereotypes of the day, they directed most substantial questions and serious discussion to the husband during the couple's selection process.[2] In contrast, Chafee exhibited no such presumptions, listening intently to both prospective clients and taking copious notes. But Chafee possessed a palpable imperious manner that surprised her potential clients. Favoring assertiveness over sexism, the couple carefully studied photographs of the generously appointed Merrill Residence in Connecticut and toured several of her more modest projects in Tucson, including Viewpoint, the Putnam Residence, and Chafee's home studio. The clients' personal friend, architect Robert A. M. Stern, had also vouched for Chafee's talent. Client Peter Salomon knew Stern from the East Coast and trusted his opinion that Judith Chafee was a serious and hardworking architect he knew from their student days at Yale University and certainly the "cream of the crop" in Tucson. Convinced

by their research that she could design a rugged desert dwelling with the texture of Northeastern refinement they expected, Chafee was hired.[3]

The Ramada House announces itself from an undulating desert floor on the drive north into the Catalina foothills along North Camino Real road. On the ascent, views of the house flash in staccato frames as the driver keeps one eye on the road and the other on the house. Just as the project is fully revealed, Camino Real takes an abrupt turn to the east. The tripartite nature of the house displays its essence immediately: the earth rising, the white mass of the house anchored to the ground, and the sheltering second roof meeting the sky with a shade trellis that makes logical sense for any home in a hot arid climate. Why not shade the house with a double roof? Primary roofs in

Exterior, looking
north (below)
and floor plans
(opposite)

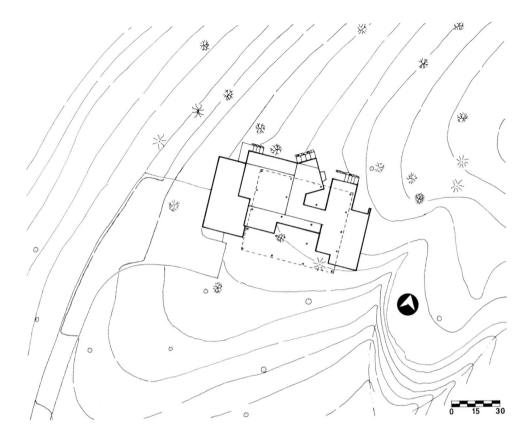

this climate typically take the full impact of the sun and heat up throughout the day, putting significant strain on mechanical cooling systems. Historically, sleeping porches were part of the summer rhythm, with families moving up to the roof or out to porches to take advantage of the significant diurnal temperature change at night in desert climates. This dual-roof strategy transforms the flat roof into a habitable room, providing a cooling effect and a psychologically comforting ceiling to the sky.

At a critical juncture in the design process Chafee wrote Stern a letter about the developing project in the Catalina foothills:

We are halfway through the working drawings on their house. I am very excited about it—a pueblo with a great cactus

rib sunshade—which though most important because of the quality of light and air motion—also saves 3 tons of air conditioning and $50 per month. Now Peter is afraid that it "looks funny," and today back from a week in San Francisco and forgetful of the summer sun they want me to remove it. And all of those Southern windows with the valley view are no longer shaded, and all those rooms planned in conjunction with the columns marching through are going to look rather pointless. And I am so disappointed it isn't going to be a really good desert house without control of light and prevailing breezes. I'm going to tell them that I sent you snapshots, please tell them it isn't funny if they ask you. It isn't.

She signs off, "come see this wilderness sometime."[4] The clients were increasingly concerned that the shade

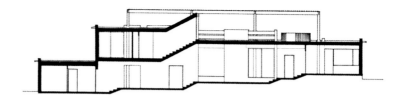

SOUTH ELEVATION

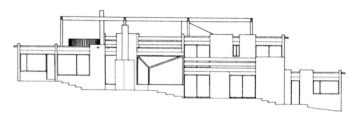

NORTH ELEVATION

roof was an unnecessary expense and might cause leakage into the rooms below. Chafee wrote Stern in an attempt to gather support for the inevitable conversation about the necessity of the shade structure. Corky Poster, an intern architect at the time, remembers a conversation in the office with the contractor George Mehl, after the bids came in high, in which Mehl argued that the ramada should be removed.[5] Chafee held her ground, the budget was raised, and the project proceeded into the construction phase.

The site for the Ramada House is large for the area, at twelve acres of open desert populated with specimen saguaro, ocotillo, and paloverde. A prickly pear forest is called out on the site plan, along with all mature trees and cacti. A site analysis drawing presents the house in a desert landscape of compound slopes with exact location and height of foliage and natural features specified, visually linking the scale of the house with landform and desert flora. The drawing also includes a detailed solar analysis including solar angles calculated throughout the year, making a strong argument for the architecture and site as fully integrated in both concept and application. The slab-on-grade foundation system is constructed with the site in mind, its mass divided into five platforms all closely following the change in topography.

The architect was presented with a highly formal list of required spaces by the clients, including separate areas for dining, living, family, library, and entry with distinct areas defined for adults and children and for sitting, study, and work.[6] Chafee noted the site was near stately foothills homes constructed in the 1930s with carefully scaled pueblo revival features built of adobe with stucco or mortar wash finishes, exposed heavy timber beams, projecting vigas, and often a small inhabitable roof area for sleeping or gathering. It was agreed that the Ramada House would respond logically to the scale and volume of the surrounding dwellings, but proceed with

a more insistent structural logic and, in response to the unrelenting climate, participate in meeting the desert with grace and intention.

Chafee references Le Corbusier in this project and directly recognizes his influence through the use of his Modulor system as a "study tool," an asset when designing the relationship between the shade roof columns and other interior building elements. She also aligns herself with "Miesian thinking" of the period of the Villa Tugendhat, with its roof patio overlooking a woodland below.[7] Even the staid entry elevation in contrast with the more dynamic rear composition is reflective of Chafee's attitude toward Mies van der Rohe, with her staggered rectangular openings, the distinctive prismatic glazing, balconies on two levels, and a cylindrical flue to the north.

The three-sided viewpoint to the Catalina Mountains provides an immersive experience of the landscape; the foreground, middle ground, far distance, and sky are brought inside as the window unit wraps above and around the spectator—a distinct and all-encompassing innovation on the traditional bay window. The building is oriented to magnetic north, which allows less sun (and therefore less solar gain) to enter the north glazing when the sun sets north of west at the summer solstice.

The presence and idea of this house struck a chord with William J.R. Curtis, author of *Modern Architecture Since 1900*:

> Even in some advanced industrial nations, there are pockets of regional consciousness, which hold out against cosmopolitan fashion. These tend to occur at the fringes where native habitats are still visible even if native culture has been undermined. In these circumstances, the best work eschews direct imitation and uses abstraction to go deeper. An example of this approach is the Ramada House in southern Arizona designed by Judith Chafee. The building stands on the edge of the desert and is formed from a protective parasol of mesquite logs and saguaro fronds that hovers above an adobe structure half buried in the ground. Seen in drawings this is an uncompromisingly modern design which descends from Le Corbusier's hot climate principle of the shading slab (e.g. the Shodhan House in India of 1951–54), but the idea has been fused with local archetypes: the simple log and twig shelters of the nomads (reinterpreted by Spanish colonial ranchers as the shading "ramada") and the pot dwellings in mud of the more sedentary communities. The result is a building of haunting poetry, its mood changing from minute to minute as light and shade dapple the walls, the roof a stable horizontal in a turbulent landscape of cacti, sand and crags.[8]

The main entrance is from the south and is often marked by a graphic light-and-shadow pattern on the white slump block concrete walls, creating a sundial effect as the sun traces its path on the house and surrounding landscape, marking the time of day and season of the year. The lattice roof extends past the southern face of the building below to maximize shading and provide a protected entry procession from guest parking to the front door—which is further protected under a small building overhang that forms a third roof plane. During the spring, a field of yellow desert wildflowers surrounds the entry path with a carpet of blooms and active pollinators. The two main sections of the plan join at the entry vestibule, with master bedroom and private library rising in elevation to the east and to the living, kitchen, and dining rooms

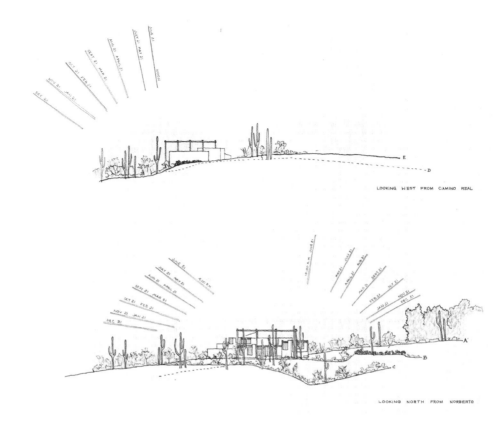

LOOKING WEST FROM CAMINO REAL

LOOKING NORTH FROM NORBERTO

located directly to the west. A small solarium and an elevation change effectively separate the entry area and the dining room via a narrow passage that requires close proximity to one of the twenty ponderosa pine columns harvested from the Catalina Mountains. The regular presence of the wooden columns for the ramada roof unifies the asymmetrical plan arrangement, with a regular column grid spaced 19 feet 4 inches east to west and 12 feet north to south. The horizontal shade structure is built out of 2-inch × 10-inch wood framing and 1-inch × 4-inch wood slats, which project an alternating broad shadow and narrow sliver of light on the surface of the building and adjacent landscape. The house was originally conceived in standard concrete block with a light-gray mortar wash for ease of maintenance and also to

encourage a monolithic reading of the building mass. The clients preferred a more distinct reading of the masonry module, which led to the selection of a rounded concrete block, known locally as "slump block," rendered in white and leading to an even more distinct graphic pattern of light and shadow on the building surface.

A central stair is placed at the intersection of two foundation platforms and leads to bedrooms on the second level and the sleeping porch above. Built-in furnishings can be found throughout the house, including seating and storage in the library and family room, and desks in the children's rooms that are adjustable to accommodate growth over time. The kitchen incorporates a movable section of countertop to allow for maximum flexibility in the arrangement of the room. The master

Exterior, looking
northwest (left),
and living room
(below)

Living room with
prism window

Exterior court,
looking skyward

View of dining area
and ramada above

bedroom fully integrates the columns as a frame surrounding the bed, an homage to the four-poster bed. Natural ventilation and daylighting strategies are evident throughout. An exterior court adjacent to the entry vestibule provides a mediated view of the exterior and full-height operable walls for air movement. It is not until guests arrive at the more formal living room to the north of the entry vestibule that the Catalina Mountains fully present themselves and draw people forward into the folded prismatic wall opening. This unique device creates an enveloping experience where one is both inside and outside simultaneously—a customized communion with the mountains that logically meets their grandeur with deceptively simple means and materials.

Judith Chafee brought a lifetime of local intelligence to the creation of the Ramada House, permeating its design with precedents from afar along with a long-term appreciation of dwelling patterns established by prior generations in southern Arizona. These time-tested lessons of vernacular building overlaid with a rigorous exploration of other desert-dwelling cultures defines Chafee's uniquely formed regionalist imperative, imbuing this house with a presence that feels both inevitable and revolutionary.

Exterior, looking
south (left) and
view looking north
from the sleeping
deck (below)

Central court,
looking toward
the Catalina
Mountains

Exterior court

Jacobson Residence

Tucson, Arizona, 1975–77

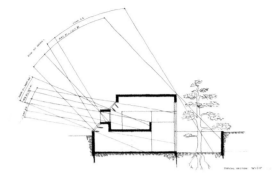
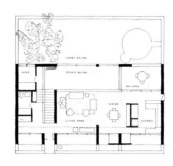

Art and Joan Jacobson commissioned the Jacobson Residence, although it is Joan who is regarded as the primary client. For Joan, a practicing weaver with grown children, this residence took on a highly personal program. She requested ample space for weaving, reading, cooking, gathering, and gardening, and a single well-appointed bedroom. Art Jacobson was a philosopher by training who organized motorcycle tours throughout the Southwest. Together, they had amassed a collection of books particular to their interests, which were essential for their creative practice. Thus the housing of this collection took on a special importance in the design of this home. Upon becoming empty nesters, the couple traded Evanston, Illinois, for Tucson's desert climate and robust art culture. After experiencing the charismatic atmosphere of Chafee's studio during the search for an architect, Joan felt an instant connection with the architect. Despite Chafee's relatively small portfolio of built works at the time of their meeting, Joan was so impressed by how Chafee revealed the various discrete spaces of her studio in seemingly choreographed fashion that she was convinced that Chafee was the architect who could realize the Jacobsons' vision.[1]

The initial conceptualization of the Jacobson Residence began as a compact, double-height, earth-sheltered,

one-bedroom residence with an expansive artist studio and library. In the first iteration of Chafee's design, an aerie and balcony anchor the corners of the building—one a cave-like room with light from the north, the other an open space with apertures on three sides, protected but open to the air and light. The main entrance from the south leads into the upper level through a skylighted vestibule into living, dining, kitchen, and balcony spaces. A central stair continues into the studio below with an adjacent sunken courtyard. A large deciduous tree and a circular pool with exterior shower define the courtyard. Detailed solar studies confirm direct light penetration or reflected light from at least two sides within all spaces in the winter, except into the courtyard, which only receives light reflected off the north wall at the summer solstice. Evaporatively cooled air is drawn into the lower levels by gravity. The weaving studio is given pride of place in the composition, with the working area appointed with two stories of glazing facing north and looking into the exterior studio court.

The inwardly focused, earth-sheltered first iteration developed into the final built form while retaining the main elements, including direct solar utilization, a courtyard organization, library, aerie, studio, and natural ventilation, but more fully integrating the defining features of the building program—all above grade. Private entry for the

Exterior,
looking south

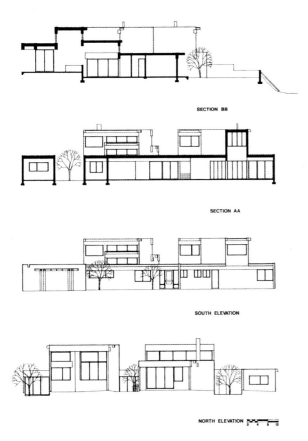

SECTION BB

SECTION AA

SOUTH ELEVATION

NORTH ELEVATION

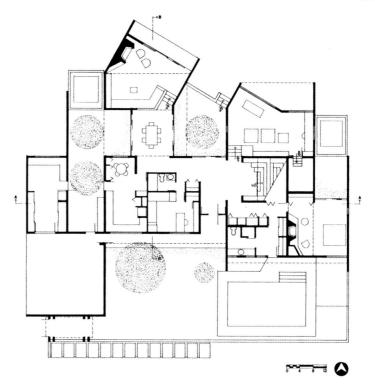

112

homeowners is through the open garage, and public access is provided via a covered trabeated gateway; both entrances open into the protected south courtyard, with its ample views to the city with the desert in the foreground. The organizing strategy for the house moved beyond one central courtyard toward a scheme of multiple courts of varying size and function, but all tuned by the architect to allow for daylighting and natural ventilation throughout the house.

A flat-panel hot-water solar array running along the southern edge of the court is assimilated into the site plan, hidden behind a low terraced wall but visible from the south as a definitive part of the linear east-west aligned composition. Water heated in the solar array is stored in a massive tank located below the entry court

and heavily insulated by the surrounding earth. The cold nighttime temperatures require heating of the pool from the solar array during most seasons. The interior is kept warm, as well, with this system, coupled with direct solar radiation in the winter. This was innovative technology for the time and place, presenting challenges in its installation, but coordination with an experienced mechanical contractor brought all the parts together into a highly effective system. Chafee often included experts on her design team, and although she certainly respected their training and specialization, she had ideas for each project that often pushed engineers' problem-solving skills into new and creative territory.

The northern courtyards are envisioned as three exterior rooms that bring outdoor desert life into the

fold of the house. The dining room is flanked by two courts with clerestory lighting above, providing a soaring, spacious quality without tending toward excess. The living room and weaving studio face mountain views and share an edge with the courtyards, allowing each room to have natural lighting from more than one direction. Opposing operable windows encourage prevailing breezes to enter the house and flush out the heat of the day.

The sacred center of the house is the library stair that leads to a secluded reading loft. The oak treads rise to over twelve feet above finish floor, its risers doubling as book storage. The intentional nonlinear arrangement of the stair provides a variety of sitting or gathering areas along with places to display sculptural artwork. During the design process, client and architect immersed themselves in conversations about bookshelves, movable shelves, sliding shelves, and high ladders. These creative discussions coalesced into the multifunctioning book steps that act as a threshold to the special hidden place above. The client's extensive collection of books could be read on the stair or aerie, which Chafee referred to in connection to Welsh and Scottish overlooks—an homage to Joan Jacobson's family roots. This sanctuary for books is constructed on top of a concrete and steel fire vault for Jacobson's textile collection, which unites two of her

passions in one construct. The architect described this multistep creation as an "involving stair," as it necessitated active engagement in the process of exploration.[2] Because the stair does not include a handrail, both ascent and descent require significant precaution not unlike scaling the great stepped pyramids of Mexico and Mesoamerica.

Throughout her career, Chafee carried on a dialogue with the architects that inspired her early development, drawing from the quiet gathering of light in the library buildings of Alvar Aalto and H. H. Richardson's lovingly detailed shingle-style buildings. In the Richardsonian house, a monumental stair tended to be visible from, or adjacent to, the main entry—a central focal point that also provides access to the upper floors and the more private spaces of a home.[3] The stair takes on the appearance of a large piece of integrated furniture or cabinetry that rises, light-filled, to the upper reaches and deftly connects floor to ceiling in one upward spiral thrust. Adjacent to the front door, the stair often accepts a formal seating area for guests at the level of the first riser. Richardson's stairs are striking because of the complexity that grows with every turn or rise—the ambition to include multiple functions in one integrated sculptural composition makes this stair important well beyond its intended use. An avoidance of applied decoration on the exterior and the

structural materials, replacing the exterior wood-spanning members seen in previous projects. The new site-cast beam strategy completes the palette of massive materials in the Jacobson Residence, allowing the house to meet the harshness of the desert with grace and force, in effect minimizing the annual maintenance of wood in exterior applications. The long north- and south-facing elevations of the house are punctuated by clerestory lights and large expanses of glass. From the interior, the edge of the beams frame the sky and mountains beyond. Viewed from the exterior, these structural elements appear effortless in their work, providing north- and northeast-facing transparency in striking contrast to the monumental quality of block and concrete.

The generous high-volume workspace of the studio was described by the client as light-filled, but not overly bright, and large, and well-appointed.[5] A room for creative work and contemplation, the space includes exterior apertures on three sides and borrowed light from the aerie, which shares light with the studio and main bedroom. The studio was a crucial part of the program, as Joan Jacobson was a weaver by avocation; she began training on the loom at Kingswood School at Cranbrook and continued creating textiles throughout her life. In Tucson, she is a founding member of the Tucson Weavers Guild. The bedroom suite is secluded from the rest of the house in the southeast corner, with deceptively high ceilings that imbue the room with abundant natural light and air movement. A personal space for the client, it is flanked by a small private court to the north and direct access to the pool and southern court.

The site plan is calibrated for solar orientation, with optimal views to the Catalina Mountains, and visual protection from future adjacent landowners. All rooms are open to air movement and views, while the east-west elevations are comparatively stark to break the western sun and block the view of close neighbors to the east. During

full integration of large elements, such as stairs and inglenooks, into a residential composition is a challenge that was met with grace by Richardson and Chafee alike. Without reverting to direct references in the work, Chafee continued in subtle conversation with her lineage of peers through the iterative development of projects over time.

Exposed reinforced concrete block creates a distinct modular pattern throughout the house and beautifully complements the fine carpentry and carefully site-casted beams, which incorporate a desert hue into the mix through the integration of sand from the surroundings.[4] The subtle surface quality of the concrete beams and textured block coursing offers a rich contrast to the softly illuminated interiors. Site-cast concrete beams were a new development in Chafee's ongoing exploration of exposed

Exterior, looking
southeast at
living room

the construction process, Diane Hastings, from Chafee's studio, climbed by ladder to the loft area after the masonry walls and beams were in place and articulated that she thought that this place was going to make a wonderful ruin. The idea that a building could be imagined as a future ruin was often discussed by Chafee and underpinned her decision to place the primary structural form of a building into a deeper conversation with the landscape, beyond program and daily concerns.

As the project neared completion, Judith Chafee gathered the client, contractor, and design team in the southern court for the planting of a shade tree. A Scottish piper could be heard approaching from the distance. Unbeknownst to anyone in the crowd, the architect invited bagpipes into the ceremony as a fitting reference to the Scottish heritage of Joan Jacobson at her new homeplace in the Sonoran Desert. On the northern edge of this same courtyard, Chafee stamped the names of everyone involved in the project, from contractor to design team, into the concrete along the client's entry procession— a reminder of origins, which, years later, assumed the character of a memento mori integrated into daily life.[6]

118

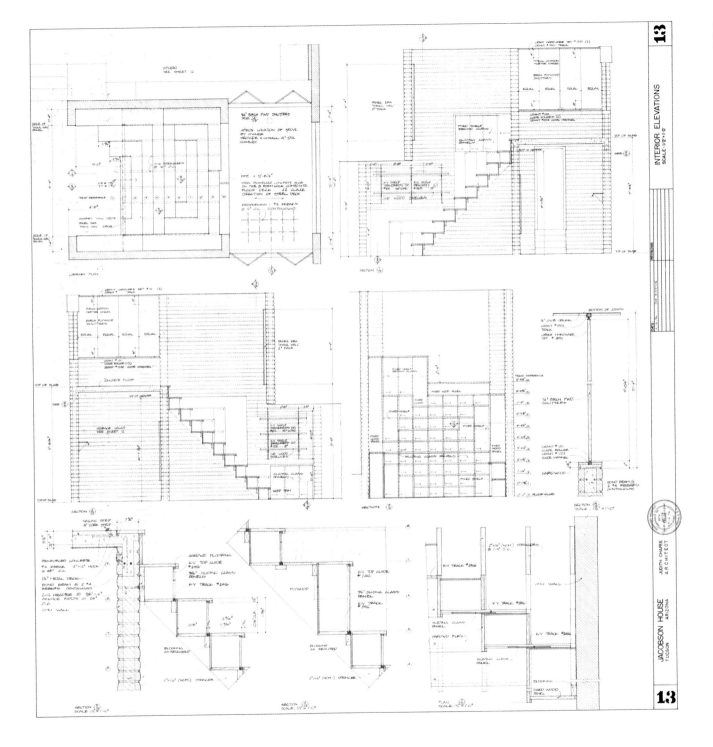

120

122

Blackwell Residence Tucson, Arizona, 1978–80

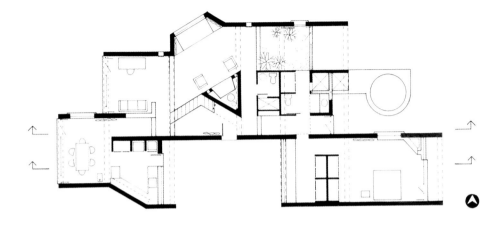

Ten years into Chafee's Tucson practice and after her work had received significant attention in notable publications, a man by the name of Jerry Blackwell, then executive vice president of Old Tucson Studios, contacted Chafee and wanted to commission a custom home for himself. The site he had in mind sat along the road approaching the entry to Tucson Mountain Park, which Blackwell passed daily on his way to work. The parcel abutted pristine protected land that the City of Tucson would years later move to subsume into the park.

At the time Blackwell first began dreaming of this house, a local artist owned the land he coveted. The site included unimproved native Sonoran Desert scrub with prominent rock outcroppings and numerous saguaro, ocotillo, and barrel cacti. Deer and other desert fauna freely roamed through the area. After Blackwell approached the artist to purchase the land, she made it abundantly clear that her property at the edge of Tucson Mountain Park was not for sale. While the artist did not herself inhabit the site, a contingent of Tucson's seasonal homeless population frequently camped on the land. In time, this peaceful tacit arrangement was broken when a murder took place there.[1] Stunned by what had happened, the artist recoiled from retaining the property and struck a deal for Jerry Blackwell to purchase it.

Finally in possession of his long-beloved site, Blackwell commissioned Chafee to design his ideal house. The timing of this project happened to coincide with Blackwell's divorce and open acknowledgment of himself as gay. This project marked the beginning of a new chapter in Blackwell's life. The client and his challenging site would require Chafee to muster skills she had honed over her time living in the desert and working with some of the most renowned architects in the world. Blackwell and Chafee's fateful meeting and agreement to build would help define Chafee's reputation as an "uncompromising artist" and a cantankerous advocate for producing architecture of dignity in Sonoran Desert landscapes.

Her project development process began with understanding the exigencies of the place and ascertaining the habits of the occupant. For Chafee, the Blackwell house grew out of the harshness and rhythms of the desert, expressing careful material distinction between interior and exterior. The house appropriately responded to the specific needs of the environment with deep-set glazing to the south, operable interior shading devices on the east, and minimal west-facing openings to mitigate the heat from the harsh desert sun. As Chafee began the design process, she explained:

Entry procession
with ramada

I like to visualize it almost like a nomadic situation first like you're camping there and putting up little tents…It's a matter of organizing all these human functions, setting them on the site, and then, in a way, making the least architecture possible to make the environment comfortable.[2]

When driving west along Gates Pass Road just past a significant rock escarpment, visitors turned onto a dirt entry drive, which led to a rustic ramada carport. Cast-in-place concrete steps directed guests up to the tall and slender steel-framed entry door with vestibule beyond. The interior arrangement and program, developed from a series of intimate working sessions with Blackwell, reflected the customized needs of this owner at a pivotal time in his life. Chafee remembered this specific conversation during the design process:

> JC: How do you feel about having guests.
> JB: Well, I live alone and like it that way.
> JC: You don't want people coming to visit?
> JB: Yes, I do, but I do not want them to stay for more than four or five days.
> JC: Then let's make the house work that way.[3]

The exposed sleeping loft adjacent to the central living space was a result of this early conversation, along with the massive fireplace/solar flue that dominated the interior volume of the house and provided a geometric center for the entire composition. A prominent steel stair joined to one edge of a triangular masonry mass led up to the loft. Chafee called this element the "Rudolph stair" in reference to Paul Rudolph's daring cantilevered single-flight stair that he designed for his New Haven residence. It is only logical that her design, which she describes here, pays homage to the master of massive concrete and block construction:

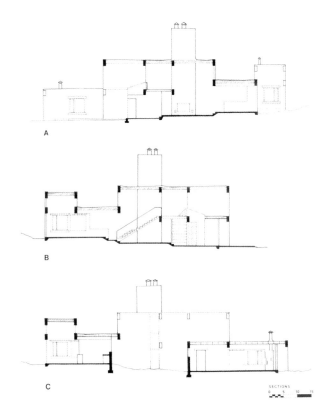

A

B

C

SECTIONS
0 5 10 15

Further development of the site-cast beam took place in this house, centered around a "solar flue." The multi-use masonry mass contains a steel fireplace flue within it and dampers for both the fireplace and solar flues. As a solar flue during autumn and spring, the sun-heated masonry is intended to draw air from the vents on the periphery of the house through the house, causing passive ventilation. In cold weather, it serves as a duct to recirculate fireplace-heated air from the high loft space back to the lower floor. In summer it is used as a duct to dump evaporation-cooled air from the roof into the house.

The site provides many natural vertical surfaces so that some interior spaces are closed spatially, not by their glass walls but by rock outcroppings or mountainside.[4]

This one-bedroom house with guest loft included a private master suite and ample space for public gathering in the central volume. A two-story-high east window looking toward Tucson was integrated into a built-in concrete seating area with an insulated cushion panel to limit direct heat gain. The massive triangular fireplace and solar flue was a prominent element at the center of the composition, separating the entry vestibule from the main living area. For the open guest loft above, Chafee removed the guardrail and provided just enough room for a bed, nightstand, and desk, which encouraged guests to move on after a few days. The floor was made of reclaimed wood from a decommissioned local gymnasium, its painted stripes visible as an abstract pattern on the reorganized wood planks. Borrowed light from glass partitions provides illumination under the loft for a bath and interior garden. Jerry Blackwell was delighted that the rough-sawn pine used on the interior ceiling and exterior soffit was sourced from a mill on nearby Mount Lemmon.

Architect Will Bruder taught alongside Chafee at the University of Arizona School of Architecture and became an admirer of the Blackwell Residence. He wrote the following:

Ever since Judith Chafee returned to the Tucson desert to practice architecture, she has created unique and thoughtful structures, which are in harmony with their desert environments. Her architecture is generally humble in its materials and details, while at times being appropriately almost monumental in its presence in the grand scale of its rugged desert settings. Her style is meant to create simple backgrounds for living in the desert, which let the occupants of her homes enjoy the dynamics of the sun, both aesthetically and climatically. While she often borrows solar and energy strategies from ancient desert architectures of the world, her own interpretations of these ideas represent very fresh and creative solutions that maximize today's technologies.[5]

In a seemingly prescient move, toward the end of the construction process, Chafee had directed the construction crew to install one of the discarded massive site-cast concrete beams in vertical orientation along the entry axis—directly west of the front door. She designated this final addition a menhir, after exploring megalithic standing stones in Puglia and Sardinia during her residency at the American Academy in Rome. She noted the ritual marking of dates in the astronomical calendar, including the winter and summer solstice, as essential to the culture. This unexpected marker in

Entry court
(left), entry door
drawing (right)

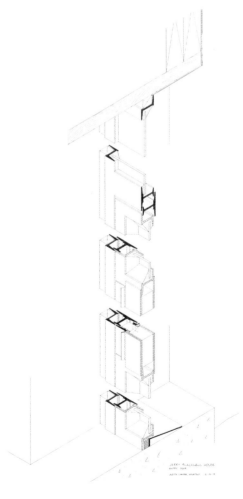

the landscape mirrored the vertical power and scale of the native saguaro but held a more speculative lineage tied to ritual inhabitation, architectural procession, and the rhythms of life and death.

For Bruder, the legacy of the Blackwell Residence was summed up in a letter he wrote for the Save Blackwell House Campaign in which he described it as "a 'living' artifact of desert magic for all to learn from and enjoy."[6] Others saw a darker side to the heritage of this desert alchemy in the altercations of its past transient occupants and the encroachment of the dwelling on a seemingly pristine desert habitat. Another long-term resident of Tucson, writer Lawrence Cheek, kept in close contact with Chafee and wrote about the Blackwell Residence from direct experience:

If the Blackwell House has metaphorical balls, it also has character. It gives off the impression of immense strength, but isn't arrogant. Instead of planting it on the top of a hill, where it would command attention like a gorilla beating its chest, Chafee nestled it between two rocky rises to the north and east. It isn't invisible from the road, but it is fairly shy....This is why the house makes so many onlookers uncomfortable: it doesn't mesh with our usual concept of architecture, which we want to be an art that creates fantasies for us.

Sometimes fantasies are an appropriate part of the script. San Xavier del Bac was a fandango of baroque ornamentation because its 18th-century architect figured it would stun the natives into adopting the God who had inspired such a building. But the Blackwell House had a very different mission. It wasn't designed to attract or enchant anyone, or to cause a

religious revolution. It is minimalist architecture, intended to let whoever lives inside to experience the Sonoran Desert as purely and thoroughly as possible.

Loveliness isn't the point of the Blackwell House; the point is integrity.[7]

The architecture culture in Arizona—Tucson in particular —is haunted by this house, which sat along the entry to Gates Pass and Saguaro National Park. Chafee designed the Blackwell Residence in the late 1970s and it was inhabited by the original client for eight years, until Pima County forced abandonment of the structure by not issuing a building permit to replace a freshwater line that had been destroyed by storm water rushing down the arroyo at the site's entry. With this administrative constraint in place, the desired land was now in reach for inclusion in the Tucson Mountain Park. Jerry Blackwell trucked water to the house for months before putting the house up for sale. After finally securing the property, the county vetted options for the site and the Blackwell Residence slowly became a ruin, as doors, fixtures, and glazing were removed or destroyed. Drug culture became rampant in the area, and layers of graffiti covered the carefully mortar-washed walls. Architects and seekers of ruin porn frequented the site for the awe-inspiring, or even sublime quality, of this brutally exposed relic. In the Blackwell Residence, Chafee struck a delicate balance between the desert environment and the architecture, which was evident in the daily rhythms of the house in its prime. When the house was abandoned, the Sonoran Desert slowly took the majority of the site back into its fold, with only the walls and roof of its ruinous form still rising strong above the land. Violence and criminal activity after dark increased on the property, and public outcry for action was evident in the daily newspaper accounts and coffeehouses. After years of provocative commentary in the local paper the house was demolished in 1998; only its foundation remains, hidden under rubble and desert sand.

The longevity of the Blackwell Residence can be measured by the lives that filled the space, the exhibitions that were staged in the house, and the parties that animated the adjacent desert and rock outcroppings. The house was a landmark along Gates Pass Road that appeared and disappeared—dreamlike—behind low hills at forty miles per hour. If you blinked, the structure could be easily missed, and if you focused too much, your car could veer into the arroyo.

Time could be measured on the weathered surface of the stacked concrete masonry units, the flush joints and rough mortar wash giving the appearance of a strange geology. The rough-sawn wood is embedded with the memory of time and the pattern of growth—its patina gives an aura of both authenticity and inevitability. Taken as a whole, the building and adjacent landscape make a

132

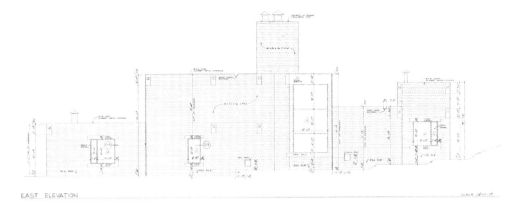

EAST ELEVATION   SCALE 1/4"=1'0"

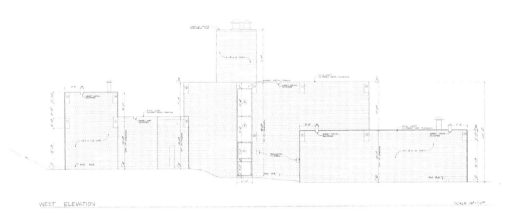

WEST ELEVATION   SCALE 1/4"=1'0"

compelling case for inhabiting this stretch of desert, with every detail of daily life considered and everything in its place for living in harmony with the desert biome. Architecture historian and critic William J.R. Curtis wrote a letter in support of saving the house to the Pima County Parks and Recreation Commission:

> Judith Chafee is one of those rare architects of high quality to have addressed the problems of living in harmony with the desert environment. The Blackwell House, in particular, is an exemplary solution to the sunny climate of southern Arizona in terms of orientation and shading. In my opinion, the subtly composed abstract forms sit well with the surrounding boulders, while the interiors offer carefully framed views of the landscape.[8]

For those unaware of the history of the Blackwell Residence, it is now difficult to even locate the site. The curb cut that marked its presence was demolished and the entry drive regraded to erase the processional trail into the site. As people gather in the evening at the nearby Gates Pass lookout area, the lights of Tucson become visible to the east. Between the lookout and the lights, a dense field of saguaro cacti populates a landscape of low rolling hills, projecting an otherworldly anthropomorphic grace. The former Blackwell land sits on a geological saddle between rock outcroppings in the middle ground of the view toward Tucson, but the house's massive Persian-inspired solar flue that marked this thoughtful desert partnership no longer rises from the center of the composition.

Dining,
looking north

133

Living room,
with Chafee on
the right (left),
and loft (below)

Late Practice

Essay by Kathryn McGuire

The second part of Judith Chafee's life and work was divided between her academic and professional avocations. In 1983, her lectures and participation in symposiums outside the academic arena, her dedication to architectural education, and her outstanding professional work earned her the national award of Fellow in the American Institute of Architects, the first woman in Arizona to receive the FAIA honor.

From 1981 to 1992, her work was well published in national and international magazines and local periodicals. Each year she averaged four to five out-of-town collaborations with professional award juries, symposiums, and lectures in academic venues and at various AIA conferences.[1] These opportunities provided connection with her peers and professional stimulation on an international platform, benefiting her office and, even more so, her college studio, as it provided influences and professional networks for her students. The invited jury reviewers and seminars induced engaging conversations with like-minded, as well as contrary, exponents, including Fay Jones, Joseph Esherick, Frank Israel, Tod Williams, Will Bruder, John Munier, and many others. This was during the time William J.R. Curtis wrote an extensive article in the *Architectural Review*, in August 1984, "Principle versus Pastiche: Perspectives on Some Recent Classicisms and Modern Transformations of Classicism," in which he noted:

> We happen to have concentrated on various species of Classicism because the matter is in vogue. But whether relevant sources lie in mud huts or mosques, in factories, cottages or cathedrals, some of the issues are surely the same. How in an increasingly industrialized world, to avoid both the anomie of meagre functionalism, and the bogus "remedy" of saccharine revivalism? How to transform lessons from history in a way that is appropriate on many levels from the organizational to the ornamental? How to achieve authenticity rather than following the easy road to the ersatz?[2]

Chafee was in agreement with this assessment of postmodernism as too often a shallow attempt to placate nostalgia and avoid real issues. She continued this conversation through the 1980s—in her teaching and in gatherings at Washington University in St. Louis, California State Polytechnic University in Pomona, and various AIA symposiums, and she referenced the subject in some of her lectures and writings during that time.

Ramada House,
*ARTSPACE
Southwestern
Contemporary Arts
Quarterly* cover,
Spring 1982

Regional Consciousness

In 1982 William Peterson, the editor of *Artspace: Southwestern Contemporary Arts Quarterly*—a successful regional arts magazine published in New Mexico—identified a need for articles from the field of architecture. After a member of the board, Robert Peters, suggested Peterson talk to Judith Chafee, it was decided she would be the magazine's first presenter of architecture. Peters was a Yale-educated, SOM-trained architect who had escaped Chicago and the postmodern "plague" to join a friend in New Mexico and decided it was a good place in which to settle.[3]

He met Chafee at an AIA regional conference there, and then again in 1989 as AIA representatives at the "International Conference on Architecture, Urban Planning and Design" in Finland; they saw work by Alvar Aalto (1898–1976), whom Chafee had met on an earlier trip with her mother. As much as Chafee admired Aalto, Peters felt that she was more influenced by the modern architects in the east. They struck up an enduring friendship, and Chafee referred to Peters as "a friendly voice out in the desert." They respected each other's work and opinions, and would discuss architecture issues during late-night phone calls. Peters observed that Chafee was "fond of concrete as an aesthetic material," and when he saw her mother's house, he remarked, "It was a nice balance with the rawness of materials and how she could see them lived in."[4]

Chafee's work received some recognition from her inclusion in seminars and publications, and the continual question of style would follow. Her early exposure to the truth found in anthropology and indigenous precedents, combined with her formal emphatic training in Chicago modern thinking, saw the notion of style as a false distraction. *Artspace* provided Chafee with a platform to declare her thoughts against categorization as regionalist and/or modernist, among other designations:

Occasionally I am asked to show the work, to "explain" it. Recently, given our state of affairs in which one could just be curious about a person and how the person saw the parts, I have repeatedly been asked to show work in relation to an attitude about "Regionalism" or "Women in Architecture." It is true that I am not a male practicing architecture in New York. Is my place or my sex less universal because I am not? Do I have any less responsibility to be a thoroughly modern practitioner with world-wide concern, or a deeply sensitive human being? What is happening when those who can't find or grow roots may steal fleeting pleasures from distant times and places, paste them on shells, and sell them to those who can grovel behind the facades, a joke that never was theirs, while they become a little more isolated from a sense of belonging in this world?

Last summer on a "Regionalist" panel, I coined one for myself: The Region of the Mindful Heart. This region is as far-reaching and as deep as my comprehension and understanding can make it. When the boundaries so set are too narrow to answer questions and problems I can perceive, then it is time to know and understand more.[5]

When Chafee began her young adulthood, she changed from desert dweller who visited the Midwest to a metropolitan dweller who visited the desert. The concept of home took on a new meaning. In Chicago she felt like an immigrant looking for her roots, an outsider learning the new language and subtleties of the region. Comfort could be found in compatible thoughts, if one was willing to wade through the modern theoretical deliberation about the arts and architecture as espoused by John Dewey (1859–1952) and Louis H. Sullivan (1856–1924), and Chafee's personal library can attest to her attempts to reconcile their idealism with her own. As her personal understanding became more clarified and as a way of remaining grounded far from home, Chafee took refuge in the interweaving of democracy and social justice, in emotional and intellectual concepts. She understood the need to consider a holistic approach at a time when science was considered the dominant reference and separated from intuitive or emotional senses. As Sullivan wrote:

> No phase of human nature can contain greater interest for the student of psychology than the history, natural, political, religious and artistic, or the successive phases for good and for ill of Objectivity and Subjectivity. They are the two controlling elements of human endeavor. They have caused in their internecine warfare misery and perturbation. They are ordinarily known and spoken of as the intellectual and the emotional, but they lie deeper, much deeper, than these. They lie in the very heart of Nature.[6]

How could Chafee, with her roots in Chicago and farther, to eastern Europe, form such a solid connection to the American Southwest that she would be compelled to return even after the connection was broken for fourteen years? There was a blend in her own nature that had been taken for granted, a modern ethos with vernacular awareness that traces back to aboriginal occurrences. The information was there, and Chafee, as a child of the desert, was eager to absorb it all—its smells, tastes, appearances, textures, and sounds—and a sixth sense called on a perception of rightness deep within her being. She had a regionalist spirit with a modernist morality.

Chafee's work was included in *A Guide to Tucson Architecture* in 2002, in which authors Anne M. Nequette and R. Brooks Jeffery wrote the following response to Chafee's Tucson work:

> The Tucson buildings of Judith Chafee are unequaled in their power and originality. She created dynamic spaces through the continuity of inside and outside, expressed the power of the structure, did not use formal references to

previous styles, and achieved balance through a limited color and material palette, echoing the modern age and the resilience of the desert.[7]

Judith Chafee, 1983

During the 1980s Judith Chafee's architectural office was experiencing a positive flow of activity in various regions, from the pine forest of northern Arizona to the high desert of Sonoita in the southeastern part of the state. In each project Chafee started by studying the land with the knowledge that something human-made would be introduced. The first question was always, how shall these new objects not only meet the needs of the client but also affect the environment? Then a choreography began between the human, the landscape, and the environment. Chafee was the astute director, one who could draw from focused observation and experience of past and present cultures, which provided ample choices for the possible technological inclusions. It may have seemed as though an intuitive nature was orchestrating her work, but Chafee had a vast depth of architectural and anthropological understanding to which she was attuned, and that music resonated in her buildings.

In an article for the *Tucson Weekly* in 2000, writer Margaret Regan included parts of an interview with Diane Hastings, an architect in Alaska who began her career working for Chafee in 1973.[8] "She wouldn't have considered (modernism) a style," says Hastings, who first served as a draftsman for Chafee and later studied under her at the University of Arizona. "It was more a commitment, the right way to design…Modernism was a moral issue to her, it had to do with the truth." Regan wrote:

> That truth had to do with the honesty of the materials. If a building is supported by steel it should say so. Its form should follow its function, and its materials should be of their own time and place; the building should relate to its site and its climate. Non-functional ornamentation is out. Hastings says the principles she learned from Chafee in Tucson are just as applicable in Alaska; likewise, Chafee's northeastern houses relate to their environment as much as her desert houses do.[9]

Pinetop and the Ramsey Canyon Preserve

Chafee's desert houses received the most prominent focus, as they were located in various terrains throughout the Tucson area. But in 1980, two houses, at different ends of Arizona, presented diverse, if not opposing, requirements: a ranch house in Sonoita in which to enjoy mild winters for the Hydemans, and a summer vacation cottage in the northern pine forest for the Dahms. The use of cedar for the house in Pinetop-Lakeside was an unexpected design choice for the Arizona context. *Artspace* was the only publication in which the house was ever featured and in which Chafee wrote the following:

> The pleasure and nostalgia of designing a wood house after years of desert houses conjured up memories of the way the geometry of Louis Sullivan's houses at Ocean Springs continuously provided parts of the living areas with opportunities to catch the breezes. The volumes are, as shingles would have them, shelf-like and continuous.[10]

The Dahm Residence completed in 1982 in Pinetop was designed for J. J. and Cecil Dahm, after Chafee had provided a unique addition to their retirement home in Tucson. The Dahms wanted to build a vacation house in Pinetop-Lakeside, a four-hour drive to a cooler pine-forest environment that would provide a sanctuary from Tucson's summer heat. The building site is located on a small lot in the forest with developed spaces for vacation houses arranged around a small golf course. The house's exterior of cedar shingles wraps around the shell-like continuous volumes that form a U-shape embracing the private woods, preserving the largest trees centered in the site. An open cedar deck completes the form around the trees and connects one end to the screened-in porch and the other to the master bedroom. The comfortable two-bedroom, two-bathroom house appears modest inside, but there is a fineness to the details that sets it apart from a traditional shingle house. Walls and ceilings of whitewashed wood

Hydeman Residence,
Sonoita, Arizona

142

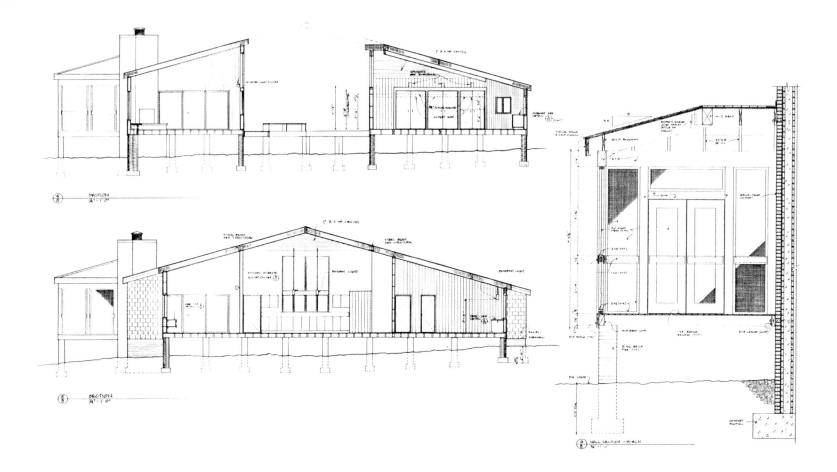

Dahm Residence,
Pinetop, Arizona,
dining and living
room

144

siding allow for the continuous flow between the spaces, and well-defined window locations capture natural breezes and introduce natural light to the interior. A horizontal band of built-in cabinets wrap around the living and dining edges, culminating at a clean-lined brick fireplace and hearth. Public areas enjoy open circulation and high ceilings while the bedrooms are given more privacy, but each space is oriented toward the big windows facing the private woods. Historic references are seen in the wood shingle detailing, and cultural references of a summer cottage are visible in the screened porch and floor plan, as they are combined with the modernist's definition of light and volume. The house's three large consecutive bays define the south and west cedar walls and provide a form that moves around to the forest views contributing to the modern functional floor plan. The exterior form echoes the traditional shingled cottages in other forested parts of the country, such as Guilford, Bristol, and Oak Park. Louis Sullivan's summer cottages in Ocean Springs and his familiar directive, often considered by Chafee, of the important relationship between function and form also come to mind: "And thus, when native instinct and sensibility shall govern the exercise of our beloved art; when known law, the respected law, shall be that form ever follow function."[11]

Soon after the Dahm Residence was completed in the northeastern part of the state, another mountain location came into the conversation. The southeast quarter of Arizona's majestic mountains are part of the Coronado National Forest, located along the Mexico and Arizona border. These high desert areas with rolling grasslands and riparian valleys contain exuberant vegetation and wildlife. These regions are so distinct in terrain and ecology that, on visiting, it is impossible to mistake where one is, be it the Huachuca Mountain Range, the Sonoita Prairie, or San Raphael River that converges into the Patagonia-Sonoita Creek region. These are places that satisfy biophilic needs.[12]

During the late 1970s, the Arizona Nature Conservancy was established to provide an active presence in preserving many significant places in these areas. In one such area, the Ramsey Canyon Preserve in the Huachuca Mountains, Tom Collazo was managing the Mile Hi Ranch and Bird Sanctuary in Ramsey Canyon Creek Preserve, where he lived with his wife, Debbie. The 1983 forest fires caused sufficient damage to create a watershed moment for the couple—it wiped out most of their domicile and the visitor center. With their once-rambling one-story cabin mostly in ruins, they needed a new home and the Nature Conservancy needed a new visitor center. There was no money in the budget, and they needed help. Then Tom remembered Judith Chafee.

Tom Collazo first met Chafee when he worked on the library cabinets for the Ramada House. He later partnered with Elliott Price for the Stanton Residence remodel project by Chafee in 1979, with Elliott as the main cabinetmaker and Tom as his assistant. Tom remembered that "her drawings were pretty clear and when we met Judith, she was smart, talented, and knew what she was doing. She had an idea of what she wanted and what the job should be. Very uncompromising— in a good way."[13]

Tom invited Chafee to visit Ramsey Canyon to see the situation. It was a beautiful forest area in the mountains, but what was left on the site was wood and rubble from the main cabin and a few small camper cabins undamaged by the flooding. "It was incredible. She offered to donate her services," he said. "She could visualize how to see a new building, get the 'spirit' of the Ramsey Canyon bird sanctuary. Everything was painted a dark 'canyon rustic' green—their standard color. Judith said it was ugly. The color should be the gray of the sycamore bark."[14]

Chafee produced simple drawings that helped raise the funds needed to rebuild the center. The intent was to design a building that would give the Nature Conservancy more visibility and credibility with the "serious nature people," and entice them to come to the preserve and engage with the environment. Debbie Collazo confirmed, "As a result, [the Conservancy] developed a boom in bird watching, with stories in *Arizona Highways*, and *National Geographic*. It helped having a good-looking visitor center."[15]

The successful visitor center was only part of the plan; providing the manager with a place to live was equally important. The old one-story building did not give the Collazos much of a private life. Chafee designed an upstairs loft space, with a high ceiling and ample windows, as their own retreat. A special large window captured views of the trees and high cliffs outside. The couple felt like they were sleeping in the trees, and it gave them a respite away from crowds to muster the inspiration and energy to keep things going. Tom said that he had a hard time reconciling the gray of the concrete block bases and the silver of the galvanized corrugated metal roof, but Chafee taught him how these colors had their own integrity. "You don't make the material design something it shouldn't be," she said.[16]

Years later, Phoenix architect Jerry Doyle's (1922–2007) expansion and restoration work on the residence and visitor center would honor Chafee's enduring work. Debbie Collazo recently remarked, "To this day, about 25,000 visitors from all over the world are greeted at the visitor center so masterfully reimagined by Judith."[17]

Points of Departure

Ironically, Chafee had better name recognition in architectural circles outside Arizona than in her hometown. Local architects were astonished that she was on first-name terms with esteemed speakers from other parts of the globe who visited the university. Chafee had spent enough time in the young professional networks of Chicago, New York, and Boston to get to know the "players" in the architectural world, from the young and driven to the mentors and sages, and photographers and publishers, too. She also participated in conferences, lectures, jury reviews, and presentations—from California to Montana, Texas to Finland, and the places in between.

Chafee approached every part of her life as a design challenge—it was the way her brain was wired. Her own lectures required considerable work: establish the main point, decide what projects to discuss, set up the slides, and write. And then there was the presentation. While one-on-one critiques or casual gatherings were usually a relaxed occurrence for Chafee, presentations made her anxious. Whether she was going to present a project description to her class or a lecture to an assembly of hundreds of people, her trepidation would increase as the time came closer. She did not want to appear weak.[18] Her presentations were focused, conscientious, clever, and to the point. As her already quiet, smoky voice became overrun with bronchial agitations, it added to her concerns for how she presented.

In March 1987, Chafee was invited to participate in a three-day symposium at Washington University in St. Louis that would include an elite and well-respected group of international architects. The event was described in the brochure:

A Symposium: "Points of Departure." Sources and evolution of architectural ideas as represented and discussed by eight distinguished practitioners and academics from throughout the world includes William J.R. Curtis from England/France, Balkrishna Doshi from India, Mario Botta from Switzerland, Wolfgang Prix from Austria, George Ranalli from New York, Antoine Predock from Albuquerque, NM, Judith Chafee from Tucson, AZ, and Peter Prangnell from Canada.[19]

Chafee spent a great deal of time, with help from employees, putting her slide presentation together, rendering presentation slides of plans and elevations, and photographing objects and old photos. It gave her time to reflect on important influences in her work and life, and she appreciated being able to express this in her presentations. Recognizing the range of languages spoken within the panels and by attendees of the symposium, she designed a masterful two-screen slide presentation with a very brief introduction only, no other words. It was image-centric with the script for the slides resembling a musical score: two beats on the left screen, one beat on the right, and hold for three. The left screen included mostly Chafee's influences—a few appropriate childhood photos, including her mother, Margaret Sanger, as well as her educational heroes John Dewey, Louis Sullivan, et al., and meaningful buildings. The right side started with some early Tucson places and experiences and then mostly showed her own work. The presentation began with a tape recorder playing soft sounds of the desert—quail chirps, distant coyotes, and rain—stopping with the slide of her Francis W. Parker School Diploma, and beginning again when slides of parched desert land and the Tucson office appeared. The presentation was visual poetry and was well received at the conference. Chafee produced this presentation, and variations of it, a few times at different colleges and universities, with a more detailed introduction and with updated work. The original introduction follows:

We have been brought together from many places in the world because we share respect and affection for one another.

(2) A lifelong fascination with anthropology and archeology.

(3) An important childhood friendship with Margaret Sanger, who, not without forethought, first introduced me to "Mr. Wright." The synthesis of steel and sensitivity which she embodied is a permanent lesson.

(4) Early training and education founded on the "Chicago School" of American pragmatic thinking—including a strong work and social ethic—and characterized by people such as Jane [Addams], John Root, Louis Sullivan and John Dewey.

(5) Related training and ethical motivation from two Weimar Republic teachers in the new world: Walter Gropius and Alexander Dorner.

(6) The teachers who provided revelations about integration of intellectual concepts and form-making: Louis Kahn and Paul Rudolph.

(7) Two architects that strike directly to my heart: Le Corbusier and Alvar Aalto.

The functional result of these elements is both cumulative and evolutionary.[20]

At this point, the desert soundtrack was turned on, and the alternating slides began to follow their precise score.

The symposium provided Chafee the opportunity to communicate with her peers and enjoy the pleasure of shared thoughts. It also brought Chafee out of the desert and reintroduced her to the East Coast. She was pleased to twice be a visiting lecturer and critic and to serve a four-year term as an adviser at MIT, and was a visiting critic at Washington University for a semester. When the architectural historian William J.R. Curtis was a guest lecturer at the University of Arizona, he was shown the Ramada House as well as other Chafee projects and determined her work merited inclusion in his second and third editions of *Modern Architecture Since 1900*.[21] The inclusion in this authoritative book introduced Chafee to an international population of students and young architects and significantly benefited Chafee's quest for her work to teach the lessons of good modern architecture.

Respect for hard work—and the affection one feels for others that speak one's own language. The language is Architecture.

Instead of translating that language into my provincial tongue and leaving you to de-code it back to Architecture, I have attempted to notate influences and some of my work directly.

While I am showing my own work, the left screen for the most part is used to show experiences, travels and buildings that have somehow become points of reference for me.

The process of making this visual notation has helped me to identify, more abstractly, the forces that have shaped my work.

Seven points summarize the influences I have seen from this presentation:

(1) Interest in the specific characteristics and history of every place or space.

Lessons from Regional Wisdom

By the late 1980s, the broader debate within the architecture community continued to be over "what kind of modernism," whether regional, critical, classical, Bauhaus, post-, and so on. But this became less of a concern to Chafee as time and experience produced other substantial issues to address. While her buildings had always reflected a rational response to the issues of sustainability, she began to notice an ever-increasing disconnect between these issues and the architecture profession. Her classes began to reflect a more overt objective of developing a knowledgeable awareness or epistemic relationship to the environment, along with ecologically appropriate materiality and technology. She imbued her students with the message that they were responsible for this world: "As an architect, I feel responsibility to help fellow citizens understand concepts that contribute to the making of a better environment… as we engineer the future, we need to look to nature."[22]

A vigorous lecture and symposium schedule provided a platform for serious talks on the subject. In 1989, the "International Working Seminar on Critical Regionalism" at California State Polytechnic University, Pomona, assembled well-known international architecture theorists and practitioners under the facilitation of Spyros Amourgis, professor of architecture (now emeritus) at "Cal Poly." While the theorists seemed only inclined to justify word usage, the presentations from practitioners demonstrated the importance of landscape, climate, light, and form. The publication of the seminar summation was released in 1991, and in Amourgis's introduction to Chafee he stated,

> Her references are strongly environmental. She recognizes the severity of the desert environment and the resulting constraints…Ms. Chafee makes a curious, but very honest and true observation, that "we all are immigrants in the desert."[23]

Amourgis continued by referencing her Spring 1982 article in *Artspace*. He also noted that her work "stays clearly away from literal formal associations, while she skillfully responds to values whether historic or environmental."[24]

In November 1989 Chafee presented her work at an interdisciplinary presentation for the "Andrew W. Mellon PhD Symposia" at the Princeton University School of Architecture. This was a different type of lecture specifically conversing with graduate students and faculty. She addressed the importance of real, personal honesty and integrity and of not fearing the "expression of openness." She reflected on her time in architecture school—experiences with Johnson, Rudolph, and especially Kahn. She mentioned Kahn's Trenton Bathhouse, a small elegant project Kahn had described to her class attending a gathering at "the Studio," Paul Rudolph's office-residence. Kahn talked about the areas where people are free to circulate and the service spaces, where inanimate objects are contained and the structure of the building honestly defined. She had additional admiration for Kahn because he was acquainted with and respected Sullivan. Chafee believed these two architects, as compared with others, represented integrity and honesty. She wrote,

> [I] enjoyed the knowledge that Kahn, too, had spent the hours in the Avery or the Burnham library with the magical holograph in his hands. I think it was "Democracy (A Man-Search)" he particularly admired.
>
> Sullivan died only a few months before Johnson checked out the Third Reich. Now Kahn is gone too. And Johnson still has parties—and causes [to] host.
>
> We know who is not really opening themselves up to all the requirements of Architecture—and laying bare an honest attempt to answer the needs of users—and the need of users to grow.

Why don't more of us admit what we see and know?

The politics, the games of skill and chance are fun. But—see how strong and almost silent the real lessons are.[25]

The Blackwell House, which was going through heated debates and being referred to as everything from "eyesore to be bulldozed" to "historically significant masterpiece." She continued her comments:

Why did people fear the Blackwell House? Were they really afraid of the freedom—and even of the closeness to nature it represented?[26]

In 1992 Chafee participated in a symposium titled "Sustainable Design: A Planetary Approach," as part of the AIA National Convention in Boston. Sarah P. Harkness (1914–2013) also participated as a presenter and coordinator. The second part of Chafee's presentation showed work that demonstrated solutions to ecological problems, but the first part showed slides of a built environment with all of its undesirable consequences. Her words at that time were serious and urgent, and are still true today:

The results of progress are clear:
· A severely lowered water table
· The development of an urban heat-sink increasing in temperature every year.
· Destruction of native vegetation
· Destruction of native habitats and their normal routes of travel
· The development of greater dependency on an artificial environment.

The impression one might have upon arrival in Tucson that no architectural tradition exists is misleading. The implication that the built environment must exist in spite of the natural environment is erroneous and destructive—even suicidal.

The severity of the climate is so extreme for both plants and animals that a very fragile balance of life must constantly be considered—very carefully.[27]

The last of Chafee's lectures was given on a return visit to the University of Texas, Austin, in September 1996, where she also participated on a jury review of the Austin AIA annual design awards and gave a presentation called "Points of Departure Revisited." It was stimulating but challenging due to her heath issues—at this point she was suffering the effects of emphysema. As a follow-up, a school project brought students from the University of Texas to Tucson to learn, measure, and build large-scale models of four of her houses, and study the compositions of the projects. A presentation of the work was exhibited at the University of Texas and later shared during a University of Arizona lecture series and building tour exploring Chafee's work and providing posthumous recognition.

Critical Mind-set

Interactions with adventuresome scholars and teaching students of all ages were very rewarding parts of Judith Chafee's life. When asked by *Tucson Weekly* what she thought was the best view of Tucson architecture, she answered, "Seated with a group of College of Architecture students high on the east side of the Tucson Mountains, looking at the spangled valley and discussing how it might be."[28]

Chafee said Walter Gropius once told her that while it is "a struggle to establish, develop and maintain an office, versus teaching…it is important to teach architecture."[29] She embraced his words, and her dedication to teaching often cut into her office schedule. Not having teaching assistants, she paid her staff or hired a student to assist part-time with additional lecture preparation and research.

Chafee was encouraged to participate in school planning activities, and she became active in bringing in guest speakers, such as Robert Peters from New Mexico, Pirkko-Liisa Louhenjoki-Schulman from Finland, William J.R. Curtis from England via Harvard and MIT, Gabriela Goldschmit from Israel, and George Anselevicius from New Mexico, and frequently offered her comfortable guest room and provided additional hosting to accommodate the budget.

After a number of years, feeling established enough and realizing the discrepancy in salaries between male teachers, even new ones, and herself, Chafee secured the support of the past deans of the architectural school, who began sending annual letters to the University of Arizona provost, requesting equity pay for her. Even when the discrepancy was specifically pointed out in writing as a male versus female pay issue, the standard response from the provost was that raises were not in the budget and instead suggested occasional merit pay bonuses.[30] Chafee did not have a litigious background, wanted to keep working with her students, and did not want to move her office to another academic location, so she settled for her annual persistence. Some years she was a little angrier about it than others.

Her teaching career culminated after twenty-five years, part of which included sabbaticals as a visiting critic for advanced students at the University of Texas at Austin, a distinguished visiting professor at MIT, and a visiting professor for the advanced studio at Washington University in St. Louis, and many lectures within the national and international spectrum.

A. Richard Williams, FAIA (1914–2016), a distinguished architect retired from teaching at the Illinois School of Architecture at the University of Illinois at Urbana-Champaign, who then taught at the University of Arizona, wrote:

> It was at that time too, that Judith Chafee, of the vintage at Yale when there were virtually no other women in architecture, brought her salty, astringent, hardy, survivor character and design talent to practice in Tucson and to be a part time critic in the school. She soon demonstrated new terms and powerful interpretations of what architecture in the desert can be, both timeless and timely in contemporary terms. She had the same no-holds-barred impact on her students, of sometimes brutal honesty and strictness but leaving no doubt that the search for rightness in the use of materials, light and shade, closeness and indigenous landscape would end up as most lasting and fulfilling, as her clients and students bear witness perhaps more strongly than for any other architect of her time.[31]

Chafee, when left to her own studio projects, was well-known for creative, and often seductive, proposals. Given that, and her long-standing, eloquent, and imaginative writing style, a faculty member was overheard making the rhetorical comment after reading one of her studio proposals, "Where does she get these ideas!" For instance, for her course Fall 1993 Design Option, she wrote the following description:

In Xanadu did Kubla Khan, A stately pleasure-dome decree: (taken from Samuel Taylor Coleridge)

The purpose of this term in design will be to exult in our growing skills as much as Architects for the purpose of creating pleasure for others. The program includes walls, pools, vapors, gardens, light and lighting, sun and shade; bathing, strolling, sketching, sitting, listening, dining and dancing. Historical precedents will be studied. The site is on North Stone Avenue.[32]

Chafee's course descriptions were particularly enticing to students willing to accept the hard work expected in her studio. One semester each school year, fourth- and fifth-year students were provided with a pin-up of individual studio options. They would list their first, second, and third preferences, and wait for the results. Although it appeared democratic, after assignments were announced, some students would complain that they were not assigned their first choice instructor, and were aware that other students were placed in that studio, even though it was their second or third choice. It was not subtle that 20 percent of students were female and very evenly distributed among all classes. One well-meaning adviser asked a student if she was more comfortable with a woman instructor, to which she answered, "No, I am not choosing her because she is a woman. I am choosing her because she is the best."[33]

Allen Freeman wrote about Chafee in the March 1984 issue of *Architecture* magazine:

She revels in the diversity of her region and its implication for architects. One of her favorite assignments for students was to "have them design something, say a conference center, requiring a lot of self-help construction on a site of their choice along the road from Tucson to the top of Mount Lemmon, a change in elevation of several thousand feet. Using materials at hand, they are supposed to respond to six climates going up the mountain, starting with the low desert where adobe is appropriate, into a rocky area, and then to the heavily timbered top where wood construction is appropriate."[34]

Judith Chafee with model, 1990

A student's first meeting with Chafee would be in design studio. They would encounter a petite woman, with her own fashion style reflecting her independence and classic southwestern culture. Her standard palette included linen or denim tunics and slacks, trim sweaters and a quilted vest when warmth was needed, a serapes as her overcoat, and desert sandals or custom-made Native American boots from the Kaibab shop in Tucson. She was definitely not an "Easterner." Her hair, which she usually trimmed herself, was very fine and straight, varied in length from chin to shoulder and parted in the middle with lighter shades symmetrically in the front and gray-brown in the back. Sometimes she pulled it back with silver Native American combs. She always had a cigarette—a long, thin, unfiltered brown Moment from a crisp red package—in one hand and a Sharpie or pencil in the other. In those days, smoking in the design studio was not unusual. The intensity of a personal critique from Judith, as students addressed her, was a "one or two cigarette crit." She was soft-spoken, with a smoker's

Student work:
Brian Farling (left),
Teresa Rosano
(opposite left),
Jack DeBartolo 3
(opposite right)

152

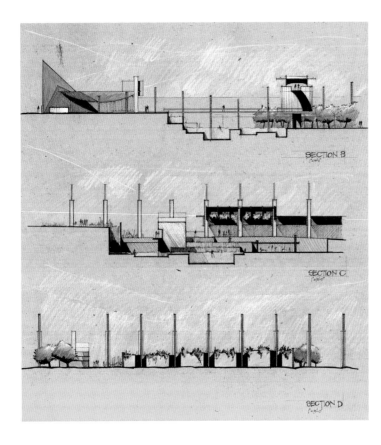

gravel, which in later years became a cough-interrupted effort. Her voice was soft enough to require the listener's full attention to hear what she was saying, whether she was talking to a class or an individual student. She spoke with absolute intent, slowly, thoughtfully choosing the right words. She always measured her comments and sometimes focused her eyes on the ash-ended "smoke" for a contemplative pause.

The studio would start with the "boilerplate school rules" followed by the project description. Additional comments, information, and encouragement would be provided, along with schedules, due dates, and presentation dates. Chafee would provide required and recommended reading lists as well as a list of significant buildings and other references. The list included well-

known architects as well as pertinent writers, including some regional ones, such as Louis Mumford, Le Corbusier, Richard Neutra, Maxwell Fry and Jane Drew, Edward Spicer, and M. T. Painter. It also included reports on sustainable housing, the Bible, and Mexican history. Such was the list of national and local influences for a community housing project for Old Pascua, a Mexican American indigenous Yaqui tribal community, located on the outskirts of Tucson. Some reading requirements were standard, while other references were customized for each project. Chafee's personal library included many of these books, which she would leave for students to borrow in the architecture school's small library.

In every project, preliminary emphasis was on getting all the site information right. Students were required to

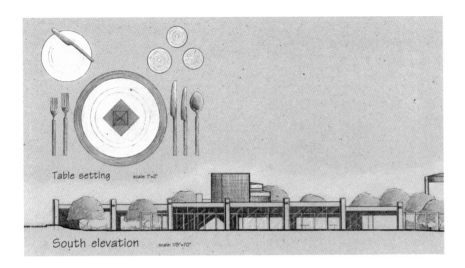

Table setting   scale: 1"=2"

South elevation   scale: 1/8"=10'

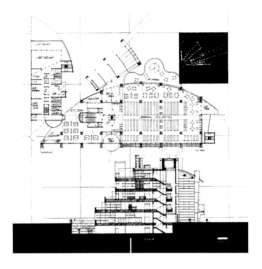

determine sun angles, wind direction, temperature ranges, drainage, topography, and views and vistas, as well as pedestrian and other traffic patterns on and around the site. These were pre-computer times, and a lot of footwork was involved. If the site was accessible, Chafee would go with the class to get a full overview. She would walk quietly through a site and note the desert's many small seasonal changes, such as the minuscule red spots on the tiny green leaves of a plant.

Studio sessions would be spent sketching, organizing information, getting a focus or big idea, and building massing models with cardboard. Work continued with refinement of drawings, revisions, and changes in perceived directions, with critiques and the occasional brief lecture in between. It was not unusual for Chafee to be in the studio helping students well after class time. Closer to a due date, the work hours became longer, and Chafee was available for additional critiques. On the way home from the office, she and her Staffordshire terrier Leda (or Leda's predecessor Bella) would stop by to see if any help was needed.

As a teacher, Chafee was a significant influence on her students' production, but their projects always reflected their own identity. Dedicated students would work their hardest in her class. Individual critiques were tough and sometimes anxiety producing, but also productive and inspiring. She was hardest on students who showed the most promise, could be dismissive with students who did not demonstrate a proper level of gravitas, and quite empathetic to students suffering from long- or short-term disabilities or family tragedies. Chafee's competitive nature was evident during the individual student presentations for school jury reviews given to Chafee and other reviewers; she gave hard critiques for students she knew could produce better work, and not much commentary on weaker students. She could become fully defensive if she felt one of her own students was getting misdirected criticism in a jury presentation. Brian Farling writes about his experience of critiques with Chafee when he was a student:

> For third year jury, she was a brutal critic. I chose the fifth year fall option, a delightful, brilliant project Xanadu, focused on what should be the focus. Part of it was a restaurant, [part of Chafee's instructions] contrast scale and details. Figure out a menu, place settings, silverware, the language and relationship and light. She instilled the belief to be fearless.[35]

Chafee brought her program for sustainable housing in the Southwest to the 1988 fall semester advanced class at MIT. She had spent time in her office gathering and creating brochures relevant to the project site in the Tucson Mountains, which would be unfamiliar to the East Coast students. Water harvesting, solar charts, prevailing wind charts, geological studies, portions of the Arizona-Sonora Desert Museum's docent study guide, southwestern building methods—rammed earth, adobe, straw-bale, double-wall systems—and cultural influences were included with selected books.

While teaching at MIT, Chafee was reacquainted with friends and associates from her early days. Sarah P. Harkness, one of the founders of The Architects Collaborative (TAC),[36] was excited with Chafee's proposal to coteach a project for the fourth-year class in Tucson. Harkness, who co-produced a study, *Sustainable Design for Two Main Islands*, conducted by the Institute for Energy Conscious Design with the Boston Architecture Center

in 1985, had been looking at cohousing projects and changes in family models, and she and Chafee found a good fit for the spring 1990 semester.[37] The class, divided into two groups, would focus on two cohousing projects, one in Lexington and one in Tucson. To save the college money, Harkness was Chafee's houseguest as she commuted back and forth from Chafee's home in Tucson to her own home in Boston. The program stated, "The integration of the physical situation, the history of the region and the personalities and needs of the clients may result in some new ideas for us all about the true identity of 'style' and 'regionalism.'"[38] Harkness was grateful for Chafee's friendship and stayed in contact, once sending her a Cambridge newspaper article about Jane Drew and Maxwell Fry with the comment, "Jane Drew appears to date from a time when architects were making sense."[39]

Technology

During Chafee's last years of teaching, the student and faculty population was experiencing political and cultural shifts and a greater global awareness, producing a paradigm shift in architectural education and the roles of the educator. From the time Chafee attended Yale and during the first half of her twenty-five-year teaching career, the professors' status was elevated within the community. Professors were the learned teachers who would guide students into the professional environment of architecture. In the early nineties, students began to develop a stronger sense of empowerment, perhaps as a result of higher tuition fees and the technical divide, whereby many students were savvier than their faculty advisers in the emergence of computer use. Chafee saw the computer as a useful drafting tool, but as a barrier to the experience of clear understanding of design principles, scale, relationship to the environment, and actual sense of space and culture.

It has long been the custom of the university to expect faculty evaluations by each student, as well as from two selected faculty members each semester. A person with a controversial persona will draw her share of dissatisfied comments from a few students, but Chafee was routinely rated as a generally outstanding and "best" teacher, albeit sometimes with communication issues.

Ronald Gourley (1919–1999), FAIA, May 10, 1989:

In addition to being the best woman architect that I have encountered in 50+ years in the world of Architecture, Judith Chafee is without question the best architect practicing in Tucson today. She is a careful programmer, an excellent design teacher and critic; she brings high level intelligence and artistry into the design studio and is admired by students for her abilities and forthrightness. Her presence as a faculty member brings distinction to the college.

Larry Medlin, May 8, 1990:

Judith—the scope of issues considered and the depth and breadth of design thinking reflected in your students' projects are always impressive and inspiring. These same qualities and a wonderfully elegant design are embodied in the residence you designed where the open house was held.[40] Your presentation at the Southwestern Center Forum was spellbinding—it inspired everyone to think about the qualities of a true southwestern / desert architecture. It is an honor for all of us to have an architect of your talents on our faculty.

Linda Sanders, May 1, 1991:

Judith: I do not know you well enough to know whether you want comments here or not. I will take the chance that you will want to hear my perceptions. Students learn from you because you have a strong design ethic and you are able to convey to them your intense commitment to architecture. Most appreciate all you offer. A few are bothered by a feeling of intimidation [sowed] when you crit projects: whether this becomes an impetus for them to improve or an impediment for growth I do not know. From a personal position, I appreciate having had the opportunity to work with you this semester, and look forward to future contacts.

Robert Nevins, April 26, 1993:

As always Judith is an excellent & respected teacher. Her programs are provocative & extremely well thought out. This semester Judith's concern for education in general & for her students in particular has been manifested by her "after hours tutorials," set up to expose her 2nd yr. students to a design-world-of-ideas she perceived missing in the curriculum. She has always attracted the most dedicated & potentially strong designers. She is one of very few teachers & designers on this faculty.[41]

A number of students were more critical of Chafee's communication and harsh style of critique.
Fall 1988:

Your thoughts and comments were very helpful. However, some comments "seemed" unprofessional and rude. Everyone should be treated politely and with respect. I wouldn't mind having you as a critique again.

Fall 1992:

Judith is brilliant as a designer and unapproachable as a person.

Fall 1992:

Although at times rude, abrupt, and abrasive, Prof. Chafee is far and above the best design instructor I have ever encountered in the college. Her ability to motivate students to do their best by accepting nothing less is refreshing in a college that seems to encourage mediocrity through the quality of design that is accepted. Her insightfulness and bluntness when dealing with students is by far her best quality. When leaving a crit the student has no doubt on how his work has been perceived, which areas are satisfactory and which are not, and how he should now proceed. Thanks Judith! P.S. Please quit smoking so future classes will be able to enjoy and learn from you as I have![42]

At a recent lecture about Chafee, two former students, John and Ann Price, reminisced about Chafee and the once-a-month evening events she held at her home. She would invite architects, contractors, engineers, and other people in business to talk about buildings and their work. The students were so accustomed to the routine of class time and college activities that they were surprised and delighted to be able to socialize and have relaxed conversations with these people.[43]

In the early 1990s Chafee's life became more unsettled. Work slowed down, she suffered deep depression over her mother's death, and with the diagnosis of emphysema her future was diminishing. Her emphysema had reduced her lung capacity to the point where she required oxygen from a portable tank full-time, yet she would still grab a quick drag from her secret cigarette stash before going into class.

During this time, a corrosive relationship with the dean became exacerbated when he sent Chafee his annual evaluation of her performance. While careful to not appear discriminatory, he drew attention to her personal struggles that year:

Judith, this seems to have been a tough year for you, health-wise and with occasional confrontations with students, faculty and staff. I received complaints that you were sometimes late for class. I also received complaints during the year that you appeared to be under the influence of alcohol during at least some of the confrontations. It is important that faculty never come to class while under the influence and I trust that you will make certain this will be the case in the coming year.[44]

Counseling helped her get some control over her situation, which included facing the heartbreak of closing her office. During her last two years of teaching, from the fall of 1996 through the spring of 1998, a new dean, Richard Eribes (1942–2013), joined the program and acknowledged her contributions to the school, finally awarding her merit pay.[45] He supported her during her health struggles and offered to team-teach to cover her class when she was not feeling well enough to get to school. She appreciated his thoughtfulness and felt encouraged to rally for a time, closing her teaching career with a positive experience. When she decided to retire, she wrote to him on April 26, 1998, to express her appreciation:

Dear Dean Eribes:

I am sorry to say that I must retire from the college, for health reasons, at the end of this term. It has been an interesting journey meandering through the ridiculous, the unsavory, and the sublime. It is ironic that I must leave at a time when I feel higher regard for the new directions for the college.

Perhaps from time to time it will be possible to participate in some way with college projects. I do plan to get back to practice, one small job at a time, and some painting and some writing.

Many thanks, and all the best wishes for your efforts. Sincerely, Judith Chafee[46]

In February 1999 Eribes, in a letter to Diana Brock-Gray, a former student and a very good friend of Chafee's as well as her executor, discussed the placement of Chafee's archives with the University of Arizona:

I once told Judith that I thought she had a very special genius that was for me a pleasure to be associated with. She was somewhat embarrassed by this accolade on my part. But I will receive a special pleasure in sharing, with researchers around the globe, a bit of her talent.

In the end, we are survived by our work. And it was damned fine work. She knew it and now others will know it.[47]

Chris Grimley recounted a brief encounter with Chafee, when he was a graduate student at the University of Texas at Austin and participated in an on-site study of the Blackwell Residence in 1997. He provides a profound realization of Chafee's focus, purpose, and impact:

It was meeting Chafee, sharing an evening with her and a day at the house that really opened my eyes to an enduring legacy that wasn't primarily based on its current fashion status. This house condensed all of the reading I had done that year into a single physical artifact. And as I stood in the now abandoned house, I observed the walls covered with graffiti, all of the windows smashed out and began to understand that this was all part of a larger legacy. Even in its current state, the house could still begin to describe all of its author's intentions, and these intentions were critical to my own cultural legacy. This was an architect working at the apex of her capabilities. And this is how she should be remembered.[48]

A Mindful Practice

Judith Chafee wrote about the recurring experience between owners and architects as a preface to a description of a residential project in *Triglyph* in Fall 1984:

> The birthing of a building, the architect's special relationship to the building, if it pleases her, and even the (sometimes justified) jealousy an owner can feel, noticing the intimacy he is not altogether a part of during creation, no matter how seriously he is respected, is a reordering of images and concerns currently in the architect's mind. This being true, no matter what the functional program may be, the building is always a portrait of the architect at that time, and only the architect knows how true and how penetrating the portraiture is. That is why we are so sensitive about our work. That is also why we must be demanding and structured in our thinking, lest the portrait start to show, blatantly, underlying decadence.[49]

This was at a time when Chafee's office was experiencing a good flow of production with residential commissions, consulting work on concrete bridges for Jerry Cannon, and projects for the Tucson Unified School District. The school projects included interior classroom cabinet work and a locker-room courtyard for Maxwell Junior High School as well as two locker rooms for girls at Rincon and Palo Verde High Schools that complied with Title IX law requiring equal facilities for female and male students.[50] Chafee was also invited to join a trip to Italy sponsored by the Marazzi Tile Company, which introduced her to a commercial tile line that proved the right application for a number of projects, including soft shades-of-gray tiles used for the Finkel Residence counters and floors, and graphically pleasing Italian tile patterns for the girls' locker rooms. Chafee especially liked to accurately boast that the locker rooms were finished on time and under budget. One would expect the successes of these projects would have led to more projects for the school district, and one of Chafee's desires was to design a school building. But the outdoor locker courtyard for Maxwell Junior High School set a different course. A roofed-over vacant space between two buildings was to be a secured location for student lockers. Chafee designed two large half-conoid light scoops, one bringing in light from the north sky and the other from the south. Lockers were arranged in plan around two opposing half circles. Chafee saw an opportunity to provide a lesson for students to experience the colors of their environment by specifying the north-facing locker colors as green, blue, and purple to mirror the palette of the north sky and mountains. South-facing lockers were painted the hot colors of the south sky: red, orange, and yellow. Bob Earl, the construction administrator from Chafee's office, noticed some of the new structure was painted red and yellow.[51] The contractor told him that the principal, who had said nothing during design meetings, told him to paint everything, including lockers, the school colors: red and yellow. Fortunately, the lockers had not yet been placed or painted, but the principal was firm on his color choice. Chafee took the issue to a school board meeting, explaining the intention of the design. The board determined that the architect should be the person who decides what colors to use on a project.[52] As local writer Lawrence Cheek described it: She won, then fumed for years. "They were so amazed," she would say, contempt dripping from her husky, tobacco-dried voice, "that anyone would think the color was of any importance."[53]

She was right, and although she had provided brilliant, thoughtful, and responsible solutions for the school board's projects, it did not call on Chafee for any more work.

Maxwell Junior High
School, Tucson,
Arizona, sections and
elevation drawing

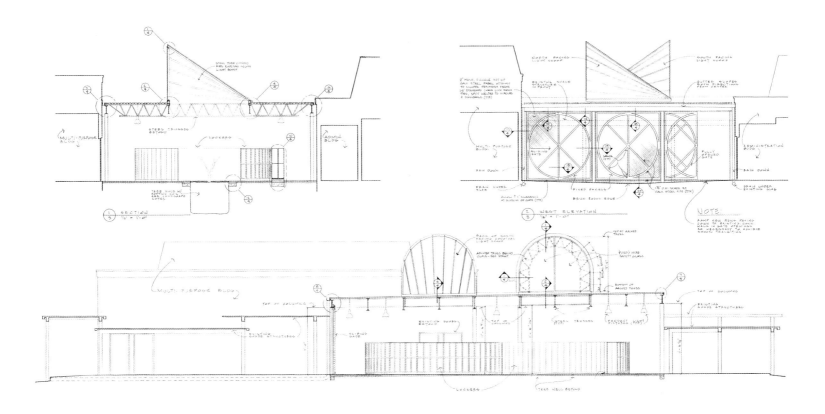

Healing Powers: The Intellect, the Hand, and the Heart

Chafee provided architectural services for three projects with clients who chose both to be their own contractor and to engage in the day-to-day work of constructing their houses. Two such projects were David Russell and Susan Randolph's adobe residence (1983) and Bill and Audrey Merriman's residence (1985). The Merrimans became interested in Chafee's work from features in numerous issues of *Sunset* magazine.[54] Audrey (1937–2016) was an art educator from Chicago who appreciated modernism and especially Scandinavian design. Bill (1937–2003) was a fourth-generation Tucsonan whose great-grandfather ran a stagecoach stop just outside town. Bill ran his own real estate business, with Audrey's assistance, and the couple owned twenty acres of undisturbed desert land northwest of Tucson, adjacent to Catalina State Park.

Chafee's methodology for working with clients would start with the first meeting, which, in many cases, was the clients' interview of Chafee and vice versa. Chafee would supply an assemblage of portfolios, each representing a specific project. If they met at the office, there would be a small Mexican platter with handmade cookies from the nearby Mexican bakery. Chafee would get a sense of which projects might have the best presentation points for the potential clients' interests, and briefly discuss the features. Then, speaking as their architect, she would discuss and ask questions about "our" project. Most clients who came to the office hired Chafee and, after occupancy of their new buildings, remained her friends. They appreciated her propensity to listen, take notes, and ask thought-provoking questions.

In an interview for the Phoenix newspaper the *Arizona Republic,* Chafee described her procedures for working with her clients:

What you try to do is analyze the site….We discuss buildings the clients like or don't like. We talk about how they will use the house, what kind of cooking they do, how they entertain and possible materials they might use. Then we start designing, keeping in mind sun angles, prevailing winds and the existing vegetation. The design must express a certain clarity.

She went on to say:

Houses, to me, are the most important architecture in the world. I think the most important thing about architecture is that it's honest on all levels.[55]

For his part, Bill Merriman said, "I would rather spend our money on you designing our house, and save money building it myself."[56] Knowing the potential to sell a few smaller parcels of the land, Chafee and the Merrimans agreed on the best location for their house. Priorities were established considering spectacular mountain views, watersheds from mountain runoff and summer rains, and hearty desert vegetation. Chafee embraced the ecology of the landscape, designing the house with multiple levels that followed the existing topography. Built for sustainability, the durable materials are concrete block walls, including a large fireplace wall unified with a thin mortar wash, polished concrete floors and steps, and interior walls and ceilings of white painted sheetrock.

Merriman Residence,
Tucson, Arizona, elevation
drawings (below) and
office hospitality (opposite)

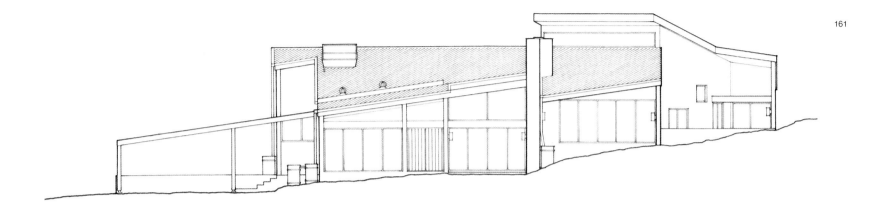

SOUTH ELEVATION

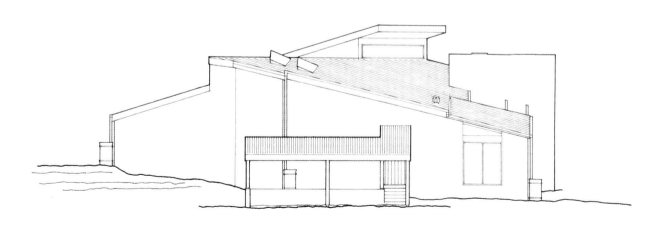

WEST ELEVATION

The large corrugated metal shed-roof system, following the distant mountain profile, includes a fiberglass extension over a small greenhouse area, a subtle echo of the Hydeman Residence. The unique framing arrangement of deep, natural-finished glulam beams supporting multilevel clerestories are 30 degrees askew of the floor plan, directing occupants toward the mountain views. North-, south-, and east-protected patios and large sliding windows extend the inside-outside living spaces, enabling views of the mountains through any part of the house. The house bears Chafee's standard of elegant natural light, spaces defined by high ceilings, and a substantial fireplace mass representing an honest modern vocabulary applied to the time and place of the building. Merriman's Danish modern furnishings were well accommodated, and Chafee provided an abundance of well-designed red oak cabinetry for the kitchen, dining, and living spaces. Bill hired master carpenter Paul Kramer to advise and help him and his three sons with the construction. After one of her site visits, Chafee returned to the office and commented, "I felt so guilty designing such a difficult roof frame, but that son-of-a-gun is doing a damn good job!" Bill had lost his right hand years earlier and would wear a prosthetic hand with a leather glove for public appearances. When Chafee saw him on the site in work mode and using a functional hook, she told him she was glad to see he had a solution that could perform work rather than the decorative hand. Audrey later told Chafee that Bill appreciated hearing that.

Many years later, Audrey said that they had such respect and admiration for Judith, they would never tell her that at one time they didn't have enough money to pay for the windows. Just as they were getting a little behind,

Bill had a successful real estate deal that brought in enough money to get the house finished.[57]

Chafee's third owner-built house came eight years later, in the Upper Peninsula of Michigan, and was designed for Adelyn Hansen and her brother Fred, who suffered from multiple sclerosis. Their efforts would provide a comforting and healing place of repose in the natural forest of the riverside location. Both Chafee and Hansen were cognizant of the standards Aalto set when he designed the sanatorium in Paimio. His concepts, as described in Dr. Esther Sternberg's book *Healing Spaces*, are still recognized as valid in the field of health care:

> Both Aalto and Neutra were explicit about the health benefits of well-planned architecture and the importance of nature and natural views in health and healing. This concept may have its roots in the tuberculosis sanatoriums of the nineteenth and early twentieth centuries, in the days before antibiotics...Indeed, the TB sanatorium designed by Alvar Aalto, built in 1929–1932 in the town of Paimio in his native Finland, became the standard for all later hospitals. It featured a patients' wing with light-filled rooms that faced south and overlooked a pine forest. The resting lounge was also bright, with a wall of tall windows looking out on forest views. Aalto was careful to stipulate that the surroundings be pleasant and tranquil.[58]

Two other Chafee houses accommodated clients' challenging health concerns: Putnam Residence was an economical design provided in 1975 for a paraplegic military veteran, and Finkel Residence introduced Chafee to new considerations for healthy buildings.

Finkel Residence: The Clean House

Drs. Miriam Finkel and Asher Finkel said Judith Chafee was the only architect with whom they spoke who listened earnestly and took Miriam's chemical and environmental sensitivities seriously. Chafee was attentive and expressed a succinct interpretation of their program needs. Today these issues are quite familiar, and many products with low or no chemical emissions are available. But this was not the case in 1983. Chafee, despite skepticism, was willing to accommodate the unusual requirements set by this Chicago couple, who wanted a modern "clean" house. Dr. Asher Finkel (1915–1988) was a soon-to-be retired physician, and Dr. Miriam Finkel (1916–1999) had been a radiobiologist in Chicago and in Los Alamos, New Mexico, during the Manhattan Project. Having been continually exposed to formaldehyde and other chemicals in her research laboratory years, she had developed multiple chemical sensitivities.

Chafee found this to be a challenging project. In addition to the usual concerns for the climate and environment was the complexity of finding appropriate building methods and materials. She began to research the chemical components in typical materials, editing out the unacceptable and experimenting with the unknowns. Miriam, as the "test pilot," would carry pieces of materials, such as drywall, around to see what kind of reaction might develop. The drywall passed, allowing for less strain on the budget, compared with full interior plasterwork. The special adaptations of procedures and products added an approximate 10 percent increase to what was considered a normal budget at the time. Chafee became an advocate for Dr. Finkel's clean built environment, as described in the construction document specifications:

> Construction of a structural steel and steel stud with stucco house, the provision of connections to sewer, electric, telephone, and water utilities.

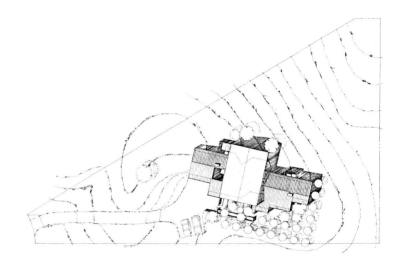

> It should be [borne] in mind at all times that the primary requirement of all construction procedures and results in this house shall be conducted in such a way as to avoid the use of many substances which are detrimental to the health of the Owner. To this end, special consideration has been given to the selection of materials. The use of any hidden or exposed chemical compounds or plastics not specifically specified in these documents is not permitted unless approved by the Architect.[59]

The house is designed to be an allergy-free building, prohibiting the use of formaldehyde or any petroleum-based products, and precluding the use of many typical building products, any wood preservatives, most glues, interior plywood, particle board, plastic laminates, premanufactured doors, most caulking, and various finishes. The best results came from inert materials, such as glass, steel, and tile applied in unusual ways. Glass with different finishes was frequently used, including sandblasted glass with a rougher frosted finish, sandblasted bronze glass, and sandblasted mirrors for store case cabinet systems, countertops, and interior doors of pocketed sliding-glass-door systems. Concrete floors require petroleum-based sealers, therefore the floors were covered with Marazzi tile and some counters

Finkel Residence
kitchen (right) and
site plan (opposite)

were set with the old method—using cement "mud" rather than standard thin-set. The steel I-beams and truss system were prominent, clearly defining the pure materials of the building. The grid of the steel frame and glass curtain walls with precise exposed steel details reflects the influence of the Fagus Factory designed by Walter Gropius. Chafee learned a great deal from Gropius, one of her early mentors, about functionality without compromising the modern solution, and how to discriminate between the essential and incidental. Jerry Cannon, the structural engineer, commented that the detailing for the steel house was like working on a fine-tuned clock, with its tight exacting details. He appreciated Chafee's intense focus, as she clearly knew what she wanted.[60]

At the time, structural grade and light-gauge steel framing was unusual for a residence, and while the construction was exposed, a fellow professor of the architecture school referred to the building as a pasta factory. Chafee had honed her steel detailing on projects during her associations on the East Coast, and her fondness for all things Italian tempered her reaction.[61] Architect Will Bruder was quoted as saying, "Judith Chafee's architecture is always worth taking time to not only enjoy but, whether you like it or not stylistically, to study."[62]

The south-facing greenhouse and courtyard were required to provide fruits and vegetables to grow free of any chemical treatments. Chafee used precise studies of sun angles to determine the height and overhang of the

166

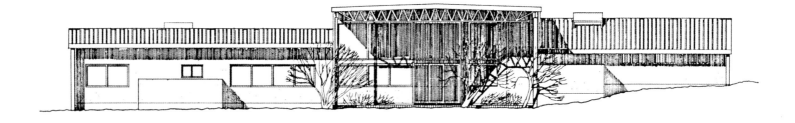

NORTH ELEVATION

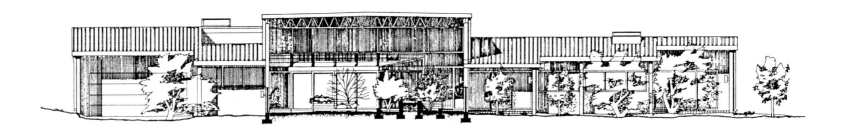

SOUTH ELEVATION

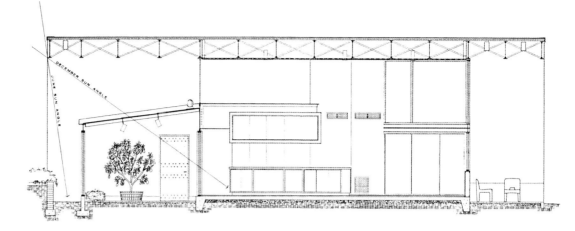

BUILDING SECTION

big roof-form hovering over the greenhouse integrated into the south glass-wall system of the kitchen and dining areas. The extension of the outside experience through the greenhouse, tucked under the big metal truss-framed roof system above, provides shade in the summer and allows for a garden year-round. The indoor-outdoor relationship viewed through the house provides visual information of time and place. Although the house is located in a well-populated community in the Tucson foothills, Chafee's precise orientation provides unobstructed views of a foreground of natural Sonoran desertscape and not-so-distant mountain views.

The interior spaces reveal one of Chafee's most ethereal projects. Her vocabulary for natural light is extended beyond normal senses, as various intensities of the sandblasted glass disperse daylight throughout white walls with anodized bronze trim. Chafee draws from Gropius's description of Japanese treatment of spaces in *Katsura: Tradition and Creation in Japanese Architecture*: "The indoor-outdoor relation between house and garden which has only been so recently 'discovered' in the West was a matter of great concern in Japan centuries ago. Openings, terraces, and balconies were placed with an eye to the landscape and far and near scenery."[63]

The image of the Katsura Imperial Villa, with the fluidity of sliding panels changing spatial definition, is taken further with Chafee's detailing of a pocket-encased sliding-glass-door system in place of the usual interior wood doors. Sandblasted glass for privacy creates a shoji-screen-like transmission of light into the corridor, while metal-backed sandblasted glass pocket sliders for closets reflect the light back into the spaces. The materiality of a glass and metal frame system was also used for all cabinets. Cabinetmaker Elliott Price remarked, "I loved the challenge of making an inert functional cabinet. So different. Great look of the sandblasted glass and it was fun working with the commercial case goods system's extruded aluminum. I really liked the upper glass cabinet suspended from the steel beam."[64]

Bathrooms had tile counters on built-in cabinets with sliding glass panels running full width, wall-to-wall. The large utility and sewing room featured the same case goods cabinets forming a work peninsula, with a frosted mirror counter that reflects natural light with a soft glow. All habitable spaces have large windows providing an abundance of natural light. Exterior hinged doors at the entry and kitchen are reminders of the human touch of the Sonoran wood doors, similar to the doors in the Ramada and Viewpoint houses, splined and cleated

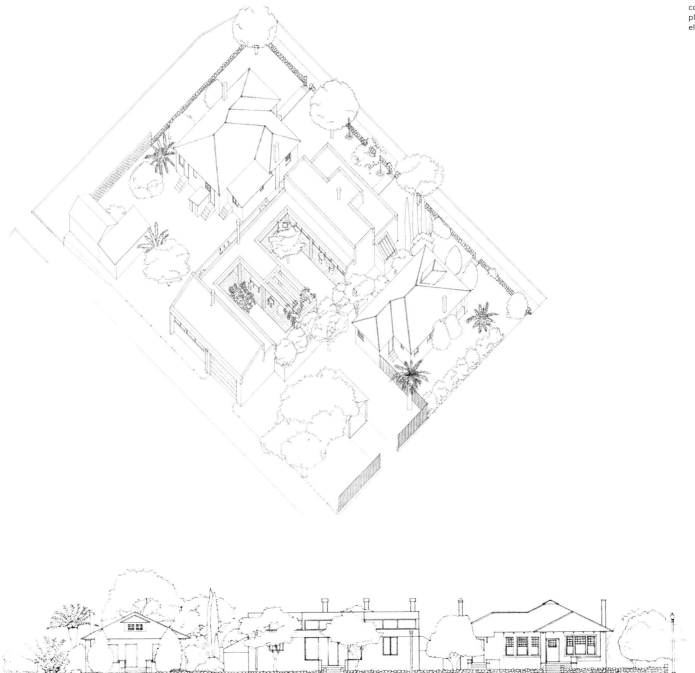

Mature Outlook
concept house, site
plan (top) and street
elevation (bottom)

one-and-three-quarter-inch solid fir, treated with linseed oil on the outside and vegetable oil on the inside. Solid untreated wood planks provide bookshelves in the library, and a special dressing table is built into the master bedroom wall.

Noticeable non-Chafee details reflect the owner's requirements, most notably the absence of fireplaces, due to air quality concerns, and a limited-access kitchen area that is reminiscent of the functional lab space Miriam Finkel preferred. Chafee was resistant to such a closed-in function for a kitchen area, but Miriam prevailed and the house was completed in 1985.

Asher Finkel died after living in Tucson for five years, and Miriam Finkel continued living in and enjoying the house that was built for her, demonstrating remarkable

improvement in her health within a year of moving in. She often assisted long-term guests trying to cope with their own chemical sensitivities. Six years later Miriam would not consider anyone else to design a guest house for her increasing number of visitors of family and friends. By that time, "cleaner" building materials were becoming available and more economical. The guesthouse does not carry the steel and glass image of the main house but is a compatible two bedroom and bath casa with very efficient and creative sleeping accommodations, and large windows with dramatic views. The little house is set on the west entrance of the small end of the pie-shaped property, a welcome into an oasis.

These two strong women had great respect for each other, and as Chafee's disabilities from emphysema became more challenging, Miriam provided helpful advice and encouragement.

Shortly after Finkel Residence was completed, Chafee was commissioned for two projects with similar challenges in historic neighborhoods. Tucson is characterized by well-maintained and historically significant older homes. For their concept house project, *Mature Outlook* magazine had chosen a vacant infill lot between houses built in the early 1900s, near the university and close to Tucson's downtown. In this context, as in the design of her own studio, Chafee's clear adeptness in integrating new modern buildings with older, venerated buildings was critical.

The other project was a new office building for structural engineer Jerry Cannon, in the historic downtown district, where his corner lot encouraged references to the corner store—a familiar commercial function in the older neighborhood built between 1880 and 1900. For each building, Chafee incorporated the modern open plans and inside-outside relationships, with different applications of interior courtyards, creating intimate natural spaces with each building's specific identity on its small urban lots. The buildings reflected the specific scale, elements, and spirit of the individual neighborhoods.

Sustainability
The Nature Conservancy:
Patagonia-Sonoita Creek Preserve

Tom and Debbie Collazo continued their work with the Nature Conservancy, and by 1990, Debbie was a major fundraiser and Tom was director of conservation. The conservancy had determined its heavily visited Patagonia-Sonoita Creek Preserve needed more than just a posted board on a pole for the 350-acre preserve with almost three hundred bird species, as well as other animals and vegetation in its diverse ecosystem. Dan Campbell, the Nature Conservancy's state administrator, saw visitor centers as additional means of raising funds and awareness, and initiated the early planning for a center at the preserve. He had appreciated Chafee's work at Ramsey Canyon, and because Tom had pushed very hard to hire Chafee, the conservancy contracted with her to design a visitor center and separate manager's house. But it immediately became apparent that this project would have considerable hurdles to overcome.

The location of the two buildings had already been considered before Chafee came on board, and the conservancy's project administrator also saw no value in spending money on buildings. It was not a good start and added to Chafee's exasperation at finding that the manager of the preserve, who was living in a trailer with his family in the nearby town of Patagonia, was working with the principals of a large engineering firm donating their "talents" to the project. To make matters even worse, the location they chose was discovered to be an indigenous archaeological site. Ever a child of the desert, Chafee commented derisively, "They should know better than to start without an architect. I could have told them there would be pot shards."[65] Chafee spoke with the preserve manager, who was dealing with a large open field of Johnson grass, an aggressive non-native species that required removal. She asked, "Why not build there?" The manager was surprised to realize that it would be a very good location, and the residence could be sited across the road. The project administrator and Chafee were still

butting heads to the extent that she was ready to walk away from the project. Tom Collazo held on to the belief that "the Preserve system could be a world class land, environment, conservation experience." He said, "I wanted the best and Judith could give us that."[66] Ultimately, Tom and Debbie took over as coordinators, and diligently moved the project along with Chafee.

Debbie was responsible for raising the funds for this as well as other projects. A fundraising event was held at the Rieveschl Residence, since the Rieveschls were supporters of both Chafee and the Nature Conservancy. The conservancy also had one additional major donor. But the project estimates came in too high. Although Debbie was able to secure more funding, Chafee still needed to trim the project. The relationship deteriorated, as Chafee, feeling overextended, made truculent comments to Debbie about her inability to raise more funds, alienating and embarrassing Debbie, who subsequently avoided the architect. Tom, however, persevered. He said he "loved the visitor center, the big metal roof, [the] clarity of the structural system, [the] simple materials." He was not thrilled with the sunken conversation pit, but said, "I wasn't going to push back, and they put it in. Years later it needed to be filled, to be more practical."[67]

Chafee's design evoked appropriate references from previous projects, as well as regional and cultural influences. Like many Patagonia and Sonoita historic homesteads, the roofline has the familiar metal hipped roof profile. The original plans included a big ramada roof with custom stainless-steel barrels, which were deemed too expensive for the project, and the roof size was somewhat reduced. Windows in the office walls are also a reference to the double-hung tall windows of historic ranch houses in the area, and provide daylight and breezes. A four-sided clerestory structure with a metal roof cap is positioned on top of the visitor center like a traditional cupola to introduce natural light and air circulation. Chafee preferred exposing structural elements when possible, to be honest about the way a building is supported. She worked with structural engineer George Stevenson to develop a system with a 4-inch-square vertical steel tube and welded plates for the junction of the four symmetrical built-up trusses. All exposed wood used in the framing remains natural and is well protected under the large roof, with the structural steel components painted red to celebrate the bold forms. Symmetry of the plan is determined by the large hipped roof system supported by 16-inch square columns of $8 \times 4 \times 16$–inch concrete block. The 4-inch height of the block provides a more human scale for the small building, and is repeated as a single-row, 4-inch-high continuous curb above which the wood baseplate of the wall framing sits, raising the wall system at least 3 inches above the finished concrete floor, to minimize buildup of water during the rainy season. Concrete block bases with redwood planks provide perimeter seating. The 6×16–foot sunken sitting area provides built-in seating for an additional sixteen people without obstructing views.

The big roof covers a 2,000-square-foot concrete surfaced area with inside and outside spaces defining function, and echoes from Louis Kahn—as in the Rieveschl

The Nature Conservancy,
Visitor's Center sections
and floor plan

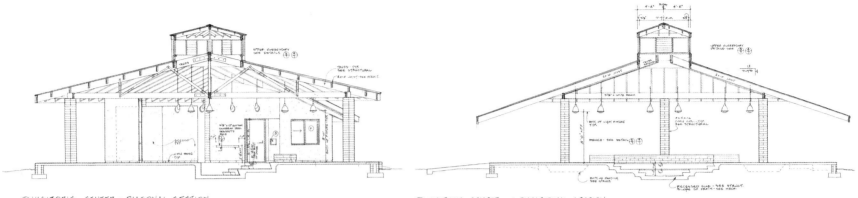

Ⓓ VISITOR'S CENTER - DIAGONAL SECTION
SCALE 1/4" = 1'-0"

Ⓐ VISITOR'S CENTER - LONGITUDINAL SECTION
SCALE 1/4" = 1'-0"

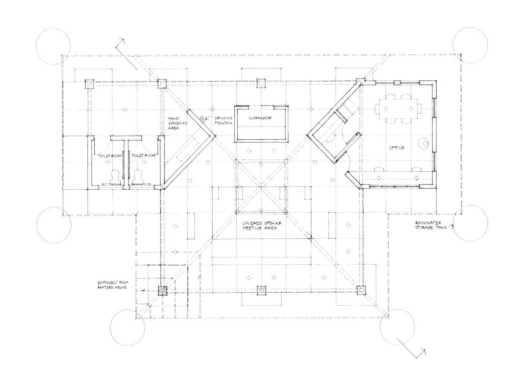

House—with three built forms of stucco-framed areas holding the objects: toilet rooms, workshop, and office. People can move around these contained spaces, benefiting from open views in all directions and breezes through the natural environment. The remarkable open area under the roof is a joyful experience.

The original design for the manager's house included a smaller version of a south-facing greenhouse for growing food, similar to that in the Hydeman Residence. The simple 1,500-square-foot floor plan starts with a traditional zaguan, a large central hall traversing the building from which the other rooms are entered. The tall ceiling and clear circulation encourage natural ventilation through the house. Modern southwestern considerations provide for one large flexible space for the kitchen, with dining and living room areas rather than smaller segmented spaces. Three 8-foot-wide sliding glass door systems on the south wall filter indirect daylight from under the deep roof overhang. These glass doors provide spectacular views of the visitor center across the road to the southeast at a 10-foot lower elevation, and to the riparian forest and mountains beyond. Fenestration on the other elevations is, as with the visitor center, expressed in the double-hung tall windows of a more traditional homestead module. Chafee was able to negotiate the addition of a small ramada on the east end of the house near the kitchen, creating the opportunity for private outside social activities.

The intent was to design sustainable buildings with low-maintenance materials: concrete floors and platform

areas, concrete masonry units, stucco walls, and corrugated galvalume metal roofing. Although hampered by a tight budget, Chafee provided a responsible and enjoyable experience for staff and volunteers living and working at the preserve as well as the many visitors.

Philip Rosenberg of PGR Construction was the general contractor and, having enormous respect for Chafee, was very patient and took great care with the project. She liked working with him and wished they could have worked on more projects, but this would be her last.

The center officially opened in April 1996. More than two decades later, Debbie Collazo still appreciates Chafee's contributions. "These buildings, with sustainable features much ahead of today's trend, can be appreciated by everyone, as they are open to the public.... Birdwatchers from around the United States and beyond visit the sanctuary, and their visits are enhanced by the attractiveness of Judith's design."[68]

173

Judith Chafee with Rieveschl Residence model, 1990

A Mindful Culture

Part of the initial information Chafee provided for a
graduate class at MIT in 1988 included this prologue,
which was her manifesto for house design work:

> As responsible, mature Architects, I wish each of us would
> have the opportunity sometime to contribute to the worldwide
> need for affordable, appropriate homes: sanctuaries that
> nurture families and individuals, providing the feelings
> of security, strength and independence that citizens need
> in order to participate in larger scale political habitats.
> As beginning Architects and participants in small firms,
> most of us become involved just in house design for quite
> privileged clients. If we view these jobs in proper perspective,
> they provide a medium in which to develop and integrate
> our perceptions and skills to make an object or place of
> great clarity.
>
> The house, after the enclosure of our own flesh, provides
> the next level of containment—holding things our body
> envelope cannot keep to itself—our voices, our emotions
> and our visions.
>
> Think of all the wonderful great houses, the crystals that
> evoke a time and an entire attitude towards Architecture
> in a single structure.[69]

Chafee ran her office in a personal way. It had initially
been her home, and retained that spirit, even when she
changed domiciles. In 1980, her mother decided to
join a number of good friends at an active senior living
complex near Philadelphia, and Chafee acquired her
Tucson townhouse in Orchard River.[70] She was glad to be
out of living in the "back room" of the studio at 317 North
Court, and the Tucson studio gained a room dedicated
for model making. The studio/office still provided relatively
comfortable work areas for the long hours spent there
with everyone working on deadlines. The front room was
fitted with two large drafting tables made from 32-inch
hollow core doors supported by two-drawer legal-size

filing cabinets on each end. A custom flat file was added
against the opposite west wall, with enough room to
walk by and review drawings on the flat door top. Chafee
would sit at the far desk facing the door and view the
whole space. A small desk on the opposite wall, which
came from one of the dormitory furniture suites Chafee
designed while working on the East Coast, accommodated
a part-time bookkeeper or whoever was responsible for
paying the bills. On deadlines, when all bodies were
needed, the bookkeeper, or even a kind-hearted relative,
might be recruited to type the specifications on the
Olivetti typewriter (Italian of course), which required Wite-
Out for corrections. Typing was left for whoever drew
the short straw.

A storage closet and second room with two additional
drafting tables rounded out the office space. When there
were two employees, one would work in this second room,
which was something of a refuge from the smoky front
room. The other table was useful for research. Two walls
of the room had 8-foot-high bookshelves enriched with
all types of product catalogs, including a treasured old
Knoll furniture binder. There were collections of writing
on solar and passive energy and books about engineering
technologies, anthropology, Native American cultures,
Aalto, Gropius, Wright, Le Corbusier, Sullivan, Rudolph,
and some newly discovered influences. Even the monthly
professional periodicals had their place, although they
often remained in plastic covers, thanks to lack of time for
reading them.

The west half of the front building was shared with
the galley kitchen, the central eating and meeting area
with its large sliding door into the open courtyard, and a
restful sitting room. The eating area was the communal
lunchroom, where Chafee would sometimes share a
special dish she made, or the crew would pitch in to make
a recipe of tamales or celebrate an occasion. Lunch could
often be a run to the nearby Mexican takeout, El Rapido, or

Sketches by Judith Chafee of her dogs, Zeus, in the 1960s (left), and Bella, in the 1980s (right)

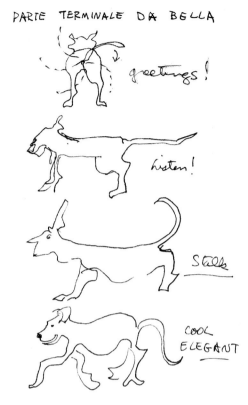

PARTE TERMINALE DA BELLA

greetings!

listen!

Stalk

COOL ELEGANT

just something brought from home.[71] The table was also the place for conversations, often relating to current events and politics of the day, and newspaper interviews. During a discussion at the table with Lawrence Cheek in 1985, Chafee related architecture to current issues, condemning revivalism as a "symptom of a people who have gone intellectually flabby." She continued, "It's very similar to what Reagan has done so successfully…You revive images from the past and hark back to a time when there was comfort and opulence. We're not willing to go through the effort of facing current problems."[72]

The large oak table had room for six to eight people to gather around. It was the place to sip champagne at the signing of a contract, share cookies at a client meeting, or hold a "salon" for students and professors (with a few engineers mixed in). And, there were always cookies for Leda, and later, her inheritor, Bella.

Chafee was accustomed to having dogs in her life. In her childhood there were large mixed breeds, and for a wedding gift, she was given a Staffordshire terrier named Zeus—whom she kept after her divorce. Chafee's dogs were family, accompanying her to the office, back home, and after-hours at the university. They were smart, spoiled, and good company. Leda's paw print is still in the office's entry threshold. One late worknight, Bella, who was "a

talker," wanted to go home and started taking Rieveschl rocks from the sample shelf and placing them on the drafting tables.[73] Chafee was also partial to other pets, and once when at a meeting at the house of a potential client, she observed the owner being "uncaring and neglectful" to his animals. She returned to the office, related the incident, and said she told the pet owners she would not work with them, then drove away. (There are many Chafee stories, some true, like this one, and some not.)[74]

When Chafee moved into her townhouse, she had Elliott Price build a long white Aalto-inspired table that she designed large enough to seat a cozy twelve people. She enjoyed the project of an occasional party, whether for six or forty-six, and assigned themes to her gatherings: Finnish, Mexican, Chinese, and Indian, among others.

Rieveschl Residence,
Tucson, Arizona,
construction site

Diana Brock-Gray, a former student, employee, and lifelong friend, remembers, "Judith's white table was like an artist's blank canvas. She would draw a plan of the table, serving dishes, plates, linens, glasses and silverware, [and] set the menu, thinking about the composition of colors and textures of the food and materials. She would have three-by-five cards noting who was coming and where they would sit."[75] Chafee hosted Christmas parties that required some office help with stringing little white lights throughout her house and courtyard. One year, she hired a piano player so she could enjoy her own Christmas party. The house, inside and outside, was filled with revelers: many clients, engineers, plumbers, electricians, cabinetmakers, students, faculty, and other friends and their children.

It was also not unusual for Chafee to pick up other hosting opportunities.

When Australian architect Glenn Murcutt was a guest lecturer at the university, Chafee put together a lovely picnic and gathered Ron Gourley (who was then the dean), Murcutt, and her office staff and drove her blue Chevy Blazer up to Kitt Peak to see the National Observatory buildings and the Tucson terrain.[76] When William J.R. Curtis was a guest lecturer for a second visit, she treated him to hors d'oeuvres and drinks at the Rieveschl Residence, when just the columns and slabs were completed. And there were "office runs," car pools to get out of Tucson for professional improvement, pleasure, and sometimes additional work—to Phoenix with Bob Earl and Kathy McGuire for AIA meetings and national design competitions, to small historic Arizona communities, and with faculty member and good friend Bob Nevins and two other friends to Sonoita to plant the Hydeman greenhouse for a photo shoot.[77]

Chafee considered professional-quality photography one of the most important tools in marketing her office's design services. She did not overtly focus on office marketing but described her awareness of the need for marketing in the noncomputer age of 1984, to Jim Morgan:

Publication was my only hope to create a respected professional image. First I had to put in the design time to make the work worth publishing. Second it had to be seen by people who could help get it published. That takes time too. Many small design firms in this region that start out to get commercial work through aggressive marketing view architectural publication as an elitist pastime. On the contrary, it has been my bread and butter. A very small firm, particularly (alas) with a woman principal, has got to have some authoritative approbation to gain credence.

Morgan stated, "Chafee points out that promoting and selling her design services has brought her an unforeseen benefit beyond designing houses and seeing them built. In most cases it has meant the owners have become friends and boosters of the practice."[78]

Changes in technology, including computer presentations and websites, soon redefined the relevance and applications of photography. Photographer friends retired, and many of the "old guard" contacts changed. *Sunset* magazine and some local publications maintained an interest in her accomplishments and published updates on the Blackwell House. But with her life divided between school and office, Chafee had neither time to invest in new associations and methodologies nor willingness to delegate decisions regarding her office's image.

By 1996, Chafee was finding it more difficult to justify the cost and necessary use of energy to maintain and commute to her office. There was barely enough work to keep student Joshua Edwards working part-time with minimal professional oversight. Corky Poster had been building his own practice and mentioned to Chafee that if she wanted to sell, he would be interested in buying her building. It was a very fortunate offer. The office was her dream, and had been her life for twenty-eight years. Giving it up was painfully difficult. Chafee knew her friend would be kind and respect what she had built. By then, she had acquired a smaller townhouse within walking distance of her own, to serve as her studio. Perhaps it was folly, but she needed to feel she still had an "office"; everything was moved from the downtown adobe and required a repository. She was not well enough to be present for the move, and the last of her staff and a few hired students whom Joshua managed to enlist moved everything to the new location. Chafee sold her building to Corky's firm, Poster Frost, in 1996.

In the fall, she wrote the following poem, reflecting her feelings about the change:

Depression   Oct. 26, '96

Back is broken,
bone can come,
Hurt is balm
and Sadness comfort.
Able to feel and move,
Coming home to myself.

Even at a very young age, Chafee paid attention to the light and the land. She was introduced to different cultures and creative people. She was always encouraged to ask questions and think critically. She learned about human relationships through her stepfather's social connections and special friendships with some of his patients, and inherited her mother's cleverness, survival instincts, and addictions. In the dichotomy of her private life the addictions to tobacco and alcohol were at the root of her chronic self-destruction, often alienating her from friends for whom she cared as well as opportunities for rewarding projects. And yet she had an epic sense of self-determination, and a genius for work that could demonstrate remarkable understanding of human needs in various environments. Barbara Grygutis, a sculptural artist who had a studio near Chafee's office, said, "She had a vision for the arts and modernism. She was very aware of who she was and what she was doing. She was her own person."[79]

Mindful Residents

Narratives and studies on architecture are often interesting, inspiring, pleasurable, and informative learning tools about time and place, methods and materials, and sometimes a suggestive program. But rarely is there much information about the owner—the initiator of a given project, be it a government, a private or public institution, or an individual—who sets the hiring of an architect. Their selection begins the process of defining the future form and its affect on the environment. Often, very little is known about these enablers unless there is an association with an illustrious entity or some kind of controversy. This is especially evident in residential architecture, where a profound synergism between the architect and the client exists. In some places in the United States including the Southwest, owners are not required to hire an architect for residential work. Chafee worked with engaging, aware, and committed clients: a New York executive who was a good family friend, a young professional family who saw the Merrill Residence and decided Chafee was the architect to hire, silent patrons underwriting a future speculative project, a young couple building their own adobe house, a young working woman who said, "Judith Chafee, you are a wonderful architect and someday I will hire you to design my house." Without these and other clients, this architecture would not be here to discuss. And, after all the struggles, complexities, resolutions, and compromises, Chafee enjoyed good long friendships with most of them. The client, friend, and owner for almost fifty years of the Ramada House told writer Lawrence Cheek, "The reason you put up with her…was that she was very, very good." Cheek's article goes on:

> The client had some misgivings about the hard-edged aesthetic she had seen in Chafee's portfolios and wanted it moderated, particularly in the interior, with warm touches, such as Mexican tile floors. "She gave me most of what I wanted inside," recalled the client. "And in return I gave

her that ramada….She saw that ramada as an intellectual challenge," said the client. But it was even more of a financial challenge: the construction bid arrived over budget and Chafee would not surrender. This was the paradox of Chafee's relationship with her clients. On one hand, if she became intrigued and challenged by the project she would go to the earth's ends to meet the client's needs, evaporating her own profits in the process. On the other hand, she was stubborn, domineering, and absolutely determined to get her own way in the matters that were important to her. Architecture was more than bricks and ramadas; it was a morality play.[80]

The original owner is the first part of bringing a project to fruition. At the other end of the process are the caretakers, curators, preservationists, and restoration activists. Many of Chafee's projects are clear representations of the original intent, withstanding the challenges of time. Viewpoint was sold within a few years of construction, after the husband of Chafee's mother died, to the Ryers family, who loved the house but needed more room for their three children. Chafee designed a unique children's house for them, which they remember as being different from their friends' houses. But then Viewpoint was sold a few more times, with each owner contributing a particular aesthetic flavor. When John Biklen and David Streeter (1929–2016) bought the house in 1994, the form and structure were intact, but the spatial clarity and materiality had been obliterated by a full variety of colors painted on the mortar-washed walls, oak cabinets, and exposed ductwork. The roof and wood trim were neglected to the point of requiring replacement. Biklen and Streeter, collectors of midcentury modern art and furnishings, spent a great deal of time and money to return the house to its original spirit.

George Rieveschl (1916–2007) enjoyed more than twenty winters in his extraordinary Tucson house before his ill health necessitated selling it. Sandra Helton and

Norman Edelson purchased the Rieveschl Residence after it had been left unattended for a few years, exhibiting damage from lack of proper temperature control and leaking roof areas. They loved the feel of the house. It was what the Chicago couple wanted—modern, clean lines, sensational views in every direction, and an interior that was special—but they did not yet realize the commitment that would be required for the needed restoration. Although they never met Chafee, their determination was generated by their respect for the architect and her work. They proceeded with significant repair work, replacing paint, most cabinets, and roof areas, exactly matching, wherever possible, what was designated in the drawings and specifications.

Three houses remain in the hands of their original owners: Ramada, Jacobson, and Russell-Randolph. Each time a building changes ownership, one may hope, but cannot expect, that the original spirit of the place be maintained. Even buildings with the most sustainable materials require some maintenance. The owners who have gleaned the specifications of their Chafee houses, continue to provide the needed care, and share their aesthetic experiences with others are owed a debt of gratitude and appreciation.

When Chafee died in 1998, Jane London, the owner of the Ramada House, Chafee's client and friend, said, "It was as though the power had been shut off forever. It was very scary to realize I was now on Earth alone in charge of this house."[81]

Chafee was a member of the board of Civitas Sonoran, a Tucson organization "dedicated to heightening awareness of the responsibilities and opportunities presented in planning and designing the built environment." A year after she died, a tour of many of the Chafee-designed houses was arranged with a detailed brochure, written by Lawrence Cheek, who had interviewed Chafee numerous times over the years for articles in local publications. He wrote:

Judith Chafee photographing Rieveschl Residence dressing area

The architecture of Judith Chafee resides in this rarefied air of righteousness. Her work, most of it private houses for secluded sites in the Sonoran Desert, responded to the land in ways that few other twentieth-century buildings managed in any place. It was usually strong and authoritative, riding the landscape with no apology for its presence, yet profoundly respectful. She seemed to revel in the paradox of designing a powerful mass for a fragile site, integrating the two so that each graced the other. The houses weren't necessarily beautiful, but they were inevitably the right object in the right place with the right skew to sun and view. They were, and are, masterful lessons in how to build in the desert.[82]

Les Wallach, FAIA, president, Civitas Sonoran, wrote in 1999, "Judith was an enigma, a complex, brilliant personality whose mastery of light, shade and form wedded inseparably to the landscape and led to the creation of meaningful architecture."[83]

Conclusion

Judith Chafee's return to Tucson in 1970 provided her the opportunity to clarify the lessons of an architecture resulting in the symbiosis of varied regions and her modern vocabulary. Her desire for a large scope of expression collided with various reasons for that not occurring—some personal concerns and other matters of timing and culture. Nonetheless, she fought hard and purposefully to get her footing. With gravitas and deliberation she chose to not invest her time in a family or other distractions. Ironically, when her aging mother moved back to Tucson, Chafee provided for her needs, to the detriment of Chafee's own work and health. But her sixty-six years were well-lived with a network of like-minded friends, stimulating travel, fulfilling projects, and the opportunity to communicate her concerns and ideas to a responsive community. Her commitment was to the relevance of architecture and its relationship with human and environmental concerns that respond to future needs with the integrity and honesty of modern principles.

He has not been taught that an architect, to be a true exponent of his time, must possess first, last and always the sympathy, the intuition of a poet; that this is the one real vital principal that survives through all places and all times.

—Louis H. Sullivan[84]

Remember Tucson in the
summer?
—
Cooler in the mesquite lone
beside the ditch?
—
And mysterious and nurturing
inside places people built
for themselves? Built the way
things were or are. Simple rooms
in rows. Rooms in rows
around a patio.
—
People come, pass through, and go.
—
People also stay. Sit at the table all night
drinking tequila, talking, and listening
to Bach.
—
The way things were—with a
lot more of the way things
are.
Bright and cool—in the desert.[85]

—Judith Davidson Chafee, 1932–1998

Hydeman Residence
Sonoita, Arizona, 1980–83

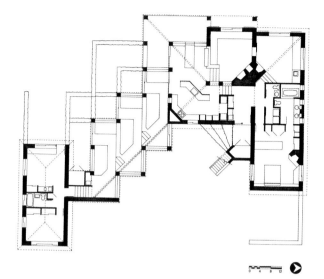

The Hydeman Residence is in Sonoita, Cochise County, in part of the Crown C Ranch, which is made up of small ranch parcels of forty acres and larger on desert prairie land. This cattle ranching country, sixty miles southeast of Tucson, is a slightly cooler area, due to higher elevations, with long rolling grasslands dotted with scrub oak and surrounded by jagged mountain ranges. One arrives at the Hydeman Residence by traveling over dirt roads through grassy hills with open grazing areas for cattle, past the small remnants of a historic cavalry outpost. It is nestled above a tree-lined ravine near an embankment, its three giant, mushroom-shaped chimney caps the first visible part of the house. Deed restrictions of view-protecting covenants prohibit any sighting of rooftops from any other property in the subdivision.

Lee and Marisha Hydeman had their main residence in the Washington, DC, area, where Lee was a successful attorney specializing in mergers for international airline companies and other corporations. Marisha, daughter of a former US ambassador, worked with several US senators. The couple also had a family summer house in Vermont and wanted a warmer place for the winter time. When building their modern Vermont farmhouse, the Hydemans worked with New York architect and sculptor Norman Hoberman, who was Lee's good friend and former roommate at Harvard. Hoberman was well respected and good friends with many of the Harvard group of architects, including Edward Larrabee Barnes, who, in 1980, recommended Chafee for the Hydeman's project in the Southwest.

Lee loved ranch work and being a cowboy, and fit right in with the locals in well-worn jeans, a crumpled cowboy hat, and hardworking boots. He and Marisha wanted to have a winter ranch to enjoy the views, have natural air flow, and embrace appropriate sustainable ideas in their home. They wanted high ceilings, a kitchen-living-dining area that was all one space, a small studio for Marisha

to enjoy painting, and a guesthouse separate from the main house. They were willing to accommodate four to six guests, including their own adult children. Built-in furniture was to be included where possible in order to save on new purchases. A greenhouse was to be part of the main house to provide additional heating.

Chafee translated the owners' desires into a habitable and pleasing environment. The best mountain views are to the west through sliding glass-door-sized windows—a familiar element in Chafee's tool box—with large sliding wooden "barn-door" panels of natural pine on the exterior providing protection from the summer sun. The low, earth-hugging structure grows out of the ground, with the corrugated metal roof lines of the traditional ranch house transitioning into the clear, corrugated, fiberglass greenhouse roof that is aligned with the slope of the land. The roof slopes into a gutter system to divert rainwater into cisterns for additional irrigation for the greenhouse vegetation. The greenhouse is secured on the south end by the two-room-and-bath guesthouse, partially sunken into the sloping terrain where the roof reverts to the corrugated metal. Also following the slope of the natural grade, polished tinted-concrete floor levels are encased by walls of poured, earth-toned concrete, incorporating local rock and inspired by the exposed aggregate walls of Frank

Entry court (below)
and floor plan
(opposite)

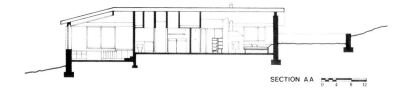

SECTION A A   0 4 8 12

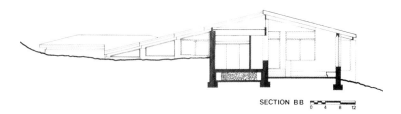

SECTION B B   0 4 8 12

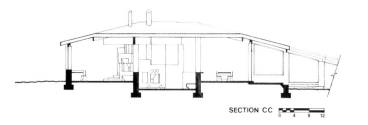

SECTION C C   0 4 8 12

184

Lloyd Wright's Taliesin West. Economy, availability of local materials, and craftsmanship determined a smaller, but no less effective, aggregate. To provide additional thermal stability, the exterior concrete walls are constructed with 4-inch-thick Styrofoam insulation, sandwiched between 6 inches of poured concrete and rock, inside and out. After testing various wall samples for the desired finish, the plywood wall forms were coated with the selected retardant for easy breakaway and reuse as the concrete cured. Snap ties were used to hold the forms together during the pour, with the usual quarter-sized holes from the ties remaining as evidence of the form work. The structural clarity is also expressed by the exposed rough-sawn 4×14–inch wood beams mounted above the grid of formed concrete columns and walls. During

construction, the formed concrete walls had the appearance of ancient archaeological ruins, reminiscent of those preserved in Casa Grande, Arizona, and the Italian vernacular relics Chafee researched in Apulia and Sardinia during her fellowship at the American Academy in Rome.

Chafee described her sense of gratification in the design and construction process of her projects in *Artspace*, writing, "If I have not said enough of how the buildings look, it is because I feel my job is to make them for you to look at as you do. I look too and always learn from and love most the building in construction. When it is finished, it is time to get to work."[1]

The remote location of the construction site for the Hydeman Residence incentivized Chafee to limit the number of subcontractors on the job.[2] Eliminating sheetrock also simplified the project and offered better protection of completed work. Ceilings are finished with rough-sawn wood planks, and interior walls with smooth wood siding. The wood ceilings and walls are painted with a 50 percent diluted whitewash to provide a lighter, reflective transition from the tinted concrete and stone wall material.

The main entrance is subtly tucked behind the open wood steps ascending to the roof deck. It is accessed through a custom-fabricated fir door with glass slits that provide natural lighting into the generous entry hall. The perpendicular corridor intersects below the hall clerestory, formed within the edge of the deck on the roof above. The north portion of the house is the private area, including the master suite and artist's studio. The studio is equipped with a poured-in-place sculptural-formed concrete fireplace, with a recirculating air system to provide additional heat. An interior sliding wood panel with a pull-handle made from a wooden trowel opens and closes to the living room for more visual and audio privacy.

The master bedroom suite has a recirculating fireplace with a more whimsical form. Made of poured-in-place

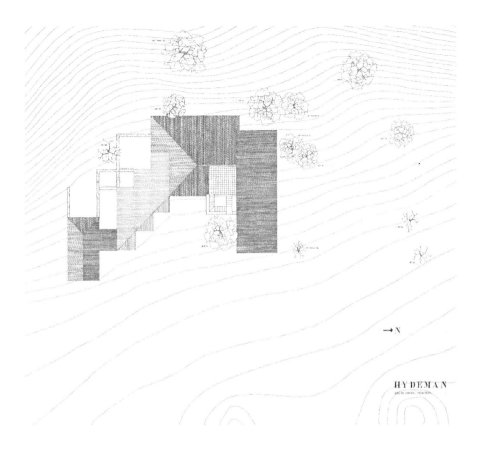

concrete, it is reminiscent of the traditional Mexican corner fireplace, and includes a row of 3-inch copper pipes below the firebox for air intake, and above the firebox for air output. A 10-foot custom-built oak cabinet, with banks of drawers on one side and bookshelves on the other, provides privacy from the entrance into the room. Cobalt Mexican tile covers the walls and counters of the master bathroom. Chafee's creative use of natural light is observed, as the bath wall receives a mysterious wash of natural light from an unseen window, hidden behind the sink counter wall.

Circulation through the house is defined by ceiling forms and the direction of exposed beams. The south corridor steps down to the kitchen and dining area; additional steps lead down to the partially recessed living room, where poured-in-place concrete seating with cushions lines the south and west walls. With no separating walls, the entire area is a well-positioned open space. The kitchen and dining areas have direct access to the greenhouse through sliding glass doors that can be opened to let in heat and closed to maintain house temperatures. Heat can also be transferred from the greenhouse to a rock bed under the kitchen slab and blown through ducts into the main house. Chafee's vision of providing natural light to interior spaces is demonstrated with an interior clerestory that brings natural light from the outside clerestory into the adjacent hall. The light washes across the poured concrete fireplace, located in the living room. This third fireplace provides a grand heat source coming out of the columnar grid.

Historic Camp Crittenden, cavalry outpost ruins, Sonoita, Arizona (left), and San Raphael Cattle Co. (below)

Air is recirculated through 6-inch terra-cotta clay pipes. Similar 4-inch clay pipes—sized to hold wine or Mexican beer bottles—are embedded into a partial-height concrete wall between the living room and dining area.

An adjacent window wall includes a notch in the concrete sill to support one end of the wood-plank built-in dining table. As requested, all furnishings are built-in except the necessary chairs for desks and tables. Enjoying shopping for a few necessary items with Marisha Hydeman at the Mexican border town of Nogales, Chafee introduced her to the pigskin chairs, blue glass dishes, and Guatemalan fabrics that add the finishing touches of comfort to this rustic modern ranch house.

At a time when the expected building form was tile roofing, arched windows, and stucco-covered hidden wall systems, Chafee was mindful of the local, traditional ranch house, using the hip roof of corrugated metal and adding deep overhangs for protection from the elements and large protected windows to provide natural cross ventilation. Modern sensibilities are introduced with the low maintenance, energy-responsive wall system, clerestory windows for lighting interior spaces, sculptural concrete for recirculating fireplaces, and the protected entry with its Aalto-inspired door panels. The roof-deck area may be a consideration of the indigenous experience of viewing beyond one's dwelling, or of the sleeping porches of later occupants of the land. In any case, it provides—with thoughtful modern conveniences—the pleasure of contemplating one's surroundings.

Chafee's closing comment in an article she wrote about the house for the journal *Triglyph* states, "Searching the portrait, looking deeply into its following eyes, I hope it shows regionalism without cant, passive solar without fussiness, and an attitude toward design that reveals dedication to the modern, yes, Modern Movement."[3]

190

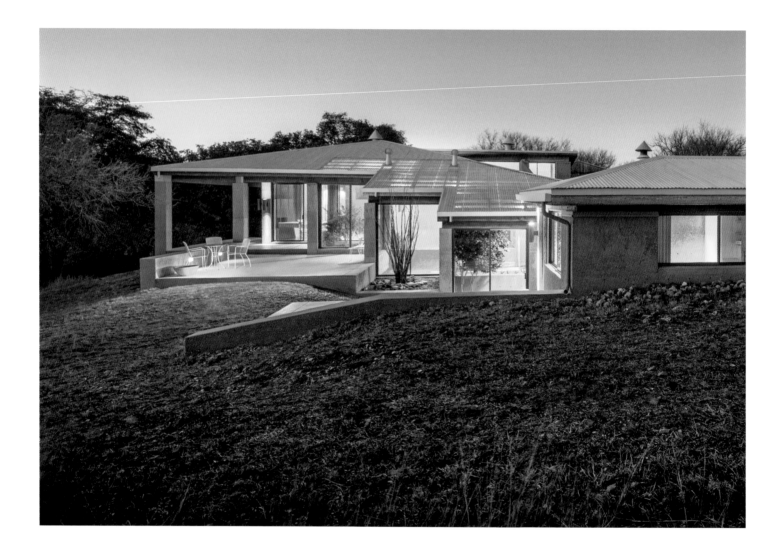

Living room
(below) and
vestibule
(opposite)

Clerestory window
(below) and kitchen
and dining room
(opposite)

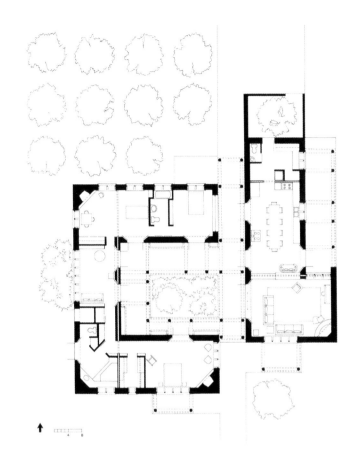

The building site of the Russell-Randolph Residence is low farming land with established mesquite groves and eucalyptus trees, in the southwestern part of Tucson. Ten minutes from downtown, the site is very near the bed of the Santa Cruz River, which seasonally becomes a small river when there is enough rain. Once a cattle ranch and farming section of Tucson, the area now has eclectic zoning, much different from the tony foothills desert area, or rolling hills of the Tucson Mountains, where many of Chafee's projects were built. She took great pleasure giving directions to the house. "When you get to the city jail complex, turn down the single road, past the trailer park and turn into the north edge of the property, 200 feet of tree-lined dirt driveway,"[1] she would say, directing visitors to arrive at a small parking plaza, paved with reused brick pavers, and surrounded by bamboo, sycamores, fig, and citrus, added for privacy screening, shade, and pleasure.

David Russell is a writer and dealer of imports, mostly pottery and weavings from Mexico. His wife, Susan Randolph, works with Jin Shin Jyutsu, a Japanese healing art, and is a special-education teacher for gifted children. They were Chafee's youngest clients, with one small daughter and another born during the building project. David Russell's parents, Ike and Jean Russell, having met in Tucson while studying at the University of Arizona, settled into a ranching area south of Tucson with their three sons, and then bought farmland close to downtown. Jean gave David and Susan a parcel from that farmland, on which they could build their house. A good friend and neighbor, Diane Hastings, told the couple, "Judith Chafee is the architect you need to hire."[2] Hastings was also a friend, student, and former employee of Chafee's.

It is not unusual for architects to have design concepts tucked away in their minds, waiting for an opportune time to work with an idea. During the initial meeting with Russell and Randolph, they expressed their desire for an adobe house, having an appreciation for the style's feel and history. Susan Randolph also liked the tin roofs of the barrio where they had been renting a house. Both Russell and Randolph felt their money was better spent on a good architect and would economize by being their own general contractor. As it was, Chafee's own youth in Tucson had been spent in an adobe house, sometimes under various stages of remodel or new construction, and upon her return to the area after Yale and East Coast work, she located her home and office in a historical adobe building. At the second meeting with the Russell-Randolphs, Chafee produced the "glass house adobe." Schematic drawings showed a glass exterior box, interior adobe walls, and an interesting, somewhat complicated,

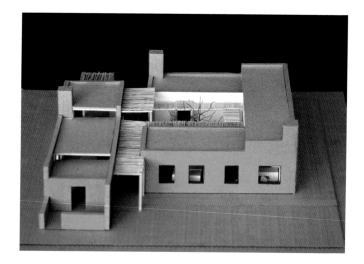

202

hip-and-gables metal roof system. The interior walls were set back far enough from the glass to utilize the heat-sink of massive adobe in the winter and to be shaded during hotter times of the year. Although this was an intriguing concept, this was not the house for Russell and Randolph. Quite concerned about the direction the design had taken, they returned with a sketch, on a napkin, of the floor plan of a very old adobe house they loved in Hermosillo, Mexico. A traditional courtyard house, one section was formed by a long, one-room-deep rectangle that was parallel to a large square, with an open corridor of separation. At the mid-area of these two forms, a square courtyard was cut out, forming a U-shaped perimeter. The house also had a flat roof. Such a design would be simple and cost effective for the clients' already challenging, owner-built adobe house project. As the design phase progressed, Susan Randolph was less eager to sit through meetings, while David Russell and Chafee had head-to-head collaborations on various concepts and details.

The existing cow pasture was designated as a flood-plain area mandating the house be built on a raised engineered-soil building pad. The footings are 36 to 44 inches wide, and 24 inches deep, below finished grade. When Russell asked why the footings had to be so big, Jerry Cannon, the structural engineer, replied, "That's

how Rome was built."[3] This required a rubble-base footing and 20-inch-high stem walls, with concrete and large rocks taken from the undeveloped property in the Tucson Mountains owned by Chafee's mother. After more than thirty-five years, the house shows no settling, even in the somewhat sandy soil, and no cracks in the polished concrete floor slab.

"The idea is to pick up the deep underlying wisdom that's come from generations of living there. Plus using your modern know-how in construction techniques," Chafee said to Margo Hernandez, writing for the *Arizona Daily Star* in February 1989.[4] Respecting the traditional adobe building modality, Chafee also provided modern solutions for environmentally responsive structures. Russell insisted on raw, unstabilized adobe and matching mortar, which he brought from Mexico, providing savings in his budget and a healthier interior product. However, most adobe products made in Arizona are stabilized with a percentage of asphalt emulsion, which makes a more durable material with better resistance to environmental challenges. Concerned about water erosion of the more vulnerable blocks, Chafee designed details for fired-brick parapet caps, concrete window headers, and sills that extend past the exterior wall plane to accept a later option of added stucco to protect the adobe. Russell has maintained the adobe walls when necessary and found additional protection from the courtyard ramadas and dense vegetation. The adobe walls are a double-wythe system, similar to the double-insulated wall system that is effectively used in the Sonoita House. The 6-inch-deep adobe block with 4-inch rigid insulation and another 6-inch adobe block on the inside as an exposed-wall system requires no painting. Interior partition walls are finished in natural pine siding.

This is a timeless adobe, wood, and glass building, extending beyond vernacular forms with adjustments for the site and climate. The strong delineation of the east

elevation is the first visible element, stepping up to accommodate clerestories, the highest of which reach 18 feet above floor level, with another 4 feet extending to the top of the chimney mass. The rectangular building provides an open floor plan in shared areas of kitchen, dining, and step-down living room, with a higher ceiling space and a clerestory. The north-facing clerestories enable natural light, occasional bobcat sightings, and a dramatic spread of light onto the patterned ceilings and adobe walls. *Latillas*—saguaro-ribbed ceilings—provide an interesting wood pattern and are used inside to minimize the view of ceiling fixtures. The same materials are repeated on the outside ramadas encircling the courtyard to provide a perforated umbrella of shade. Clear corrugated fiberglass covers the wooden ribs and

protects the wood and area below from getting wet, while still permitting slits of light into the circulation areas.

Chafee was familiar with the use of courtyards with protected perimeters providing a microclimate with cross-ventilation inside and outside in arid regions such as Mexico, the Mediterranean, and China. But this courtyard is different, with its small, centered arboretum and well-defined circulation to all interior spaces. It also provides a means of assigning public and private spaces, with bedrooms and the library in the U-shaped building, protected by the courtyard vegetation. The buildings are a single room in depth, with a suggested interior corridor along the courtyard walls, creating a rich layering of inside and outside spaces, light and dark spaces, and some doors for optional privacy.

Exterior custom doors and windows are inserted into the 16-inch-deep walls, and the wood casement windows are set within full-depth wood trim. Chafee's elegant detail for the French doors includes the wood jamb set in a 35-degree slice in the wall to enable a full opening of each 2-foot-wide door panel. The wood trim is shiplap fir and relates to other wood-finished interior walls, eliminating sheetrock work. The tall French doors open from every room into the courtyard with a precisely located wood colonnade, an homage to the colonnade of the University of Virginia and Susan Randolph's lineage to Thomas Jefferson.[5]

Because Randolph and Russell knew very little about building a house, Chafee recommended they hire James Hamilton, a building contractor with whom she had worked, to consult. He recommended his best subcontractors, including an excellent senior mason, master carpenter, plumber, and experienced electrician. This was invaluable, and allowed Russell to feel comfortable with the people working on the job. But as work proceeded, he became more concerned about continually increasing costs for Hamilton's consulting work. As Russell tells it, he took Hamilton to lunch, and after a delightful meal at a longtime favorite French restaurant, he said, "James, I have to tell you, you are fired." Hamilton sat quietly, seeming a bit surprised, and then said, "Well, Dave, I didn't think you would catch on so quickly."[6]

Continuing to work with the experienced specialists, Russell traveled to towns in Mexico to hire adobe masons and carpenters. Little houses across from the site were rented for the men, and Susan prepared three meals every day for the crew as they stayed and worked on the house. Some of these workers are still family friends.

Joe Breen, a senior mason, complained about what he called the 16-foot-high "shitter" in the plan, a small bathroom next to the library. "How about a library loft?" he suggested.[7] Having worked on Chafee's Jacobson Residence, he knew about its library steps and loft. Russell recalled that Chafee said cutting a library loft into the high bookcases would interrupt the axis. Although he wasn't sure what she meant—perhaps she meant breaking up the space formed by the bookcase walls—he figured out a way to continue the verticality of the bookshelves and stay true to the high library space Chafee designed by building a subtle access up to a small, hidden reading loft. The east-facing clerestory brings uninterrupted morning light to illuminate the harmonious reading room and library.

At one point Chafee lamented to Russell about her lack of work. He observed, "For you to not have work is like Picasso not having oil paint," and hired Judith to design a visitor's tower and loft, separate from the main house.[8] This was intended for guests who often stayed over from late-night barbeques, for which Russell would place large metal grills on rocks near the east porch and host gatherings around the fire.

Joseph Wilder, a friend of Chafee's and of Russell and Randolph, and the longtime editor of the University of Arizona publication the *Journal of the Southwest*, expressed a familiar conflict occasionally sensed within the local community:

> She was a driven intellectual. I have a hard time responding to Judith Chafee's houses. They are brutal, harsh, and cold, and out in the middle of the desert. So, when I saw Russell House, I said that it is one of her finest buildings. She had an aesthetic vision, the materiality, the modern line combined with the adobe; an ensemble of modern line with softer material and I realized she had that language of modern southwestern architecture.[9]

Others, more attuned to modern forms and functions would not have agreed with Wilder's assessment, describing her work as vernacular, regionalist, modernist, and industrial. But Chafee rejected labels, especially if they ended with "ist" or "ism." She had a modern ethic and considered the work of architecture to be about finding the truth for each building by understanding what is happening on and around the site, what is needed, and how best to provide clean, honest solutions.

Living room (below)
and library book
tower with reading
loft (opposite)

210

Library book
tower

Centrum House   Tucson, Arizona, 1983–84

214

A unique feature of this project was the absence of both a client and a specific site—only a general location in Tucson, Arizona. The program was a speculation (spec) house, designed from a kit of parts to be adaptable to various site applications and owner options. The original idea came from builder James Hamilton, with whom Chafee had worked on a number of projects. The project description, as produced by Hamilton with Chafee's input in the early 1980s, stated the intent,

> to market well-conceived pre-designed houses by several local Architects. The belief that this was an important need stemmed from the low design standards of pre-built houses in the region and sometimes prohibitive time periods involved in planning an architecturally designed house from the beginning. Why couldn't a well-designed house be repeated, with the related savings, just as a well-designed piece of furniture or equipment can be repeated with dignity? These house designs were to be offered to the public on a limited edition basis, each design being constructed no more than twelve times. Each design would have a somewhat different program. Each would also have to adapt to a variety of site conditions, since no pre-selected lots were involved.[1]

Centrum House was the first house built for the Limited Editions product line. The program was determined for a three-bedroom, two-and-a-half-bath residence. Potential buyers might be a retired couple with children out of the house, or the moving-up or growing family. The geometric three-dimensional forms are the delineation of one square and one circle incorporated in a multirectilinear plan. The house is expressed in simple building materials, with painted stucco—the color of the shadow cast on a white wall—over insulation and wood framing, and painted drywall inside. The roof has a minimal slope with parapets capped by bronze metal, emphasizing the geometric forms. A high pyramid

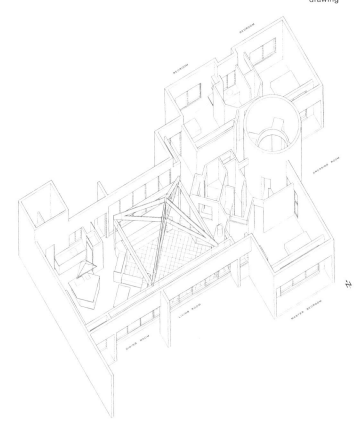

form defines the central area, which is covered in a bronze standing-seam metal roof with a cutout for triangular clerestories. Bronze anodized frames for sliding doors and windows complete the simple geometric lines. The exterior stucco half-circle wall of the circular dressing room, an unusual undertaking for the carpenter to execute, provides a sculptural form for the exterior.

The challenge of providing a flexible design that accommodates various site conditions was met brilliantly by Chafee. She indicated numerous options to reset the 3,100-square-foot floor plan. The option of either mirroring or flipping the north and south glass wall orientations, as well as the east and west elevations, can be best determined once the site is chosen. The garage size can be attached along the east wall or west wall, preferably

Living room,
looking south

216

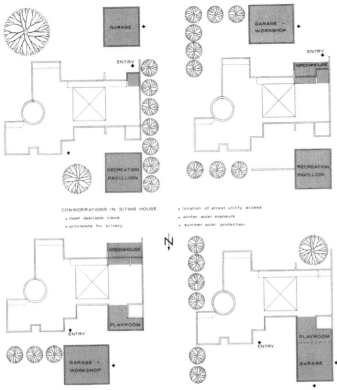

CONSIDERATIONS IN SITING HOUSE:
• most desirable views
• provisions for privacy

• location of street, utility access
• winter solar exposure
• summer solar protection

EXAMPLES SHOWING USE OF OPTIONAL ADDITIONS

next to the kitchen, or as a separate or semiattached building, and can vary in size. A small rectangular workshop, playroom, or greenhouse can also be added, and the entry can be placed on the north or south wall planes of the central rectangle between several spaced wall fins.

A tenacious focus is directed toward the center of this house. Four steps go down to the central core, recalling a kiva, the main meeting area in traditional indigenous homes, found often in archaeological sites. Four round, Danish-blue steel columns support steel brackets and a combination of natural-finished rough-sawn beams and wood trusses, to form a pyramid roof with two triangular clerestories and a whitewashed, fir-paneled vault. The remaining ceiling heights are flat for economy and ease of placement for utilities. Built-in oak cabinets embrace the sunken living space, which includes Chafee's signature sculptural-formed concrete fireplace and three locations for concrete steps. The living, dining, and kitchen areas form the open plan with brown-tinted polished concrete floors, more concrete work, steps, fireplaces, and banquettes. Only the sunken living area is surfaced with tan Marrazzi tile, set on a diagonal axis to emphasize the significance of the space and one's circulation through it. Chafee had admired the tile while traveling as a guest of the Italian Association of Ceramic Tile Manufacturers. The living room's almost square area is set within the big rectangular room, with full glazing on north and south exterior walls and interior and exterior spaces, with a view to the garden areas and mountains. A triangular

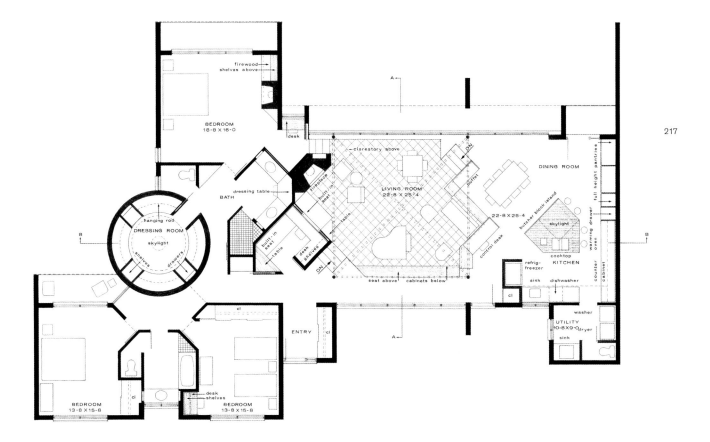

skylight illuminates the five-sided kitchen island, topped by a maple countertop with a pivoting raised leaf to hide clutter. The island blends into the dining space, with small activity areas and private alcoves assigned to numerous built-in oak cabinet sections. Cabinetmaker Elliott Price later described the work as very challenging:

> The cabinets defined the living space, ringing around the top of the sunken living room. Cabinets were different sizes, functions and had to look perfect on all sides. Every cut had to be clean and accurate. I learned a lot about how to use my equipment, as an exercise in what it could do. As my helper and I were easing the last cabinets into place, Judith came by with her dog, Bella, and said, "What's the matter, couldn't get them to fit?" with a jokingly wry smile.[2]

Bedrooms and bathrooms are located opposite the kitchen and dining area. Rather than a basic house with three bedrooms and a hallway, here, one side of the corridor is formed by the rounded wall of the large circular dressing room and closet. A bronze-framed glass door at the end of the hall is tucked behind the curved wall, distributing a soft wash of light along the curvaceous form. The main bedroom passes the glistening travertine bath and brings into view the second fireplace wall of poured-in-place concrete. An intimate reading nook leads to obscured steps to the living room and quick access to the kitchen. The study appears as a small bonus room, until the flush wooden wall panels are opened to expose a comfortable crow's nest with a view into the living room and beyond.

SECTION A-A

SECTION B-B

The one-acre building lot for the Centrum Model House was acquired in Cimarron Foothills, a desert development in the northeast part of Tucson. The house was built and displayed for about one year, with precise modern furniture provided by a local store, Copenhagen Imports.

The landscape around the house was sparse. The north front yard of the house has a minimal desert landscape, with well-formed paloverde trees. Low concrete retaining walls and a small cascade of matching concrete steps for the stroll to the protected entry area are part of the original landscape completed to show the house. The south yard is at the back of the house, and is a cleaned-up desert area, with a small arroyo and trees east of the building site.

Despite positive responses at various open house tours, no Limited Edition houses other than this one are known to have been built. The fact that this was a semicustom house with the feel of a custom design may have contributed to the lack of sales; even Frank Lloyd Wright's Usonian houses proved difficult to sell, and this promotion may also have suffered from poor timing in a weak economy.

When the Centrum House was purchased in 1985 by Ann and Jerome Shull, they wanted outside areas for quiet lounging, a place to enjoy a south-facing garden, a place to entertain with a grill and patio area, and perhaps a fountain. They appreciated Judith Chafee's design talent and hired her to finish the house.

Just as the house had clear zones of activity, Chafee applied the same tactic to the landscape, with rich areas segmented for different uses in the outdoor spaces. The main bedroom has a porch and 12 feet of glass sliders along the south wall. Steps lead down into an Alhambra-inspired water garden, with a private lounging area surrounded by a narrow water canal. An opening in the privacy wall leads to a sculpture garden, with shade trees and lower, terraced earthen areas providing a tranquil view from the living room. Continuing west on a paved brick walkway outside the kitchen and dining room glass sliders, the brick winds into a 12-foot-square aromatic herb garden. Here the area opens into a large entertaining patio that includes a brick-encased grill area and a continuing water channel around the perimeter that leads to a cobalt blue ceramic Barbara Grygutis water sculpture centered on the back wall. Grygutis created the edgings of the water channels, grill area, and masonry work with edge bricks glazed in shades of blue to purple in response to Chafee's request. Within this area is a bronze-painted steel ramada that reflects the house structure and is topped with a bronze pyramid pergola.

The varied-height stucco perimeter walls around and in between the landscaped areas suggest the plan of a building without a roof. It is a true outside living space that has almost the same square footage as the main house. In the climate of the Tucson desert, an inside-outside house is a desirable way to enjoy life.

Kitchen and
passageway,
with sculpture
by Seymour
Sabesin

View from garden,
looking north

222

South bedroom

223

Living room
(opposite and
below)

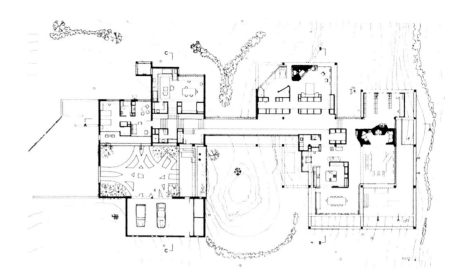

The Coronado mountain ranges in the Sonoran Desert form the northern boundary of the valley that contains the city of Tucson. The foothills provide a luxurious array of vegetation: splendid saguaros and stiletto lines of ocotillo, ironwood, paloverde and mesquite trees, shrubs, multicolored wildflowers, ground-covering prickly pear cactus, and an array of the smallest desert vegetation. The Rieveschl Residence defines the top of the foothills, a desirable location on which to build, with its north views along the mountain side, its long east views of protected canyons and distant mountain ridges, and the south view, with eye level set above distant rooftops toward the nighttime sea of city lights. The site is spectacular, and Chafee compared the route to the Rieveschl Residence to the rendering made by Delacroix in his travel journal of a caravan's passage through a steep, narrow, winding path to a walled village atop a hill.

Dr. George and Joan Rieveschl met Chafee after appreciating an extensive renovation of the foothills house of friends Rose and Edgar Stanton, who were also supportive friends of Chafee. George Rieveschl, a scientist who had developed Benadryl, said he and Joan "admired her handling of natural light and her craftsmanship."[1] George had worked with Alexander Girard on building a house in Michigan and was familiar with the process of working with an architect. The Rieveschls spent short winters in Tucson; the rest of their time was spent in Cincinnati, Ohio, where they were generous supporters of the arts, academia, and the cultural scene of the city. They owned acreage at the top of the Tucson foothills subdivision, where they also owned a modest house closer to the golf course. What they envisioned was a more substantial modern house sited on the east side of the lower granite hillock.

Chafee described the overview of the project this way: "The philosophical goals of disturbing the ground as little as possible and of living directly on the site determined the structure."[2] A broad part of the building area, including the driveway, was designated to be surveyed. All saguaro cactus, exceptional outcroppings, and any other significant vegetation were noted along with the usual topographical information. As a result, some areas where the floor plan jogs or turns in an unexpected direction are often due to the presence of a saguaro. Only one saguaro of nineteen documented was lost to construction work.

The west side of the house has the presence of a protected pueblo. The central courtyard is bound by the south building block, an enclosed place for vehicles, and a workshop, and sits level with the entrance. Minimal

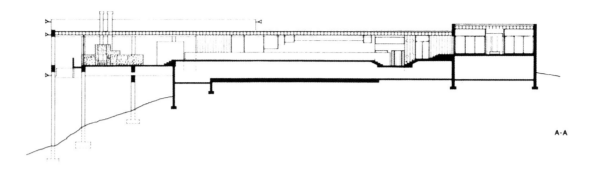

A-A

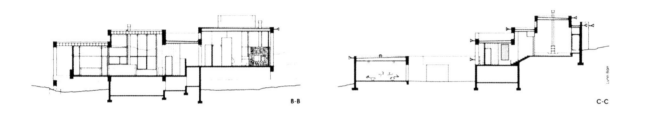

B-B   C-C

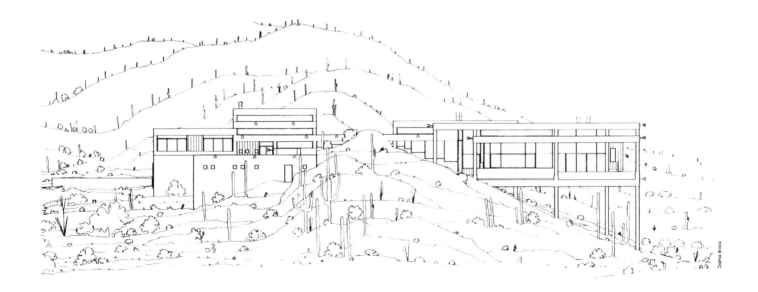

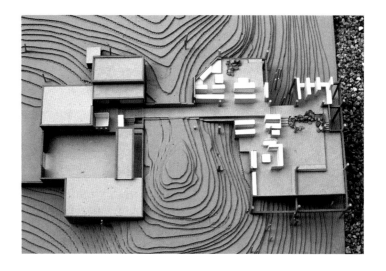

square windows are punched into the south wall for daylight, and no windows occur on the west side of these buildings, except one intentional square opening for the second-level patio that encourages a cross breeze and provides a west view with minimal heat gain. The courtyard surface is unique, with concrete paths defined by tire trails made by the owner's car. Between the trails are small site rocks that form a tight infill, reminiscent of a paving technique Chafee saw at the Summer Palace in China. The back of the courtyard celebrates a wall of chiseled granite, formed from the edge of the hill, which separates the west and east sections, the public from the private areas.

An abstract model with detailed topography and nine potential layers for occupancy—the levels following natural elevations on the site—was mailed to Cincinnati. It demonstrated that the east side of the hill cascading into the canyon was too steep and not suitable for all the functions the owners wanted. Chafee suggested locating site circulation and public activities on the more accessible west side, with a more manageable five layers, while supporting the private, contemplative areas on the east side. Horizontal building lines stretched through the natural saddle formed by the granite hill and the continuation of the side of the mountain. The Rieveschls sent back their message: "That looks great! Let's do it."[3]

Chafee flew to Cincinnati to gain a better understanding of the Rieveschls' lifestyle and the sense of scale they wanted to experience in their new house. After seeing their extensive art collection, she asked what pieces they planned to bring to Tucson, to ensure they would be accommodated. Finally, Chafee was able to gather the necessary information to develop the program. She returned to her Tucson office and announced that the square footage was to be doubled in size to approximately 7,200 square feet. When George was asked about the budget, the answer was, "Let's see how it goes." On one hand, this allowed Chafee the freedom to create the best concept and expression of work, but, on the other hand, there would be concerns throughout the process that a decision might end up being determined as excessive.

Chafee's team had had some larger commercial projects, with much simpler engineering needs, but this was its largest residential project. It took about twenty months, with intermittent client meetings, for design and construction documents to be completed. The bid came in higher than George and Joan Rieveschl desired, and after some substantial changes to material choices and downgrading some very high-end appliances, an acceptable budget was achieved. The square footage, floor plan, windows, and elevations remained as originally

230

specified. The west side of the building area had been designed as concrete block, faced with beautiful granite rocks from the site for a rough stone masonry wall system. Stucco painted over the block walls was approved as an alternative, sacrificing some material continuity from the west to east ends of the building.

The primary materials in the house are concrete, steel, and glass, all low- and no-maintenance products that continue to hold their integrity. The standing-seam wall covering system of Terne-coated stainless steel is used on exterior walls (inside and out) and adjacent interior walls. Chafee called it the "pin striped suit" of the building. The glass framing is a storefront system, providing sturdy frames and double-glazed units. Initially, Chafee proposed red metal frames, noticing that Joan Rieveschl wore red-framed glasses. Frank Lloyd Wright was also known to have used red window frames for Fallingwater. But the Rieveschls were not convinced and opted for the clear anodized aluminum frames.

Concrete abounds throughout the house: poured-in-place concrete is the dominant material for panel-formed retaining walls, polished concrete floors, majestic concrete columns, and bush-hammered concrete beams, some with dual functions, such as the concrete beam guardrail around the outside deck. While concrete work is typically assigned to a subcontractor, the scope of the concrete work for this residence required a contractor experienced with constructing parking garages. Ulmer Construction was selected and worked in concert with the general contractor, James Hamilton. Design limitations were determined by the available technology: the allowable location of the farthest column (at 40 feet high, one of the tallest) in the southeast corner was determined by the farthest reach of the concrete truck's pumper arm. A network of interwoven rebars for the horizontal components and outstretched vertical rebars, similar to the appearance of the ribs of a saguaro cactus skeleton, made it a challenge to direct the concrete pour.

The Rieveschl Residence's design is about the sequential journey to and through the building. At the end of the courtyard, a low concrete planter, which doubles as a bench, is backed by intentionally sparse greenery. The main feature of this space, the 18-foot-high chiseled granite hillock, was the result of a serendipitous event with a talented backhoe operator named Sissy, and David Eisenberg, a savvy job superintendent. The back wall was being gouged flat to accept a concrete block retaining wall to match the adjacent garage wall, because the expectation was that the hill would have too many pockets of soil to be stable. To everyone's surprise, it was

beautiful, solid, raw granite. Upon the discovery, Eisenberg called Chafee's office to suggest that she come take a look. Ultimately, the granite was left in place and no retaining wall was needed. Chafee went back to the office and announced, "That gal is so good, she can dust my house with that backhoe!"[4]

The stunning granite wall leads one to the left, toward the entrance, with its four stepped platforms terminating at a streamlined door of stainless steel and glass. The entry sequence offers choices of direction. Up a rhythm of concrete steps to the west end is the guest suite, with a kitchenette, sitting area, full bath, storage, and bedroom. The area is gifted with generous shaded south windows facing the city and north windows that look out on the mountains, and enjoys a north patio with a geologically

formed outside wall. Between the entry and guest quarters is a turn and another set of concrete steps ascending north to a large studio with natural light streaming through the high clerestory and an intimate "poet's corner" with the only interior west view and where the owners can observe winter sunsets. The central area of the entry is an intricate juxtaposition of concrete steps and landings, reflective of the Buddhist temple compounds Chafee saw during her travels in China. She appreciated how spaces were revealed in stages of consciously paced experiences.

From the entry, two paths also lead to the east, parallel but at different levels. At the entry level is an open passage intended for "the red wagon express," a means of transporting various items and/or people to the east-side pantries and kitchen, which are all at the same level.

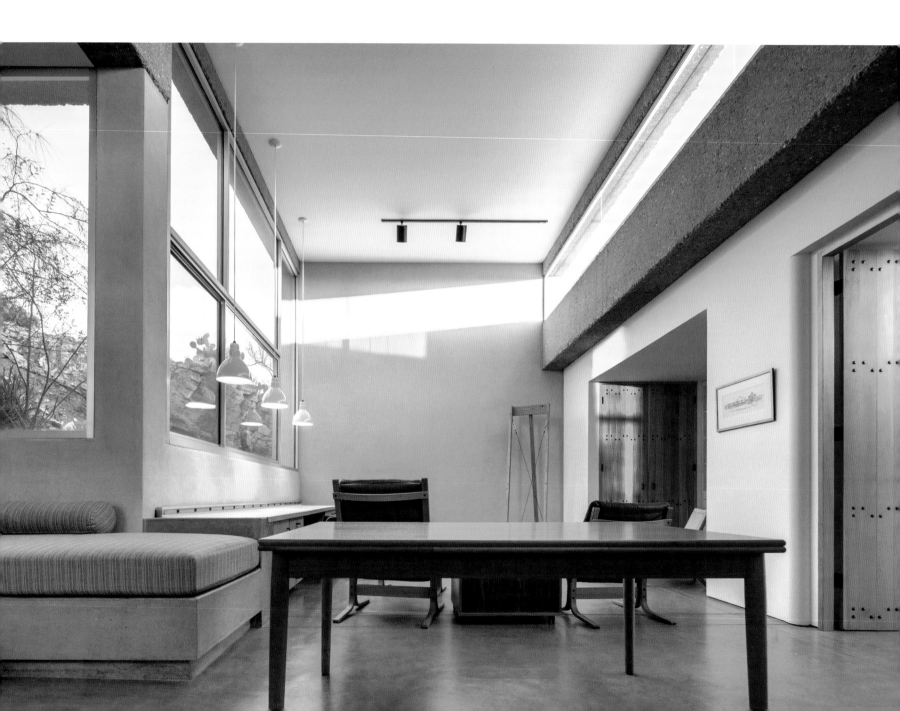

An enclosed passageway is adjacent to this open runway. All the infrastructure of the house is contained in this tunnel, accessible from the carport on the west end and an outside mechanical room door on the east side below the kitchen floor area. Stainless-steel-wrapped chimney tubes extend from the mechanical room furnaces, through the kitchen counter sill, and on through the roof. Knowing the Rieveschls would not be occupying the house on a full-time basis, Chafee established this method by which various maintenance workers could maintain and provide repair work without needing access into the main building.

The other path to the east is the ceremonial ascension of the concrete steps, leading to a sublime art gallery corridor that is the horizontal spinal column of the house. Unobstructed by the utilities and mechanical underpass below, the gallery is a grand corridor through the natural saddle formed by the mountainside and granite hillock. The concrete guardrail between upper and lower floor levels is notched with small lighting channels at handrail height and at toe level, and extends for the entire distance of the gallery. Natural light is reflected on the ceiling from high, narrow windows that increase in size as the outside grade level lowers.

The master suite extends north from the gallery, its polished concrete floor slab partially on grade as the east side, supported by columns, hovers over the sloped hillside. Parallel to the art gallery corridor, behind the privacy of elegant cherry doors crafted by Chafee's cabinetmaker Elliott Price, is the silver and mirrored dressing room gallery. Beyond the dressing room is the

master bedroom and bathroom, separated by a rock masonry wall structure with two fireplaces. The partition wall provides for the head of the bed, which has views to the mountains, and is an undulation of cherry tambour, inspired by admiration for Alvar Aalto's curved wood ceiling treatments. Double interior clerestories light the spaces—the first brings light from the gallery corridor into the dressing room gallery, and the second shares light from the master bedroom and bath into the dressing gallery. Natural light is transferred completely through the spaces from the north and south windows.

The gallery transitions between levels into the library space and the naturally lit main area of the east end. The ceiling-height bookstacks are lacquered a soft dark blue, carefully matching the blue of the distant mountain ridges to the north. The casework is aligned in progressively shortened widths, facilitating the pathway to the built-in desk, which has stunning views of the mountains and desert below, as well as interior views across the lower living space, through the house, and out to the city views at night. Pivoting between the library and lower living area is a second formation of masonry work using rocks gathered from the site, this one larger than the master suite structure. Opposite the window seat in the library is a small fireplace, emerging from the low back wall of the rock mass. The inglenook from the Connecticut house becomes a coyote den in the Arizona house. Looking across the top of the coyote den, the sight of the massive formation might remind one of ancient native ruins. But this is not an attempt to mimic the physical attributes of

southwestern ancestry. Being mindful of the provenance, Chafee infused the spirit of the stonework into these rock formations, providing an enriched space within a modern framework. A room-within-a-room, the coyote den displays a generous fireplace accompanied on each side by seating long enough to recline on, with reading lights recessed in the rocks, a detail similar to one discovered by the authors during a visit to Chafee's childhood home on Martin Avenue. A small viewing window of desert flora and fauna peeks through the bottom of the masonry work to the ground below. These colorful rocks were gathered from the site and installed by the Saenz family of master masons. Chafee wanted the mortar to appear almost invisible, as if the rocks were simply dry-stacked in place. At the start of the project she brought books about the Ancestral

Puebloan ruins of the Southwest to show the masons how the work should look. She worked with them to scoop out mortar until it was recessed enough to appear almost invisible, providing a semblance of stacked rocks. The masons were intrigued by this method and soon became expert with it. Stainless-steel-encased chimney flues for the four fireplaces reflect the verticality of the concrete columns and metal glass frames as well as their modern functional image.

The living areas of the main plateau enjoy 18- and 14-foot ceiling heights and are defined by 11-foot-high enclosures of the pantries and preparation areas. These free-standing, three-sided, white objects allow open circulation and views between and around them. The kitchen preparation area is a large stainless steel control

Southeast outside
corner and exterior
looking south (right)
and southeast
outside corner
(opposite)

center surrounded by other cabinet forms and surfaces of wood, Corian, plastic laminate, and tamboured closures of custom-made sliced ApplePly with solid layers facing outward. Cabinetmaker Elliott Price said this was the project that made him start to think of himself as a master craftsman. At the time, it was the biggest project he had worked on, and he was coordinating with his own subcontractors for the stainless-steel counter and hood, the Plexiglas surround for the bar top, the slate countertop in the dining room, the counters and shower in the master bath, and all the wood doors. He even supervised the interior framing of walls to assure he had straight surfaces to which he could attach his cabinet work. He welcomed the challenge of crafting the large-scale sliding panel doors that hang from the overhead

concrete beam between the kitchen and dining room.[5] The living and dining room areas are bounded on two sides by lower concrete terraces, on and over the site, with cool breezes and seasonal experiences of sun and shade. The intimate west garden and sitting area, as well as west-facing windows, are completely protected from unwanted solar exposure by the granite hill formation. The extended overhead roof provides additional shade protection as part of the weather enclosure system.

Chafee incorporated lessons learned from Le Corbusier's application of the processional path—a ceremonial route through a sequence of spatial relationships between a site and building—as part of her methodology. The Rieveschl Residence is a celebration of living in the desert, engaging the sojourner with a

242

controlled entry into an assemblage of stairways that ascend into a defined art gallery corridor, emerging into the greater overview through a magnificent open space to the mountain and city views beyond. It is a completely open viewing plateau that brings acute awareness of the geographic placement of the house and the spectacular vistas of the city and mountain. The granite rock formations create small, protective, outside areas to sit and enjoy soothing weather, and the coyote den provides front-row seating for watching dramatic summer lightning shows and rainstorms moving across the valley floor. Rain escaping from oversized copper canales, based on the traditional Sonoran custom-made trumpets that direct the rainwater off the roof and onto the desert below, adds a delightful sound.

Considering the placement of a large house in a pristine desert site, with a sloped terrain that ranges from a moderate workable slope on part of the west to a steep canyon on the east with a central saddle for connections and circulation, Chafee determined that suspending platforms above the desert would require a very disruptive and costly system. She drew inspiration from the rational, concrete master designers of her lineage—Le Corbusier and Paul Rudolph—and called on the desert floor to accept the supporting concrete columns that stand carefully in the dynamic desert ecosystem.

Living room and coyote den (left and below) and south viewing deck looking southwest (opposite)

Hansen Residence   Crystal Falls, Michigan, 1991–94

This project brought Chafee back to a region she knew from her younger days: the shoreline of the beautiful Paint River in the Upper Peninsula of Michigan. Chafee spent happy adolescent summers at Camp Kechuwa on Lake Michigamme, less than an hour from Crystal Falls, in a very similar environment. Summers in the southwestern desert are hot enough to encourage anyone who is able, to leave for cooler parts. The Bloom family, with its ties to Chicago, stayed in comfortable hotels near the city area, while Judith joined close friends in the cooler mountain areas farther north. She was very familiar with the terrain and its history. Presenting a lecture about this project at the University of Texas in Austin, she noted:

> In the late 1800s, a sturdy extended family of Finnish
> farmers; [*sic*] uncles, aunts, cousins, etcetera (depending
> on your place in the genealogy), came to this shore with this
> view. They had Sisu. Whole books have been written about
> this word. This is a mystical Finnish word which has to do with
> a Finnish national characteristic of courage and special skills
> to overcome adversities...In passing, let us remember that
> not too much later, Michigan became the new home of some
> very urbane Finns, such as the Saarinens at Cranbrook.[1]

In this early Scandinavian community, each house was built parallel to the river, on a deep parcel of farmland. Historical photography indicates a hierarchical layering of the site starting from the river shoreline, with the log farmhouse placed in the cleared area by farm fields and meadows beyond, and forested areas at the back. Eventually, most of the log cabins were demolished and farmland was divided and sold. The Hansen family had reduced their lot size, keeping the original cabin as their modest summer vacation home. Adelyn Hansen described the building, which over the years had increased in size with "all manner of lean-tos" without footings. Everything was covered in layers of green Masonite siding and

asphalt shingles. Interior walls were covered in various types of fiberboard and more Masonite.

Adelyn Hansen and her brother, Fred, were the remaining owners of the property. As a young intern in interior design, Adelyn worked under the direction of Chafee's mother, Christina Bloom, when she was head of the modern interiors department known as the Scandinavian Shop in the upscale Chicago department store, Carson Pirie Scott. Adelyn said she was extremely grateful and appreciative to work with Christina, also known as "Cricket," whom she described as a brilliant, creative professional. When Christina retired, Adelyn became the director of the department and eventually established her own successful career. She met Judith Chafee and told her how much she admired the house

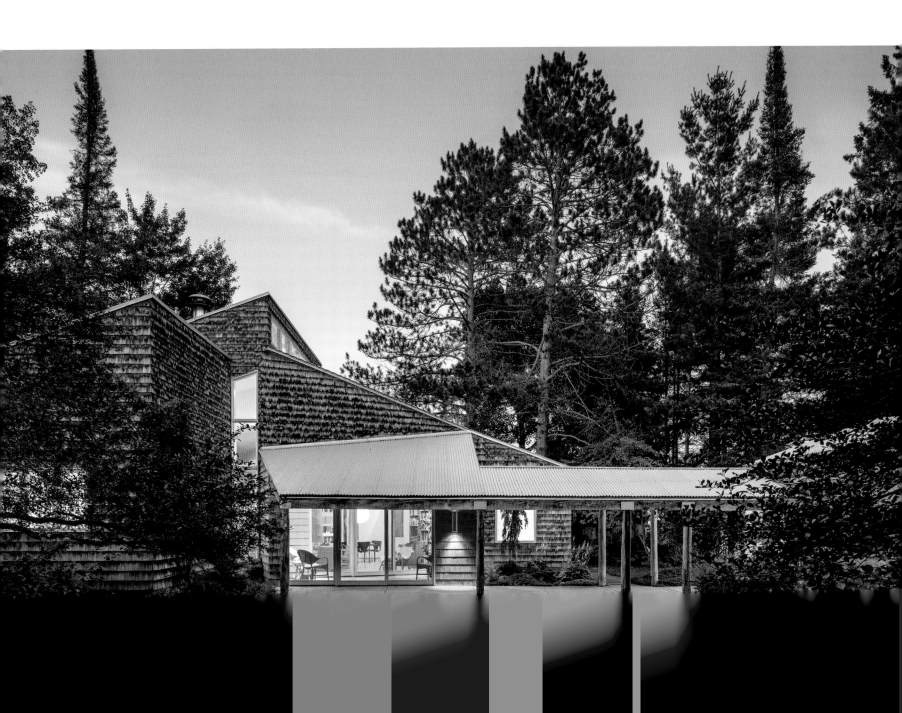

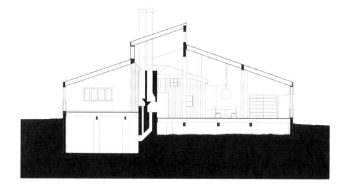

248

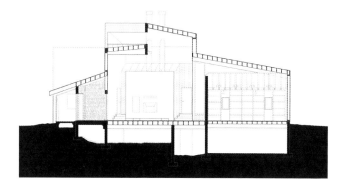

Chafee had designed in Connecticut. She told Chafee, "You are a wonderful architect, and someday I am going to hire you to design a house for me." Thirty years later, Chafee was surprised to receive a phone call in her office in Tucson. It was Adelyn Hansen, who said, "Judith, I am ready for you to design my house."[2]

The story of this house is one of dedication. The project was to be a new house on the family site that was slightly larger than one acre, with shoreline on the Paint River. On the site was the small, much-altered family vacation home where Adelyn and Fred had spent memorable summers. After a career in the air force, Fred developed multiple sclerosis, a terrible neurological disorder affecting the muscular and immune systems, which progressed to requiring full-time care. Facing

a grim prognosis, he placed himself into the Veterans Administration Hospital. Adelyn, no longer married and with grown children, promised her brother she would provide a home, and care for him. Ready to retire, she sold her Chicago condo and called Chafee.

Chafee said this site was the only place she had ever designed a building where "north is north," meaning where true north and magnetic north coincide, which can be very helpful in land and building design. During her first visit to the site, she noted the river was 20 degrees off the north-south axis, and the river's edge defined the site's edge, producing an "interesting geometry" for getting ideal river views and good southern solar exposure.[3] The surveyed boundaries formed an L-shaped lot, with the wider boundary on the river. A number of site challenges, including recent local rulings that limited areas for any new construction and a new requirement to build a minimum of 100 feet from the river's shoreline, created significant design problems for Chafee. These also involved a matter of community aesthetics and the desire to protect scenic views of the river, which was over 60 feet lower in elevation than the house.

A new house would have been required to comply with current setbacks, which diminished most of the views and limited the square footage due to the narrowing lot's shape. To retain the beautiful views of the river from the house, a different strategy was required. Rather than tear down the old family vacation house, it was reduced to the size of the original rectangular log cabin, approximately 18 by 26 feet—decades worth of additions to the structure were removed. A new, 2,700-square-foot "addition," albeit a substantial one, was added to the existing building, which allowed for the application of the earlier setback requirements, which were grandfathered in. When the former add-ons were removed to expose the original log cabin, they discovered, much to everyone's surprise, that the logs had been set in a vertical position.

Elevation drawing

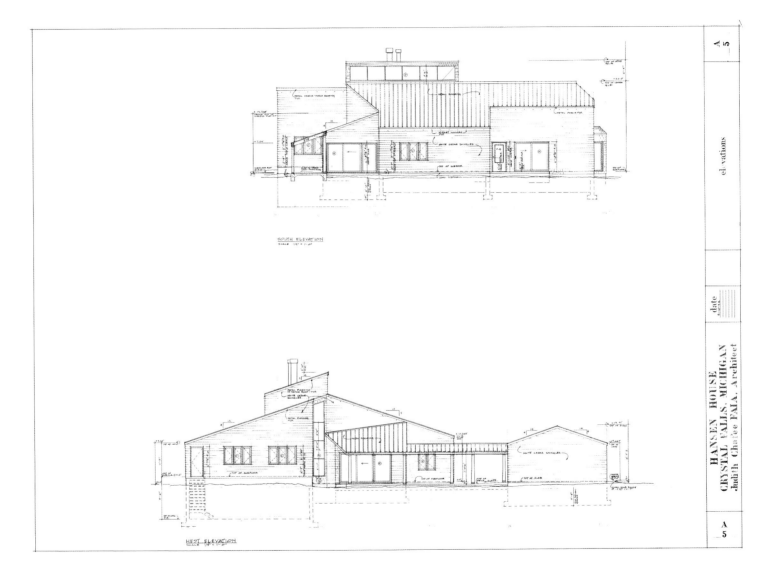

SOUTH ELEVATION

WEST ELEVATION

A
5

elevations

date

HANSEN HOUSE
CRYSTAL FALLS, MICHIGAN
Judith Chafee FAIA, Architect

A
5

250

South patio,
looking skyward

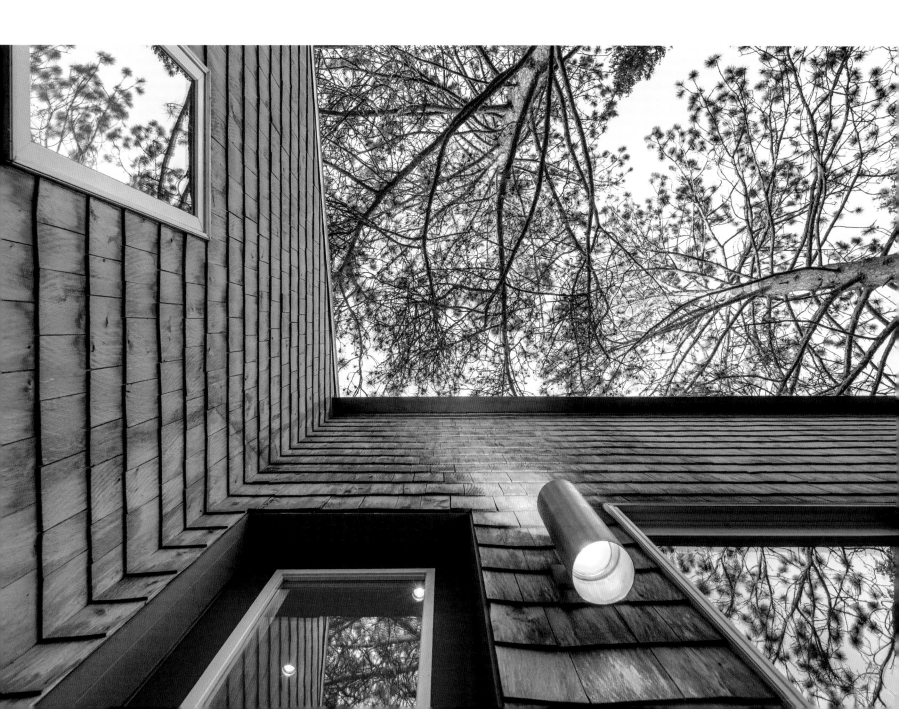

252

Visiting the site, Chafee, expecting to bury an existing ugly duckling, was very pleased to find that the ancestral log cabin was a gem. The new house would form around the heart of the settlers' family homestead.

This house-within-a-house, the original 468-square-foot log cabin, upgraded by cleaning and chinking where needed to match the existing material, is now a gourmet cook's kitchen and casual eating area that enjoys a direct view of the river. Natural-finished wood shelving is surface-mounted to expose the interior log walls. Counter-level shelving folds out for optional counter-depth work surfaces. Chafee kept the original roof system of minimal hand-hewed trusses, rather than disturb the historic construction. The large metal roof of the new building extends around the cabin roof for full protection from the

elements. The new wood floors are supported by concrete piers with wood beams, allowing the wood flooring to cantilever to the older building without any structural impact. The original storage and root cellar beneath the cabin floor is adequate to contain the necessary mechanical equipment.

The complicated geometry of the house plan, which enables river views, natural ventilation, and solar orientation for natural light and heat, clearly defines the living areas. The corrugated metal shed roof, with its silver-colored, natural galvalume finish and separated ridgeline formed by beamed clerestories, defines the spaces and provides dynamic beams of light into the interior. The area nearest to the river views is the master suite for Fred, with hospital-grade accessible bathroom and doors, a

sunporch, and a bedroom/studio for caregivers. Chafee perceptively described her design concerns for this part of the house:

> Since Fred had loved the river since childhood, it was important now that he be able to see it, the geese flying in for the night, the changes of seasons, etcetera, from his hospital style bed and from the places he is wheeled to dine in a cumbersome high wheelchair.[4]

The central space, also accessible to Fred, provides a dramatic dining and living area. A massive double fireplace wall, with stainless-steel flues piercing the high ceiling, is adjacent to the vertical logs of the once-exterior cabin wall. Double clerestories with substantial natural-finished glulam beams rise to 20- and 24-foot heights, with a supporting column made from one large, peeled pine tree from the nearby forest. Chafee and the Hansens named the column Alvar. The south clerestory floods sunlight onto the fireplace mass and an interior clerestory above the fireplace wall brings additional daylight into the other master suite. This third area, which houses the master suite for Adelyn, a shared bath, and guest room, steps up from the main floor to rise with the natural grade of the site. Generous windows focus on the landscaped borders and adjacent woodland.

The major building material for this region is wood, appropriate for the climate and the history. Here more than forty years after her memorable summer-camp experiences, Chafee returned to a familiar materiality,

Kitchen shelving (right) and kitchen (opposite)

using white cedar shingles, not unlike the palette of the Merrill Residence in Connecticut, her first significant project. Because of the harsh climate that boasts severe freezing and thawing sequences, she determined a good metal roofing system would be more resilient to the elements in Michigan's Upper Peninsula. The sharp angled forms of the metal roofline maintain the modern Scandinavian sensibilities while preserving a mindfulness of the settlers' legacy.

From a small country road, one enters the property at the narrower area of the site, accessing the cedar-shingled garage with its simple metal gabled roof. A short transition from the garage along a colonnade of the low metal roof supported by adequate, local, peeled tree posts is adjacent to an intimate and protected garden area. The entry is through a greenhouse space, which allows one to adjust from the outside, where snow drifts can build up to 6 feet high, to a welcoming interior. The greenhouse provides a dense, green, vegetated area, even on the coldest winter days, and from its intimate scale leads into the striking living room space. Chafee's genius for bringing in natural light,

using dramatic spatial proportions, showing clarity of structure, elegantly siting the building, and combining relevant old and new forms is indisputable in this preeminent project.

Chafee's health had presented too many challenges for her to visit when the house was completed in 1994. Adelyn sent her numerous construction photos, as well as photos of the completed house. Chafee praised Adelyn's collection of classic modern furnishings and art. She was very thankful to have a client who understood the intent of the drawings and who held the subcontractors accountable in an area where capable craftsmen were scarce. At the time, she did not realize that this would be her last significant residential project.

Most of Chafee's work is site- and program-specific, resulting in buildings that look quite different from one another. But all her projects reflect the integration of her building concepts and form-making principles. This house responds to the very specific needs and parameters of the location and the inhabitants, and provides spaces that enable a comforting and nurturing environment in which to live a full life.

256

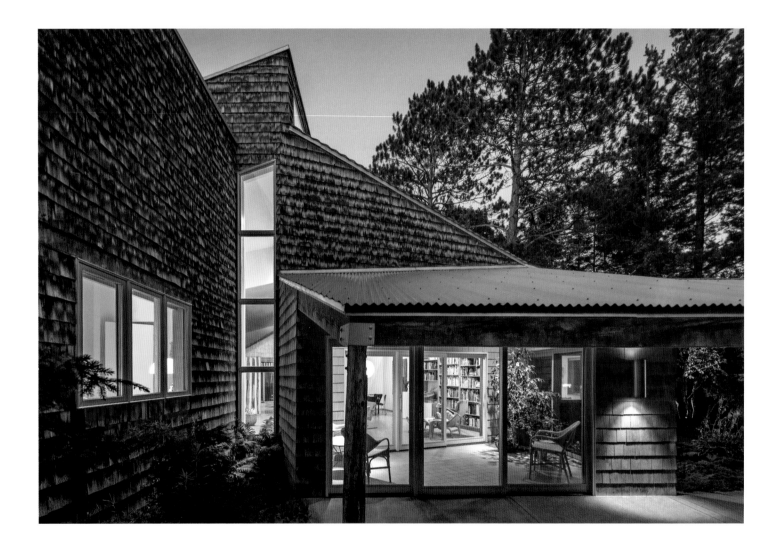

Notes

Introduction

1 For Mies van der Rohe's notion of framing and intensifying "nature" through a modern concept of space, see, for example, William J.R. Curtis, "Mies van de Rohe (1986–69) Reputations," *Architectural Review* (November 2011).

2 In 1986, I wrote to Judith Chafee: "I must say that I do find the Ramada House very fine. Complexity of effects engendered through simplicity of means, and a building with a real grammar based in traditions (vernacular and modern), in climate, habitation, materials etc.…To cut a long story short, Phaidon have asked me to put another chapter on the end of *Modern Architecture Since 1900*. I probably have room to illustrate about twenty buildings and would very much like to include the Ramada House" (Letter WJR Curtis to J Chafee, Fall 1986, Judith Chafee Papers, Special Collections, University of Arizona Libraries).

3 In 1987 I revisited Tucson and got up to date on Judith Chafee's projects. I have vivid memories of visiting the half-constructed Rieveschl Residence with Judith Chafee, Kathryn McGuire, and Bella the dog.

4 Judith Chafee, Note on the Salomon (Ramada House), 1973. This reveals Chafee's sensitivity to the client's needs and to "the unrelenting climate," sun angles, shade, the natural flow of air in the microclimate, etc. (Judith Chafee Papers).

5 William J.R. Curtis, *Modern Architecture Since 1900*, 1st ed. (Oxford: Phaidon Press, 1982). See especially chap. 25, "The Problem of Regional Identity," 331ff., chap. 27, "Modern Architecture in Developing Countries Since 1960," 356ff.

6 William J.R. Curtis, "Towards an Authentic Regionalism," *Mimar 19* (January 1986).

7 William J.R. Curtis, *Modern Architecture Since 1900*, 2nd ed., (Oxford: Phaidon, 1987), 394. See also Curtis, "Contemporary Transformations of Modern Architecture," *Architectural Record* (June 1989).

8 Ibid.

9 William J.R. Curtis, *Modern Architecture Since 1900*, 3rd ed. (London: Phaidon, 1996), 637–8.

Essay: Early Practice

1 "Record House," *Architectural Record* (Mid-May 1970): 66–69 (cover).

2 "Stage Star in Radcliffe Tells Girls of Footlight Thrills," *Boston Evening American* (March 8, 1928).

3 *Annals of Medical History*, in Chafee / Bloom Family Archive.

4 Photographs in the Chafee / Bloom Family Archive document travel throughout the American Southwest and Mexico. Christina, Benson, and Judith are also depicted at a visit to the architecturally significant 1939 World's Fair in New York.

5 Judith Chafee quote from Lawrence W. Cheek, "Courageous Architecture for a Fragile Land," *Tucson Citizen*, October 8, 1988.

6 Judith Chafee quote from Margo Hernandez, "Uncompromising Architect Is Shaping Dreams," *Arizona Daily Star* (1989): 1B, 2B.

7 Joseph Wood Krutch. *Baja California and the Geography of Hope* (San Francisco: Sierra Club, 1967), 154, from essay "One Spring Again" written in Tucson.

8 Margaret Sanger and Edward Spicer were both patients of Dr. Benson Bloom in Tucson.

9 Betsy Babb (formerly Betty Babb) interview with C. Domin and K. McGuire, November 25, 2014.

10 "Jesu Fimbres" poem, Judith Chafee Papers, undated.

11 Zachery LeBolt interview with C. Domin, July 24, 2015.

12 Judith Chafee confidants noted a palpable sadness that was impossible to breach on her daughter's birthday. Judith would often be overtaken by a deep state of melancholy during this time of the year.

13 James McNeely interview with C. Domin, March 25, 2015.

14 Robert A. M. Stern and Jimmy Stamp, *Pedagogy and Place: 100 Years of Architecture Education at Yale* (New Haven: Yale University Press, 2016), 156–59, 168–69.

15 David Niland, interview with David Niland, *GA Houses* 13 (March 1983), 70–71.

16 Paul Mitarachi interview with C. Domin, April 29, 2015.

17 Richard Spofford Chafee interview with C. Domin, August 20, 2014.

18 John J. Molloy interview with C. Domin, March 13, 2015.

19 James McNeely, from unpublished diary entry (digital version), Collection of James McNeely, February 15, 1960.

20 The Mr. and Mrs. Sidney Friedberg Residence in Baltimore, Maryland, is an unbuilt project. A set of construction documents is located in the Judith Chafee Papers.

21 Judith Chafee, "The Region of the Mindful Heart," *Artspace Southwestern Contemporary Arts Quarterly* (Spring 1982): 27.

22 Richard Spofford Chafee interview with C. Domin, August 20, 2014.

23 The Pan Am Building in New York was a collaborative project designed by Emory Roth and Sons, Walter Gropius, and Pietro Belluschi.

24 Gordon Meinhard interview with C. Domin, July 16, 2015.

25 Gene Festa interview with C. Domin, July 25, 2015.

26 Edith Rose Kohlberg, "A Battleground of the Spirit," *Mademoiselle,* (May 1966), 162.

27 In the Edward Larrabee Barnes office list of employees, no woman is indicated as a partner or associate in the firm's monograph *Edward Larrabee Barnes: Architect* by Peter Blake (1995).

28 Judith Chafee letter to Edward Larrabee Barnes (Thanksgiving Day, 1966), 8, in Chafee / Bloom Family Archive.

29 Joan Geller interview with C. Domin and K. McGuire.

30 In 1969 Yale University announced a competition for the design of the Yale University Mathematics Building with architects Charles Moore and Edward Larrabee Barnes as advisers and final jury members. Kevin Roche and Vincent Scully are also listed as part of the final jury. The competition process and documentation of the winning entry by Venturi and Rauch, Architects is compiled in *The Yale Mathematics Building Competition* by Moore and Pyle. Chafee's concern about a changing of the guard in the Northeast and the rising influence of what would be known as "Post-Modernism" in architecture is in evidence throughout the organization and outcome of the competition. In Chafee's opinion, a portent of a coming storm.

31 Judith Chafee, "The Region of the Mindful Heart," *Artspace Southwestern Contemporary Arts Quarterly* (Spring 1982): 27.

32 Judith Chafee letter draft to Sergio Pace, in response to correspondence from Pace dated November 12, 1997, in Chafee / Bloom Family Archive.

33 Judith Chafee, "The Region of the Mindful Heart," *Artspace: Southwestern Contemporary Arts Quarterly* (Spring 1982): 27.

34 Susan Lobo correspondence with C. Domin and K. McGuire, October 24, 2014.

35 Ibid.

36 Charles (Corky) Poster, essay written for Chafee memorial gathering at the Franklin Auto Museum, in her childhood neighborhood of Richland Heights (December 1998).

37 Poster, December 1998. Confirmed in interview with C. Domin and K. McGuire, October 7, 2014.

38 Jim Morgan, "Block-like Forms Nestle into Berkshire Woods." *Architecture Record* (November 1972): 119.

39 Correspondence from Ray Barnes to C. Domin dated November 7, 2018.

40 Ibid.

41 Ibid.

42 Judith Chafee Papers.

43 William J.R. Curtis, *Modern Architecture Since 1900*, 2nd ed. (Oxford: Phaidon, 1987), 637.

44 Yung and Ming Wang interview with K. McGuire, July 13, 2014.

45 Ibid.

46 Edward Larrabee Barnes, architect, letter to the American Academy in Rome, dated April 14, 1976, Judith Chafee Papers.

47   Judith Chafee application for Mid Career Fellowship in Architecture at the American Academy in Rome, in Chafee/Bloom Family Archive, August 19, 1976.
48   Ibid.
49   "To Louis Sullivan" poem, in Chafee/Bloom Family Archive.
50   Diane Lewis interview with C. Domin, November 18, 2015.
51   Letter from Diane Lewis, dated November 22, 1978, Judith Chafee Papers.
52   Charles Bowden, letter to "Save Blackwell Campaign" undated (probably early 1989).
53   "House in a Remote Area" poem, in Chafee/Bloom Family Archive.
54   The "Arizona School of Architecture" was first introduced by Lawrence Cheek in Architecture magazine, May 2002.

Merrill Residence

1   "Record House," *Architectural Record* (Mid-May 1970): 66–69 (cover).
2   Yale classmate Paul Brouard noted that this neighborhood was developed in the 1960s and contained many houses designed by young architects trained at the Yale School of Architecture. From interview with C. Domin, March 12, 2015.
3   Judith Chafee, "The Region of the Mindful Heart," *Artspace: Southwestern Contemporary Arts Quarterly* (Spring 1982): 29.
4   See *Paul Rudolph: The Florida Houses* by Christopher Domin and Joseph King for examples of movable or kinetic building components in the early work of Paul Rudolph.

Judith Chafee Studio and Residence

1   A Maynard Dixon painting in the Bloom Family Collection was sold to finance the Chafee Studio and Residence renovation project. This painting is now in the permanent collection of the Phoenix Museum of Art in Phoenix, Arizona.
2   Correspondence from Ray Barnes to C. Domin, dated November 7, 2018.
3   "Architect's Office Distinctive," *Arizona Daily Star* (June 21, 1981): 1K.
4   Correspondence from Ray Barnes to C. Domin, dated November 7, 2018.

Viewpoint

1   Formerly Christina A. Bloom.
2   Earl J. Johnson retired as editor of United Press, where he worked for thirty years. His reputation as

a gifted editor was well known, and his mentorship influenced a generation of correspondents and writers, including Joe Alex Morris, Merriman Smith, Walter Cronkite, Eric Sevareid, Robert Manning, Harrison E. Salisbury, Eugene Patterson, and William H. Lawrence.
3   "A Study in the Use of Light," *Los Angeles Times: Home Magazine*, cover (March 30, 1975): 7–8, 16.
4   "Architectural Record Houses of 1975," *Architectural Record* (Mid-May 1975): 82–83.
5   "A Study in the Use of Light," *Los Angeles Times: Home Magazine* (March 30, 1975): 7, 8, 16 and cover.
6   Olivera H. Jorge, "San Xavier Del Bac: Spanish Mission or Moslem Mosque?" *Dove of the Desert: A Newsletter to the Friends of San Xavier Mission* (Winter 1989, Number 4): 1–6.
7   The original configuration of the house provided views to the south. Judith Chafee later designed an additional structure and courtyard to the south for the second owners of the home.
8   Undated document in Judith Chafee Archive, University of Arizona Special Collections.
9   Undated document in Judith Chafee Archive.

Ramada House

1   Peter Solomon interview with C. Domin, February 11, 2015.
2   Client interview with C. Domin, April 18, 2011.
3   Peter Solomon interview with C. Domin, February 11, 2015.
4   Judith Chafee letter to Robert A. M. Stern, in Chafee/Bloom Family Archive (March 20, 1974).
5   Charles Poster interview with C. Domin and K. McGuire, October 7, 2014.
6   Judith Chafee, undated Ramada House project description in Judith Chafee Archive.
7   Judith Chafee, "The Region of the Mindful Heart," *Artspace: Southwestern Contemporary Arts Quarterly* (Spring 1982): 30.
8   William J.R. Curtis, *Modern Architecture Since 1900*, 2nd ed. (New Jersey: Prentice Hall, 1987).

Jacobson Residence

1   Joan Jacobson interview with C. Domin and K. McGuire, April 30, 2014.
2   Judith Chafee, "The Region of the Mindful Heart," *Artspace: Southwestern Contemporary Arts Quarterly* (Spring 1982): 31.
3   The H. H. Richardson design for Stonehurst Residence near Waltham, Massachusetts, includes a surprisingly complex stair design that meets all the basic circulation needs but integrates into the stair a variety of other functions.
4   Jerry Cannon interview with C. Domin and K. McGuire, September 9, 2014.

5   Joan Jacobson interview with C. Domin and K. McGuire, April 30, 2014.
6   The list of participants' names stamped into the concrete cannot be found in any other Judith Chafee building site, which is a testament to the uniqueness of the project and her fondness for the client.

Blackwell Residence

1   Dennis Decker interview with C. Domin and K. McGuire, October 15, 2015. This story was also confirmed by Kathryn McGuire as told to her by Judith Chafee.
2   Judith Chafee quote from Margo Hernandez, "Uncompromising Architect Is Shaping Dreams." *Arizona Daily Star* (1989): 1B.
3   Ibid.
4   Judith Chafee, "The Region of the Mindful Heart," *Artspace: Southwestern Contemporary Arts Quarterly* (Spring 1982): 32.
5   William P. Bruder, letter to "Save Blackwell Campaign" dated January 4, 1989.
6   Ibid.
7   Lawrence W. Cheek, "By Design, Structural Integrity," Tucson Weekly (June 2–8, 1993): 37.
8   William J.R. Curtis, letter to "Save Blackwell Campaign" dated January 8, 1989.

Essay: Late Practice

Many of the details in this essay are written from the experiences of Kathryn McGuire. As she was graduating from the University of Arizona School of Architecture, McGuire asked Professor Chafee if she had any job openings in her office. Chafee said there was nothing but would keep her in mind. One late evening McGuire's phone rang. "Hello," said Kathryn, and a familiar voice on the line said, "When can you start?" "Judith?" and the caller impatiently said, "Yes, when can you start?" McGuire said, "Tomorrow?" "9:00." And so it began with quick introductions to Bob Earl and Susan Engelsberg and a young Bella the dog, happy to meet her new walking partner. Starting as an intern, then project manager and associate, McGuire worked with clients, engineers, and other advisers. There were no computers at the time, so all drafting was done by hand, with Chafee providing the initial concepts and direction, laboring over many rolls of yellow tracing paper to get the idea just right. The work was challenging and so was Chafee. McGuire studied with Chafee, then became an employee, associate, and friend over more than twenty years. The work on this book has produced gratifying reminders, deeper understandings, and surprising realizations as one is able to stand back and review the past. Kathryn McGuire gladly shares these experiences with the reader.

1   American Institute of Architects is a national not-for-profit organization.
2   William J.R. Curtis, "Principle versus Pastiche: Perspectives on Some Recent Classicisms and Modern Transformations of Classicism," *Architectural Review* (August 1984): 11–21, 39–46.
3   Skidmore, Owings & Merrill, founded in the 1930s with their headquarters in Chicago, is one of the largest architecture firms in the world. Many well-known architects and building projects have been associated with SOM.
4   Robert W. Peters, FAIA, interview with C. Domin and K. McGuire, August 26, 2014.
5   Arizona Society, American Institute of Architects, Fall Conference on "Regionalism," Phoenix, Arizona, 1981; Judith Chafee, "The Region of the Mindful Heart," *Artspace Southwestern Contemporary Arts Quarterly* (Spring 1982): 27.
6   Louis H. Sullivan, *Kindergarten Chats and Other Writings*, (New York: George Wittenborn, Inc. 1947), 194.
7   Anne M. Nequette and R. Brooks Jeffery, *A Guide to Tucson Architecture* (Tucson: University of Arizona Press, 2002), 263.
8   Hastings began working for Chafee in 1973. Prior to that, she attended Rice University, where she grew tired of the architecture school faculty telling her that she did not belong there and would not receive any attention.
9   Margaret Regan, "Master Builder, Architect Judith Chafee Melded Sleek Modern Design to Sonoran Desert," *Tucson Weekly* (February 3, 2000): unpaginated.
10 Chafee, "Region," 33.
11 Sullivan, *Kindergarten Chats*, 208.
12 Biophilic need is the desire to enjoy natural pleasure that comes from being surrounded by living organisms in a natural environment.
13 Tom Collazo, interview with K. McGuire, November 18, 2014.
14 Ibid.
15 Debbie Collazo, email message to author, February 20, 2018.
16 Tom Collazo, interview with K. McGuire, November 18, 2014.
17 Debbie Collazo, email message to author, February 20, 2018.
18 Author Kathryn McGuire was a student, employee, and friend of Chafee's for more than twenty years. Some commentary throughout the book is from firsthand knowledge.
19 Washington University in St. Louis, School of Architecture, "Points of Departure" brochure. The March 26–28 symposium was presented in

an inspiring building by Eric Mendelsohn. The synagogue was built in 1949 and had a change of use by the 1980s as one of the university's performing arts buildings.
20 Judith Chafee Papers.
21 William J.R. Curtis, *Modern Architecture Since 1900* (London: Phaidon Press, 1996, 3rd ed.), 637–38.
22 Judith Chafee, "To Arizona, Designing in the Desert," American Institute of Architects, "Frank Lloyd Wright Symposium," Phoenix, March 1990, 7.
23 Spyros Amourgis, *Critical Regionalism, the Pomona Meeting-Proceeding* (Pomona, CA, College of Environmental Design, California State Polytechnic University, 1991), 54.
24 Ibid.
25 Judith Chafee, Nov 10, 1989, for Princeton, Judith Chafee Papers, University of Arizona Libraries: 7.
26 Judith Chafee Papers, University of Arizona Libraries.
27 Judith Chafee Papers, also included a tape recording of her presentation.
28 "One of Tucson's Best, Judith Chafee," *Tucson Weekly* (October 6, 1993): unpaginated.
29 Walter Gropius (1883–1969) was chair of the Department of Architecture at Harvard when Chafee first met him through their mutual friend Alexander Dorner. The accentuation he placed on architectural education had a significant impact on Chafee's life plan.
30 Judith Chafee Papers. There are numerous files of letters, document comparatives, and records that attest to the continuous effort by the Architecture School to establish an equitable salary for Chafee.
31 A. Richard Williams, *Archipelago Critiques of Contemporary Architecture and Education* (Champaign: University of Illinois Press, 2009), 232.
32 Judith Chafee Papers.
33 K. McGuire.
34 Allen Freeman, "Reinterpreting Regionalism: Arizona," *Architecture* (March 1984): 113.
35 Brian Farling interview with C. Domin and K. McGuire, December 9, 2014.
36 The Architects Collaborative was formed in 1945 in Cambridge, Massachusetts, and closed in 1996. Chafee worked on some projects with Sarah Harkness and Ben Thompson from 1962 to 1963.
37 A study conducted by the Institute for Energy Conscious Design (Boston Architectural Center, 1985).
38 Judith Chafee Papers.
39 Judith Chafee Papers; Jane Drew and Max Fry were English modern architects who worked with Le Corbusier in Chandigarh, focusing on social housing. They were progressive leaders in urban planning and housing in desert areas such as Nigeria, Ghana, Iran, Sri Lanka, and West Africa.
40 An open house celebration provided by the Rieveschls.

41 Judith Chafee Papers.
42 Ibid.
43 Ann Price and John Price conversation with K. McGuire, March 13, 2018.
44 Judith Chafee Papers.
45 Ibid.
46 Ibid.
47 Ibid.
48 Chris Grimley, "Judith Chafee, An Abandoned Modernism," *Loud Paper*, 3, no. 4 (2004).
49 Judith Chafee, "House in Sonoita, Arizona," *Triglyph* (Fall 1984): 21.
50 Title IX is a federal civil rights law passed in 1972 stating that no person in the United States shall, on basis of sex, be excluded from participation in, be denied benefits of, or be subjected to discrimination under any education program or activity receiving federal financial assistance. This law affected the Tucson public schools athletic facilities.
51 Bob Earl worked as the construction administrator, among other jobs, in Chafee's office.
52 Dale Frederick, assistant supervisor of Tucson Unified School District, consulted the school board, suggesting it was feasible for the architect to determine the colors for a project.
53 Lawrence Cheek, "Judith Chafee," *Civitas Sonoran* (1999): unpaginated.
54 *Sunset* magazine is a monthly publication that focuses on the West coast and Southwest life-style, featuring travel, food, and housing.
55 Ann Patterson, "Architect Custom-Fits to Environment," *Arizona Republic* (Phoenix), May 28, 1989, S12.
56 Bill Merriman, as heard by K. McGuire.
57 Audrey Merriman interview with C. Domin and K. McGuire, April 1, 1914.
58 Esther M. Sternberg, *Healing Spaces, The Science of Place and Well-Being* (Cambridge, MA: Harvard University Press, 2010), 5.
59 Judith Chafee Papers.
60 Jerry Cannon interview with C. Domin and K. McGuire, Tucson, Fall 2014.
61 Chafee, while in the Saarinen office with Roche and Dinkeloo, worked on the Cummins Engine Factory in Darlington, England, a multiuse building with complex exposed steel framing.
62 Ann Patterson, interview, May 28, 1989.
63 Walter Gropius, Kenzo Tang, and Yashuhiro Ishimoto, *Katsura: Tradition and Creation in Japanese Architecture* (New Haven: Yale University Press, 1960), 5–6.
64 Elliott Price phone interview with K. McGuire, January 26, 1916.
65 Chafee conversation with K. McGuire.
66 Tom Collazo, interview with K. McGuire, November 18, 2014.
67 Ibid.

68 Debbie Collazo, email message to author, February 26, 2018.
69 Judith Chafee Papers.
70 Christina Johnson, Chafee's mother, returned to Tucson in 1986; many of her elderly friends were dying. She bought a townhouse near Chafee so she could have help when needed.
71 Small family-owned business and Bob Earl's favorite lunch place.
72 Lawrence Cheek, "Courageous Architecture for a Fragile Land" *Tucson Citizen* (Tuesday, October 8, 1985): 1B, feature article.
73 Chafee's dogs each were her beloved companions, starting with Staffordshire terriers: Zeus at Yale and East Coast, then home and office with Leda, Bella (Bellisima), and, finally, Coonhound Jam.
74 K. McGuire, who worked in Chafee's office until November 1998.
75 Diana Brock-Gray interview with C. Domin and K. McGuire, Phoenix, January 19, 2014.
76 Chafee was an admirer of Murcutt's functional Australian-outback architecture.
77 Robert (Bob) Nevins graduated from Yale a few years after Chafee. He described her as "formidable and scary." When he moved to Tucson to teach at the architecture school, he "rented" a desk space at Chafee's office while he settled in. He earned his "stripes" as a longtime friend and, after a celebratory birthday party he threw for her, Chafee wrote a thank-you poem:

Fifty
The unimagined task of gaining age,
then being feted, made to think it out,
involved some finding of an unknown gauge
to seek out what my life might be about.

Anxiety of recognition gone,
A dreadful peace descended on my soul
and many doubts of worth or strife or wrong
were lifted from the sight of: Judith whole.

A sober, gentle rock-hard sense of gain
made every single thing my prize from growth,
and past and future seemed to meet the same
beliefs and hopes and love of open ends,
and who could say this without you as friends?

78 Jim Morgan, *Marketing for the Small Design Firm* (New York: Whitney Library of Design, 1984), 32–33.
79 Barbara Grygutis interview with C. Domin and K. McGuire, February 17, 2015.
80 Cheek, "Judith Chafee."
81 Ibid.
82 Ibid.
83 Les Wallach, *Judith Chafee* (*Civitas Sonoran*, 1999); unpaginated.
84 Sullivan, *Kindergarten Chats*, 199. Chafee carried a "simpatico" recognition and connection to Sullivan, a solitary modernist.
85 There is no date for this poem.

Hydeman Residence

1 Chafee, "Region," (Spring 1982): 33.
2 The general contractor for this project was Bill Bowman, a retired structural engineer and neighbor. He respected Chafee's work, and later hired her to design his own house in Sonoita.
3 Judith Chafee, "House in Sonoita Arizona," *Triglyph* (Fall 1984): 21.

Russell-Randolph Residence

1 Kathryn McGuire, while working in Chafee's office, overheard Chafee make this comment many times.
2 David Russell and Susan Randolph interview with C. Domin and K. McGuire, April 28, 2018.
3 Ibid.
4 Margo Hernandez, "Uncompromising Architect Is Shaping Dreams," *Arizona Daily Star* (February 19, 1989): unpaginated.
5 Susan Randolph had admitted to Chafee that her family from Virginia had an ancestral relationship to the Randolphs of the Thomas Jefferson lineage. Thomas Randolph, father of Archibald Cary Randolph, was the brother of Jane Randolph, mother of Thomas Jefferson. Archibald Cary was a first cousin of Thomas Jefferson and was her (Susan's) great-great-great grandfather, making Thomas Jefferson her first cousin five or six times removed.

6 D. Russell and S. Randolph interview with C. Domin and K. McGuire, April 28, 2018.
7 Ibid.
8 K. McGuire, while working in Chafee's office, heard David Russell make this comment while visiting Chafee. He was looking at a potential office to rent in a nearby location.
9 Joseph Wilder interview with C. Domin and K. McGuire, November 25, 2014.

Centrum House

1 Centrum Statement, Judith Chafee Papers (MS 606).
2 Elliott Price phone interview with K. McGuire, January 26, 2016.

Rieveschl Residence

1 Michael Smith, "Streamlined Majesty," *Phoenix Home and Garden* (November 1993), 41.
2 Judith Chafee Papers.
3 K. McGuire, while working in Chafee's office, overheard as part of a phone conversation between George Rieveschl and Chafee during the program development phase of the Rieveschl Residence.
4 Ibid., during the construction phase of the Rieveschl Residence.
5 Elliott Price interview with K. McGuire, January 26, 2016.

Hansen Residence

1 Visiting Lecture at the School of Architecture, University of Texas, Austin, September 9, 1996, copy in the Judith Chafee Papers.
2 K. McGuire, while working in Chafee's office, overheard as part of a phone conversation, after which Chafee hung up the phone, said "I'll be damned," and described her earlier experiences with Adelyn Hansen.
3 Visiting Lecture at the School of Architecture, University of Texas, Austin, September 9, 1996.
4 Ibid.

List of Projects

264

The Tilt Chair
New York / Chicago, 1956–60

Merrill Residence
Guilford, CT, 1967–69

Bennington College, Three Dormitories, Interiors Consultant
Bennington, VT, 1968

Radcliffe College, Currier House Interiors
Cambridge, MA, 1968–70

Yale Mathematics Building Competition
New Haven, CT, 1969

Judith Chafee Studio and Residence
Tucson, AZ, 1970–71

Funking Residence
Stockbridge, MA, 1970–72

Viewpoint
Tucson, AZ, 1970–72

Knauth Meditation Barn
Rushville, PA, 1970–74

Mining Club of the Southwest (unbuilt)
Tucson, AZ, 1971–72

De Havilland Residence (unbuilt)
Hillsdale, NY, 1972–73

Yankee Stadium Remodel (unbuilt)
Bronx, NY, 1972–73

An Evening Dinner Theatre
Elmsford, NY, 1972–74

Wells Residence (unbuilt)
Tucson, AZ, 1972–74

Putnam Residence (Pool House)
Tucson, AZ, 1972–75

Best Residence (unbuilt)
Patagonia, AZ, 1972–79

Planned Parenthood Proposal
Tucson, AZ, 1973

Ramada House
Tucson, AZ, 1973–75

Wells Residence Remodel
Tucson, AZ, 1974–77

Jacobson Residence
Tucson, AZ, 1975–77

Meyers Residence
Tucson, AZ, 1975–77

Dahm Addition
Tucson, AZ, 1976

Viewpoint / Reyers Addition
Tucson, AZ, 1976–77

Cannon Residence Remodel
Tucson, AZ, 1978

Cromwell Addition
Tucson, AZ, 1978

Pioneer Paint Store (unbuilt)
Tucson, AZ, 1978

Stanton Residence Remodel
Tucson, AZ, 1978–79

Tucson Museum of Art Historic Restoration for Stevens House
Tucson, AZ, 1978–79

Kollar Residence
Tucson, AZ, 1978–80

Blackwell Residence
Tucson, AZ, 1978–80, demolished 1998

Bishop Residence Remodel
Tucson, AZ, 1979

Downey Residence Remodel I
Tucson, AZ, 1979

Schneider Adobe Office Remodel
Tucson, AZ, 1979

Tin Roof Dinner Theater (unbuilt)
Tucson, AZ, 1979

Kelsik-Vishner Residence Remodel
Tucson, AZ, 1980

Chafee Residence Orchard River Interior Remodel
Tucson, AZ, 1980

Johnson Residence Interior
Pennswood Village, Newtown, PA, 1980

Unity Church Proposal
Tucson, AZ, 1980

Zeches Residence Remodel
Tucson, AZ, 1980

Stanton Guest House
Tucson, AZ, 1980–81

Dahm Residence
Pinetop, AZ, 1980–82

Hydeman Residence
Sonoita, AZ, 1980–83

Daniels Addition (unbuilt)
Tucson, AZ, 1981

Strachan-Piccone Residence (unbuilt)
Tucson, AZ, 1981–82

Russell-Randolph Residence
Tucson, AZ, 1981–83

Bridge Design consultant for Jerry Cannon
Pima County, AZ, 1981–84

Marks Addition
Tucson, AZ, 1982

Fred Chaffee Addition
Tucson, AZ, 1982–83

Maxwell Jr. High School Locker Court
Tucson, AZ, 1982–83

Schlosser Residence Remodel
Tucson, AZ, 1982–84

Bowman Residence
Sonoita, AZ, 1982–84

Yanker Guest House
Tucson, AZ, 1982–84

Merriman Residence
Tucson, AZ, 1982–85

Funking Addition (unbuilt)
Stockbridge, MA, 1983

Centrum Limited Edition House
Tucson, AZ, 1983–84

Garfield Residence Addition + Remodel (unbuilt)
Tucson, AZ, 1983–84

Jones Residence
Avra Valley, AZ, 1983–84

**Palo Verde High School Remodel for
Girls Varsity Sports**
Tucson, AZ, 1983–84

**Rincon High School Remodel for
Girls Varsity Sports**
Tucson, AZ, 1983–84

Finkel Residence
Tucson, AZ, 1983–85

Rieveschl Residence
Tucson, AZ, 1983–88

Centrum Gardens for Ann & Jerome Shull
Tucson, AZ, 1985

**Arizona Nature Conservancy, Mile-Hi / Ramsey
Canyon Preserve Renovation and Addition**
Huachuca, AZ, 1986

**Mature Outlook, Concept House for
Marilyn Hadley**
Tucson, AZ, 1986

Cannon Office Building (unbuilt)
Tucson, AZ, 1986–87

Nendza Residence (unbuilt)
Tucson, AZ, 1986–87

Zephyr Building (unbuilt)
Tucson, AZ, 1986–88

Downey Residence Remodel II
Tucson, AZ, 1987

Genser Residence (unbuilt)
Tucson, AZ, 1988

Oehrle-Steele Addition
Tucson, AZ, 1988

Schlosser Residence Remodel II
Tucson, AZ, 1988

University of Arizona Press Feasibility Study
Tucson, AZ, 1988

Hutchinson Stables
Tucson, AZ, 1988–89

Spencer-Sanders Master Plan (unbuilt)
Tucson, AZ, 1988–89

An Evening Dinner Theater II
Elmsford, NY, 1988–90

Brown Residence Remodel
Tucson, AZ, 1989–90

Finkel Guest House
Tucson, AZ, 1990–91

Trueblood Residence
Sonoita, AZ, 1990–93

**Arizona Nature Conservancy,
Patagonia-Sonoita Creek Preserve**
Patagonia, AZ, 1990–96

Hessler Pool Court
Tucson, AZ, 1991

Kollar Residence Addition (unbuilt)
Tucson, AZ, 1991

Hansen Residence
Crystal Falls, MI, 1991–94

Tracy Residence Addition
Tucson, AZ, 1993

Russell-Randolph Residence Addition (unbuilt)
Tucson, AZ, 1994

Chafee Studio Orchard River Interior Remodel
Tucson, AZ, 1996

Joan Rieveschl Land Use Study
Tucson, AZ, 1996

Meyers / Bendt Remodel (unbuilt)
Tucson, AZ, 1996

Murli Dhar Agarwal
Rameen Ahmed
Ray Barnes
Lynn Barr*
Jean Beck
Diana Brock-Gray*
Howard Chandler
Jules J. Chatot
Clarence Coyle
Eleanor Davico
Robert Earl*
Joshua Edwards
Susan Engelsberg-Moody*
Glenn Robert Erikson
Rudolf J. Graessle (Rudy)
John Greene
Chuck Hall
Nancy Harris
Diane Hastings (a.k.a. Schwalbe)*
Scott Howard
Shannon Hyland
Liz Jheeta
Szu Fu Jiang
Russell Johnson
Dan Kundiff
Mel Lazar
Timothy Lowerre
Richard Luckett
Brian McCarthy
Robert McDougal
Kathryn McGuire*
Charles M. Poster (Corky)
Claudia Shwide
Myron B. Silberman*
Thomas Spendiarian
Anissa J. Tooley
Julius Zappa

*Long-term project
associates

Based on records in
the Judith Chafee Papers,
Special Collections,
University of Arizona
Libraries.

Timeline

1928 Christina Johnson (neé Affeld) marries
Percy B. Davidson

'32 Judith Chafee (neé Davidson) is born in Chicago,
Illinois, August 18
'34 Christina Johnson (then Davidson) marries
Benson Bloom and moves to Tucson, Arizona
Judith is adopted by Bloom; becomes known
as Judith Davidson Bloom

'48–50 Francis W. Parker School, Chicago, Illinois

'50–54 Bennington College, Bennington, Vermont
'52 Christina and Benson divorce; Christina Bloom
moves to Chicago
'54 Judith Chafee's (then Bloom's) daughter born
in Boston and is adopted
Bachelor of Arts Degree, Bennington College
'54–56 Work in New York City
'56 Yale University School of Architecture, New Haven,
Connecticut
'57 Christina Johnson (then Bloom) begins work at
Carson Pirie Scott in Chicago
'59 Married to Richard Chafee
Award for Hospital Design

'60 Bachelor of Architecture Degree, Yale University
Tilt-Chair Patented
Master of Architecture Degree, Yale University
(retroactive)
'60–61 Office of Paul Rudolph, New Haven, Connecticut
'62 Travel to Denmark, Sweden, Finland, USSR,
Norway
'62–63 The Architect's Collaborative, Cambridge,
Massachusetts
'63–65 Office of Eero Saarinen & Associates, Hamden,
Connecticut
'64 Divorced from Richard Chafee
Travel to Germany, Holland, England
'65–69 Office of Edward Larrabee Barnes, Hamden,
Connecticut
Travel to Italy, Germany, England
'66 Established Office of Judith Chafee, Architect,
Hamden, Connecticut
'68 Consultant for Edward Larrabee Barnes
Three Bennington Dormitories—interiors
'69 Returns to Tucson, Arizona
Merrill Residence
Yale Mathematics Building Competition

'70 Establishes Office of Judith Chafee, Architect,
Tucson, Arizona
Record House Award: Merrill Residence
Funking Residence
Christina Johnson (then Bloom) and Earl Johnson
move to Tucson
'71 **Chafee Studio and Residence**
Viewpoint
'73–76 University of Arizona, Visiting Critic
'74 **An Evening Dinner Theatre**
'75 Travel to Mexico City
Ramada House
Record House Award: Viewpoint
Putnam Residence
Burlington House Award: Viewpoint
'76 University of Texas, Austin, Visiting Critic
'77 Travel to Rome, Sardinia, Italy
Jacobson Residence
American Academy in Rome
Meyers Residence
'77–98 University of Arizona, Adjunct Professor
'78 Travel to Mexico City
AIA Housing Award: Ramada House
American Concrete Institute Award:
Jacobson House
Tucson / Pima County Historical Commission
Award: Judith Chafee Studio and Residence
'79 Record House Award: Jacobson House
Stanton Residence Remodel

'80 Christina Johnson moves to Pennsylvania
Chafee moves to Orchard River Condominiums
Blackwell Residence
'81 Travel to Italy, Marazzi ceramic tile trip
Stanton Guest House
AIA Phoenix Conference on Regionalism
'82 Travel to Finland
Dahm Residence
"The Region of the Mindful Heart," *Artspace:
Southwestern Contemporary Arts Quarterly*
'83 Fellow of the AIA
Hydeman Residence
Russell-Randolph Residence
Maxwell Junior High School Locker Court
'84 Travel to China
**Rincon and Palo Verde High Schools Girls
Locker Rooms**
William J.R. Curtis, Visiting Lecture at University
of Arizona
Bowman Residence
American Concrete Institute Award: Hydeman
Residence
Centrum House

'85 **Merriman Residence**
Finkel Residence
'86 Christina Johnson returns to Tucson
Mature Outlook concept house
MIT Visiting Professor
**Arizona Nature Conservancy, Mile-Hi, Ramsey
Canyon Preserve**
'87 Washington University Symposium, "Points of
Departure"
William J.R. Curtis includes Ramada House in
Modern Architecture Since 1900
'88 Mortar Board Citation from University of Arizona
Rieveschl Residence
MIT Visiting Professor, Fall semester
Washington University, Visiting Professor
'89 Travel to Finland, Conference for Urban Planning
and Design, Helsinki
Critical Regionalism Seminar, California State
Polytechnic University, Pomona
Princeton University, Andrew W. Mellon Symposia

'90 University of Montana, lecture, "Architecture
of Place"
Finkel Guest House
An Evening Dinner Theatre II
'91 **Hessler Pool Court**
'92 Christina Johnson dies, January 12, 1992
AIA National Convention, Boston, lecture,
"Sustainable Design: A Planetary Approach"
'93 **Trueblood Residence**
'94 **Hansen Residence**
'96 University of Texas, Austin, Lecture and jury
participation
**Arizona Nature Conservancy, Patagonia-Sonoita
Creek Preserve**
Chafee Studio building sold; Chafee moves studio
to Orchard River
'98 Retires from teaching at the University of Arizona,
April 26, 1998
Judith Chafee dies of complications from
emphysema, November 5, 1998

1954 Judith Bloom, "Shower Song," *Silo: Bennington College '53–'54* (volume 1, number 3, 1954): 34.

Judith Bloom, "The Still Sleeping Beauty," *Silo: Bennington College '53–'54* (volume 1, number 3, 1954): 36.

'59 "Chapel St. Woman Receives Award for Roof Design." *New Haven Register* (October 11, 1959): 13.

'66 Edith Rose Kohlberg, "A Battleground of the Spirit." *Mademoiselle* (May, 1966): 162–63, 209–11.

'69 "Collegiate Geometry: Three Dormitories at Bennington." *Progressive Architecture* (April, 1969): 94–97.

'70 "Record Houses." *Architectural Record* (Mid-May 1970): 66–69 and cover.

'71 "At Journey's End: The House She Couldn't Find." *House Beautiful,* editors Nancy Craig and Melissa Sutshen (April, 1971): 114–21, 117.

'72 "Unique Solutions." Kitchens & Bath, *House & Garden* (1972): 82.

Jim Morgan, "Block-like Forms Nestle into Berkshire Woods." *Architectural Record* (November, 1972): 118–120.

'74 "Sleeping Car Bunks Leave Major Space for Living." Second House, *House & Garden* (Spring–Summer 1974): 26–29.

Karen Fisher, "Women in Architecture." *Arizona Architect* (October–December 1974): 9.

'75 "A Study in the Use of Light." *Los Angeles Times, Home Magazine* (March 30, 1975): 7, 8, 16, and cover.

"Record Houses of 1975." *Architectural Record* (Mid-May, 1975): 82–83.

"Building Guide." *House & Garden* (Spring–Summer 1975): 88–93 and cover.

"Outdoor Showering." *Sunset Magazine* (June, 1975): 65.

"Door Pull Is a Float Handle." *Sunset Magazine* (August, 1975): 74.

'77 "Tree-to-Tree Canal System." *Sunset Magazine* (March, 1977): 100.

'78 "Sun Shades." *Sunset Magazine* (March 1978): 148.

"Display Shelves for Old China and Sewing Counter Does Much Else." *Sunset Magazine* (June, 1978): 116.

"Odd Shape Is What Makes the Room." *Sunset Magazine* (July, 1978): 102.

"Ground-hugging Desert House." *Housing* (August, 1978), AIA First Honor Housing Award.

"Southwest Architecture: Bold and Sheltering." *Building, House & Garden* (Fall 1978): 150–153.

'79 "Desert House Revives Region's Traditional Form." *Architecture Record* (February, 1979): 107–110.

"Delivering Winter Sun and Constant Views." *Building, House and Garden Building Guide* (Spring, 1979): 71–75.

"Adobe Gets a Pardon." *Remodeling, House & Garden Spring Remodeling* Guide (Spring–Summer, 1979) 102–103, office and home

"House in the Southwest, Record Houses of 1979." *Architecture Record* (Mid-May, 1979): 104–107.

"House in Southern Arizona." *Nikkei Architecture* (September, 1979): 105–107.

"Western Home Awards." *Sunset Magazine* (October, 1979): 79–80.

"Jacobson House." *The ToshiJutaku* (November, 1979): 46–50.

'80 "Ready for the Eighties." *Yale School of Architecture* (January, 1980): annual banner.

"Cabinets Step Down the Wall, Add Storage Space." *Sunset Magazine* (April, 1980): 124.

'81 Ann Patterson, "Women Are Leaping Barriers into the World of Architecture." *Arizona Republic* (Sunday, June 14, 1981): SL 1, SL 10.

Judith P. Smith, "Architect's Office Distinctive." *Arizona Daily Star* (June 21, 1981): 1K.

"Sideboard for Bottles to Stand Up, Lie Down." *Sunset Magazine* (September 1981): 117.

"Lazy Susan Spins Contents of 2-Way Drawer." *Sunset Magazine* (October, 1981): 118.

"Hinged Panel Converts an Open Sink into Useful Counter Space." *Sunset Magazine* (November, 1981): 181.

'82 "They Pushed Out the Porch, Raised the Roof." *Sunset Magazine* (February, 1982): 126.

"Natural Light for Dressing Table." *Sunset Magazine* (May, 1982): 175.

Judith Chafee, "The Region of the Mindful Heart." *Artspace: Southwestern Contemporary Arts Quarterly* (New Mexico, Spring, 1982): 27–33 and cover.

"The Big Windows Are Sliding Door Panels." *Sunset Magazine* (September, 1982): 120.

"Bella Still Has a Little Trouble Getting the Key in the Lock." *Sunset Magazine* (October, 1982): 119.

"A Team-Built Concrete House." *Arizona Daily Star* (December 26, 1982): 1J, 4J.

'83 "With Windows behind Them, Cabinets Seem to Float." *Sunset Magazine* (June, 1983): 133.

"Signing One's New House Project." *Sunset Magazine* (October, 1983): 186.

Donald Watson, *Climate Design for Home Building* (New York, McGraw-Hill Publishers, 1983).

'84 Jim Morgan, *Marketing for a Small Design Firm* (New York, NY, Whitney Library of Design, 1984): 18, 19, 32, 33, 49, 54, 77, 83, 103, 111, 133, 146.

"When Your Book Collection Grows Too Big for a Bookcase." *Sunset Magazine* (January, 1984): 56–57.

Allen Freeman, "Reinterpreting Regionalism: Arizona; Forms That Change the Situation." *Architecture* (March, 1984): 112–119.

Judith Chafee, "House in Sonoita, Arizona." *Triglyph,* Marcus Whiffen editor (Arizona State University: Fall, 1984): 21–23.

"Distinctive Idea for the Discerning." *Arizona Daily Star* (Sunday, October 14, 1984): 1I.

Bob Womack, "Architects Take Dim View Of Tucson." *Arizona Daily Star* (Sunday, October 28, 1984): 1I, 7I.

'85 Lawrence W. Cheek, "Courageous Architecture for a Fragile Land." *Tucson Citizen* (Tuesday, October 8, 1985): B1, feature article.

"Counter Skirt Swings Up or Down." *Sunset Magazine* (October, 1985): 172.

"The Counter Lifts Up into a Drawing Board." *Sunset Magazine* (November, 1985): 163.

'86 "Their Wine Cellar Is Cast in Concrete." *Sunset Magazine* (January, 1986): 108.

"Getting More Light into the Bathroom." *Sunset Magazine* (May, 1986): 169.

"Rooms without Walls." *Sunset Magazine* (July, 1986): 119.

Sonya Hepinstall, "Eastern Architects Help Preserve Arizona Traditions." *Arizona Daily Star* (Sunday, July 27, 1986): 8.

"Adjustable Bedside Lamps." *Sunset Magazine* (September, 1986): 133.

Elizabeth Brewster and Nancy Goode, "The Possible Dream 2." *Mature Outlook* (November–December, 1986) 26, 27, 32–35.

Deborah Latish, "After Twelve Years, County Finally Will Get Crucial Gates Pass Acreage." *Tucson Citizen* (Wednesday, December 17, 1986): 1B, 2B.

'87 William J.R. Curtis, *Modern Architecture Since 1900,* second edition (Oxford, Great Britain: Phaidon Press Limited, 1987): 394.

Michael Munday, "Design for Desert Light." *Tucson Magazine* (December 1987/January 1988): 71–74.

Jim Kemp, *American Vernacular,* Regional Influences in Architecture and Interior Design (New York, NY, Viking Penguin, Incorporated, 1987): 93, 102.

"Concise Design, Ample Light." *Home, Creative Ideas for Home Design* (February, 1987): 94.

"Arizona Firebox Sculpture." *Sunset Magazine* (March, 1987): 128–129 and cover.

'88 Lawrence W. Cheek, "The Good, the Bad and the Ugly." *City Magazine* (April, 1988): feature article on Tucson architecture.

'89 Fran Feldman, *Fireplaces and Wood Stoves, Sunset Books* (Menlo Park, CA, Lane Publishing Company, 1989): 40.

Margo Hernandez, "Park Officials Face Dilemma over House Touted as 'Special', but Targeted for Razing." *Arizona Daily Star,* (Friday, January 20, 1989): 1A, 2A.

Mary Bustamante, "Eyesore Will Get Reprieve." Tucson Citizen (Wednesday, February 15, 1989): 1C, 6C.

268 Margo Hernandez, "Parks Board Order Study on Cost of Keeping or Razing Blackwell House." *Arizona Daily Star* (Thursday, February 16, 1989): 1B.

Margo Hernandez, "Uncompromising architect is shaping dreams." *Arizona Daily Star* (Sunday, February 19, 1989): 1B–2B.

"Blackwell House Fits Well within Its Desert Home." *Arizona Daily Star*, Susan Albright, Editor, Viewpoints column by Judith Chafee (Sunday, April 9, 1989): 3.

"Blackwell House, Special Structure Requires Special Response." *Arizona Daily Star*, Susan Albright, Editor (Thursday, April 19, 1989): 10 (featured editorial).

Paula Panich, "Tucson Blackwell House: Eyesore… or Legend?" *Phoenix House and Garden* (May, 1989): 44–46.

Ann Patterson, "Architect Custom-Fits to Environment." *Arizona Republic* (Phoenix, Sunday, May 28, 1989): SL 1, SL 12, SL 13.

William J.R. Curtis, "Contemporary Transformations of Modern Architecture." *Architectural Record* (June, 1989): 114.

Ann Patterson, "Shades of History: Papagos Inspire Home's Famous Roof." *Arizona Republic* (Phoenix, Sunday, June 18, 1989): 1S, 3S.

Pat Conner, "Santa Fe or Santa Fade?" *Arizona Daily Star* (July 4, 1989) 1B, 7B.

'90 "Want a Huge Operable Window? Try a Door." *Sunset Magazine* (September, 1990): 80.

"Beton-Oase Arizona, Avant-garde in der Wuste." *Ambiente Magazine* (November, 1990): 86–94.

"Living Space: Contemporary Western Architecture." Exhibition in conjunction with the 1990 AIA Western Mountain Regional Conference, Gallery of Contemporary Art, University of Colorado (Fall 1990).

Posy Piper, "Exciting Plans Coincide with Silver Anniversary of Area Wildlife Preserve." *Panaorama, Nogales International* (Wednesday, December 5, 1990): 17, 20.

'91 Spyros Amourgis, *Critical Regionalism, The Pomona Meeting—Proceeding* (Pomona, CA, College of Environmental Design, California State Polytechnic University, 1991): 54–60.

"Sliding Barn Doors Provide Sun Control and Security." *Sunset Magazine* (September, 1991): 83.

John Rawlinson, "Gates Pass House Pact at Last Opens Way to Restoration," *Arizona Daily Star* (Monday, December 2, 1991): 1B, 2B.

"Blackwell House; Simple Steps Could Have Prevented Damage." *Arizona Daily Star*, Susan Albright, Editor (Wednesday, December 4, 1991): 12, featured editorial.

'92 "Tall Bath, Tall Towel." *Sunset Magazine* (June, 1992): 91.

Faye Bowers, "Sustainable Design, Hot Topic for Architects." *Christian Science Monitor* (June 30, 1992): unpaginated.

"They'll Be Sleeping in the Clouds." *Sunset Magazine* (September 1992): 128.

Chris Limberlis, "Blackwell House Is Spruced Up as Part of U of A Preservation Drive." *Arizona Daily Star* (Monday, November 23, 1992): 1B, 2B.

'93 "Built-in Headboards as Bedroom Sculpture." *Sunset Magazine* (February 1993): 91.

Lawrence W. Cheek, "By Design, Structural Integrity." *Tucson Weekly* (June 22-June 8, 1993): 37.

"One Of Tucson's Best, Judith Chafee." *Tucson Weekly* (October 6–12, 1993): special feature article, unpaginated.

Michael J. P. Smith, "Streamlined Majesty." *Phoenix Home and Garden* (November, 1993): 38–43.

'94 "Fall Winter." *House & Garden Building Guide* (1994–1995): 94.

'96 William J.R. Curtis, *Modern Architecture Since 1900*, third edition (London: Phaidon Press, 1996): 637–638.

'98 W. Jesse Greenberg, "Rocks, Glass, Concrete, & Cow Dung." *Tucson Guide Quarterly* (Winter, 1998): 82–87.

Blake Morlock, "County Could Raze House It Bought." *Tucson Citizen* (Tuesday, June 2, 1998): 1 (front page).

Blake Morlock, "County Votes to Raze Blackwell House." *Tucson Citizen* (Wednesday, June 3, 1998): 1 (front page).

Hipolito R. Corella, "Blackwell House to Be Demolished within Two Months." *Arizona Daily Star* (Wednesday, June 3, 1998): 1B.

Hipolito R. Corella, "New Blackwell House Ideas May Be Too Late." *Arizona Daily Star* (June 19, 1998): 2.

Pila Martinez and L. Anne Newell, "Blackwell House Architect Chafee Dies; Was 'Straightforward' in Word and Work." *Arizona Daily Star* (Tuesday, November 10, 1998).

'99 Lawrence W. Cheek, *Judith Chafee* (Tucson, Civitas Sonoran, 1999): unpaginated.

2000 Margaret Regan, "Master Builder, Architect Judith Chafee Melded Sleek Modern Design to Sonoran Desert." *Tucson Weekly* (February 3, 2000): 16–21.

'02 Anne M. Nequette and R. Brooks Jeffery, *A Guide to Tucson Architecture* (Tucson: University of Arizona Press, 2002): 41, 230, 244, 247, 248, 262, 263, 291.

Lawrence W. Cheek, "The Arizona School of Architecture." *Architecture* (May 2002): 92–93.

'04 Chris Grimley, "Judith Chafee, an Abandoned Modernism." *Loud Paper* (volume 3, issue 4, 2004): unpaginated.

'09 A. Richard Williams, *Archipelago Critiques of Contemporary Architecture and Education* (Champaign: The University of Illinois Press, 2009): 232.

'12 Ann Gilkerson, "*Viewpoint*" (Tucson), SAH Archipedia, editors Gabrielle Esperdy and Karen Kingsley (Charlottesville: University of Virginia Press, 2012).

'15 *Pedagogy and Place, Celebrating One Hundred Years of Architecture Education at Yale*, Yale School of Architecture (December 3, 2015– May 8, 2016): 12.

'16 Arizona Public Media, *Arizona Illustrated: The Architect: Judith Chafee.* Film produced and edited by Andrew Brown (October, 2016).

'17 Christopher Domin, "Judith Chafee: The Influence of Place and Character." *Tucson Modernism: Tucson Historic Preservation Foundation* (2017): 5–9.

'18 Darci Hazelbaker, "JC Real Things." *Territory Magazine* (issue number 2, 2018): 62–79.

Index

Contributors

Christopher Domin is an architect, educator, and international lecturer focusing on regional critical practice and technological innovation. He is co-author of *Paul Rudolph: The Florida Houses* and *Victor Lundy: Artist Architect*, published by Princeton Architectural Press. At the University of Arizona, Professor Domin specializes in teaching design studios and material technology courses. His research is supported by grants from the Graham Foundation for Advanced Studies in the Fine Arts, the J. B. Jackson Endowment, and the Paul Rudolph Foundation.

Kathryn McGuire is an architect practicing in Tucson, Arizona. Her essays for the book are written from direct experience first as a student, employee, and a friend of Judith Chafee for over twenty years. Starting as an intern, then project manager and associate, McGuire worked with clients, engineers, and other advisers with Chafee. McGuire's practice is based on many of the principles experienced in the Chafee studio, dedicated to desert-adapted building strategies and regional modern architecture.

William J.R. Curtis is a historian, critic, artist, and photographer who has taught worldwide. His best-known books include *Modern Architecture Since 1900* and *Le Corbusier: Ideas and Forms*. Other books include *Balkrishna Doshi: An Architecture for India*; *Denys Lasdun: Architecture, City, Landscape*; *RCR: Aranda Pigem Vilalta Arquitectes*; *Teodoro Gonzalez de Leon*. Curtis's critical texts appear regularly in *Architectural Review* and *El Croquis*. A retrospective *Abstraction and Light, Drawings, Paintings, Photographs by William J.R. Curtis* took place in the Palace Carlos V, Alhambra.

Image Credits